The Concept of Empire
in Western Europe
from the Fifth to the Fourteenth Century

by

ROBERT FOLZ

Professor in the Faculty of Letters at the
University of Dijon

translated by

SHEILA ANN OGILVIE

J. & J. HARPER EDITIONS
HARPER & ROW, PUBLISHERS
NEW YORK and EVANSTON

THE CONCEPT OF EMPIRE IN WESTERN EUROPE
FROM THE FIFTH TO THE FOURTEENTH CENTURY
Printed by arrangement with Edward Arnold
(Publishers) Ltd, London

© Edward Arnold (Publishers) Ltd, 1969

Authorised translation from the French
L'Idée d'Empire dans L'Occident du Ve au XIVe siècle

First Published 1969

First Published by
Aubier, Editions Montaigne, 1953

FIRST J. & J. HARPER EDITION 1969
Printed on long-life, acid-free paper, with reinforced bindings
Library of Congress Catalog Card Number: 77–101226

Contents

BOOK IV

THE CONCEPT OF EMPIRE BEYOND THE
REALM OF REALITY

DOCUMENTS

Foreword

The concept of empire was a legacy from ancient times and it has been one of the dominant themes of human development. To study its history in the Middle Ages is to become aware of its strength and to see how the succession of factors contributing to the concept have fascinated the minds of men. In the Middle Ages nothing that happened was ever regarded as absolutely new: more usually each development or event was seen as a renewal of a former state of things. By studying the concept of empire during that period, therefore, we can try to understand how, in effect, it caused political structures to be formed which could be claimed, in different degrees, to be a continuation of the Empire of Rome; and we may also discover the influence which these creations in turn exercised on its substance.

The difficulties of a study of this kind are multiple and not hard to perceive. Some arise from the movement of the concept of empire through space and time: certainly, different eras and different human environments took different views of the meaning of empire. In this study, time is represented by some ten centuries (about 476 to about 1350), the first of which are still very close to ancient times and therefore strongly influenced by the memory of the Roman Empire, its survival in Byzantium and the hope of seeing it resurrected in the West. The Carolingian Empire was, at least to some extent, the result of this aspiration. But from the middle of the ninth century the formation of future European nation-states began to be perceptible – how far could an empire be integrated into such a development? From that moment, with an ever-increasing intensity, the history of the concept of empire was to be that of a divorce between theory and reality or, put in different words, that of a compromise between the unlimited and the possible. This process continued until the middle of the fourteenth century when, losing all contact with reality, the concept of empire dissolved completely and what remained was no longer anything but an aspiration.

The problem becomes even more complicated when one takes account of the fact that during the Middle Ages the concept of empire in the West never had the internal unity which it demonstrated for nearly a thousand years in the Byzantine Empire. The main reason for this absence of unity is the fact that the heritage of the Roman Empire was claimed not only by certain political bodies but also by Western Christendom. As early as the century which followed the triumph of the new religion, the West knew not only the emperor but also the pope-emperor. Two concepts of empire were thus in existence, which were never to achieve complete harmony: this was all the more the case because it was the universality of the papacy alone which proved capable of imposing itself, in theory at least, on the whole of Western Christendom, whereas the concept of empire, in the proper sense of the word, had inevitably to be adapted – even at the time of its most brilliant successes – to accommodate the forces which were dragging the West in the direction of an ever-increasing differentiation between them.

In addition to these basic problems the nature of the documentation at our disposal makes our study doubly difficult. It is relatively plentiful and varied: chancellery records and deeds, pictorial representations, liturgical ritual, external evidence (clothing and emblems) – these, along with certain narrative texts, are our main sources of information for the first part of the Middle Ages, when symbols were definitely more important than theory in the expression of political formations. In the twelfth century the revival of juridical studies began to play an ever-increasing rôle in the furnishing of documentation – the texts of debates and controversies, providing new sources of information, appeared at the time when the decline of the Empire as a reality was taking place, and continued long to survive it.

The evidence available to us reflects the diversity of the concept of empire. For convenience, therefore, it is grouped in chapters corresponding to different aspects of the concept of empire during different periods or within specific human situations. Yet we must recognise that we are very unequally served on this subject. The ideas of certain popes are indeed well enough known to us, but how we wish we could have at our disposal indications as precise on the views held by such and such a ruler! This gap is mentioned here and now, once for all, and must be borne in mind by the reader throughout the book: we are better informed about the speculations or dreams of clerics and notaries, of lawyers and of poets, than on the ideas of political leaders or ordinary people. Yet, throughout the whole of the period we are studying, we can at least discern one collective dream, one aspiration towards an ideal state of things which people called Empire and which, in Germany if not elsewhere, was prolonged long beyond the Middle Ages.

Such varied circumstances compel us to approach our subject with the utmost prudence. It goes without saying that it can only be outlined in these pages. Our aim is that, in spite of unavoidable gaps, this book may guide the reader through one of the most interesting chapters in the history of the intellectual and spiritual conceptions current during the Middle Ages.

Since all that is best in this study is due to those which have preceded it, the author can do no better than dedicate it in homage to all who, living and dead, have advanced our knowledge of the Empire and mediaeval thought in general.

Acknowledgements

Thanks are due to Mr V. H. H. Green for providing the reading list of books in English. The translator also wishes to thank Mr John Benton who kindly read the proofs and suggested a number of valuable improvements.

List of Abbreviations
Used in this Book

C.I.L.   *Corpus Inscriptionum Latinarum*

M.G. (or *Mon. Germ.*)   *Monumenta Germaniae historica*

P.L.   *Patrologia latina (Patrologia Cursus Completus, series latina,*
        ed. J. P. Migne)

S.R.G.   *Scriptores Rerum Germanicorum in usum scholarum ex*
         Monumentis Germaniae Historicis recusi

BOOK I
The Chief Elements of the
Mediaeval Concept of Empire

1

How the Concept of Empire Survived the Fall of the Western Roman Empire

The deposition by Odovaca of Romulus Augustalus in 476 spelt the end of the Western Roman Empire. It had been steadily shrinking since the beginning of the fifth century; one by one its provinces had fallen into the hands of the barbarians: the events which took place in Rome were only the most spectacular act of the drama. Nevertheless, though it had ceased to exist in fact, the Empire still lived on in the minds of men – 'imaginarie', to quote the expressive word used by the Goth historian Jordanes. In the sixth century, Justinian achieved a partial restoration, but this lasted for only a brief period. Ultimately the Western Empire survived in certain regions of Italy alone, and not for much longer even there: in the middle of the eighth century, events occurred which gave birth to the papal state and simultaneously caused the northern and central regions of the peninsula to fall into the hands of the Franks. In this chapter we shall study the period between the two dates – 476 and 774 – and attempt to discover the various elements which constituted the concept of empire current during those years.

I. THE IMAGE OF THE ROMAN EMPIRE

The concept of empire existed at several levels, but at the risk of over-simplifying, it can be said that the two most important of these were the realm of religious and philosophical thought and the realm of political realities.

A. *The realm of the mind – universalism*

The belief that the Empire was universal was essentially Hellenic in conception and outline. The Greek philosophers, in particular the Stoics, stressed the notion that all mankind formed one community, partaking of universal reason. To them, influenced by Alexander's conquests, it seemed plain that Greek civilisation had a universal mission: they regarded it as human civilisation at its best, dominating the *oikoumene* on the outskirts of which barbarism reigned. It was, indeed, the Greeks who from the second century B.C. had regarded the Roman Empire and the *oikoumene* as one: Panaetius, friend of Scipio Emilianus, considered that the Roman conquest would lead to the realisation of a union of all civilised peoples; its purpose, and at the same time its justification, was to give peace, order and justice to mankind. Ideas such as these made a deep impression on the minds of the political and intellectual élite of Rome, and through their influence the two notions of *orbis terrarum* and *imperium* came to be regarded in the first century as identical: from then on no distinction was ever made between them.[1]

This concept of an empire which was the hearth and home of civilisation was reinforced and sublimated by the Christian religion, which had an essentially œcumenical mission.[2] At first there was a conflict between the universalism of Christianity and that of Rome, but by the end of the second century Christians no longer treated the Empire as an object of systematic hostility: on the contrary, they said prayers for it and regarded it as having its place in the design of Providence. Indeed, they thought it was probably the fourth and last of the monarchies foretold by Daniel, at the expiry of which the Kingdom of God would be established. Speculation along these lines took on a sharper definition during Constantine's reign, for at that time the Empire became more and more officially Christian and simultaneously the Roman aristocracy, brought up on the concept of empire, began to penetrate ecclesiastical circles. From then on, the conceptions of *orbis christianus* and *orbis romanus* coincided: it was easy

---

[1] Countless pieces of evidence; see for example Livy, Book I, chapter xvi; the *Aeneid*, vi, 852–3; Rutilius Namatianus, *Itinerarium*, v, 63; Claudian, *De consulatu Stilichonis*, iii, 150–4.

[2] See Documents, I, p. 177.

4

to pass from one form of universalism to another, as did Leo the Great, for example, in his 82nd sermon, *in Natali Apostolorum* – a brilliant synthesis of the ideas current at the time.[3]

The instrument which preserved and propagated the theme of universalism, both Roman and Christian, was the liturgy. Indeed, in the oldest known forms of religious service we can read prayers for the Emperor in which Roman and Christian ideas are inextricably intermingled: God is the protector of the Empire; He is invoked in order that He may guarantee Roman peace, safety, freedom and devotion, that is to say, the essential qualities of the Roman race of men. These had become identical with Christianity and the Empire acted as its framework.[4]

Thus the Empire survived in men's minds both as a cultural ideal and as a quasi-religious notion. The second of these soon proved to be much the stronger and, as a result, the idea of an *Imperium Christianum* began to evolve. At first conceived as a synonym for the Roman Empire, the term came to stand for something much wider, and ultimately to mean all the countries collectively in which Christianity reigned. Once this interpretation was accepted, it was evident that the Empire need no longer be ruled by one single emperor, much less a Roman emperor.

B. *The realm of politics*
These were the ideas developing in men's minds, but, in addition, much instructive information, which cannot be ignored, has descended to us from the fifth century in the form of pieces of evidence surviving from the machinery of the imperial government. Faithfully collected by contemporary witnesses, they were seized upon later by historians, who then applied them to the political situations which they saw around them. They differ from the ideas analysed above, in that they are actual facts.

First of all, there is the very notion of *Imperium*, evocative of some kind of authority possessing an essential superiority, the authority wielded by rulers outside Rome before becoming, in its most perfected form, the essential attribute of the Emperor. Then there is one particular aspect of this authority, namely, its military character, and hence the rôle of the army in conferring it: the picture of the victorious

---

[3] See Documents, II, p. 177.
[4] Numerous examples of prayers in G. Tellenbach, *Römischer und christlicher Reichsgedanke*.

general proclaimed *imperator* by his troops, and – scarcely distinguish-able – the imperial acclamation proper, the one which made the Emperor. Now, from a constitutional point of view, the importance of the latter had grown progressively and, by the third century, the visible fact of an emperor created by the army alone had become so common that St Jerome was able to utter his frequently quoted remark: *Exercitus facit imperatorem.* What is equally instructive is the fact that numerous emperors who were so acclaimed by their legions did not become genuine 'Augustuses' (i.e. rulers over the universal empire), but had to be content to exercise power over a limited part of that empire, and even – for example those in Britain – in a region which was outside the *orbis romanus* proper.[5] Isidore of Seville informs us most pertinently that such empires were not the real Empire when he notes that: 'From the moment when the senate observed that the generals were assuming the title of emperor, they decided that it should be reserved to the Augustus Caesars, so that they might thereby be dis-tinguished from the kings of other nations.'[6] This definition is a good illustration of the most conspicuous feature of the notion of empire: the empire is to be distinguished from kingdoms. Can we determine how those two terms were related to each other in the fifth century?

Geographically speaking the term *Imperium* used to be applied to those lands which were subject to the rule of the Roman people, and, later, of the Emperor: the unity, and indeed the unique character, of the Empire did not permit of a multiplicity of *regna*. Little by little, however, this sharp distinction became blurred and the two terms drew closer in meaning. Several facts combined to cause this, the most important of which was the advent of the invading Germanic tribes, who installed themselves on the soil of the Empire, turning provinces into *regna* and recognising, at least at the outset, the superior authority of the Emperor. This process steered the concept of empire towards the notion that the Emperor had supremacy over the kingdoms. As to the inner significance of this pre-eminence, it must be admitted that a good deal of uncertainty still exists; however, it does seem clear that it had some similarity to one of the fundamental notions of the classical principate, that of *auctoritas*, i.e. moral superiority, inherent in either the person or the institution to which everyone[7] was subject

[5] The credit for having thrown light on this fact belongs to C. Erdmann, *Forschungen,* who also gives numerous references to the history of the terms *Imperium* and *Regna,* which are discussed below.

[6] *Etymologies,* ix, 3, 14.

[7] Numerous pieces of evidence: i.a. see that of Augustus in the *Testament of Ancyra: auctoritate omnibus praestiti* (J. Gage, *Res gestae divi Augusti,* Paris 1935, p. 146).

and that it was very different from the *potestas* of public authority which was exercised through the machinery of the law.

After the fall of the Western Roman Empire, this image became crystallised in the Eastern Empire, where the chancellery drew up a detailed scheme of a complete hierarchy of different types of ruler, over all of whom the Emperor presided. In the West this hierarchy was already familiar: 'The Roman Empire, of which other kingdoms are dependencies', as Isidore of Seville[8] put it. The forms of religious service current in the sixth and seventh centuries contain prayers that the Empire may surpass all kingdoms. The most significant proof that this was the accepted picture is a treatise on public duties which seems to have been drawn up in Merovingian Gaul before the middle of the eighth century and which contains the following statement: 'The Emperor is he who is pre-eminent in the whole world; the kings of other kingdoms come under him.'[9] Although this definition was inspired by the factual situation then existing in Rome, it was nevertheless novel in that it did not suggest that the concept of empire was inseparably bound to Rome: it thus opened up the possibility that a non-Roman sovereign might accede to the Empire, if he actually possessed hegemony.

II. THE EMPIRE AND THE CHURCH

A. *The antecedence of the Empire: the sacred nature of the monarchy*
The person of the Emperor was heavily wrapped in tradition, itself inherited from ancient times. The Roman Empire had, it must be recalled, gradually adopted Hellenistic and Oriental notions concerning the personal power of the sovereign, and a progressive evolution of these ideas led emperors first to imitate and finally to identify themselves with the gods: the cult of the empire was centred on the Emperor, as a god on earth. This conception borrowed much from Christianity and vice versa. On the one hand, there is no doubt that Christianity was steeped in an imperial atmosphere: the picture of Christ evolved in ancient times was that of Christ-Caesar, a brilliant sun, victorious over darkness and death, *Kosmokrator*, head of the militia of his faithful followers, enthroned among the splendours and pomp of the World Beyond, surrounded by a senate of the saints. On the other hand, although the Deity was thus clothed with the majesty of the world

---

[8] *Etymologies*, ix, 3, 2.
[9] G. Baesecke, *Gradus Romanorum, Festschrift für R. Holtzmann*, 1933, p. 5.

below, a parallel tendency in the opposite direction is perceptible from the fourth century onwards: henceforth the Emperor was regarded as being the image of this God of glory, the vicar on earth of Christ Triumphant. As a result of this development the Empire was able to preserve its holy character, without the need for any doctrine to justify it: all that was required was that it should be exteriorised in a sumptuous liturgy, the many forms of which were each in turn survivals from the ancient imperial cult of this empire, now Christianised. Court etiquette at the Sacred Palace in Constantinople included *inter alia*, the act of prostration (*proscynesis*), which the Church tried in vain to have abolished; annual festivals with rites closely related to religious celebrations; the wearing of symbolical vestments and emblems; processions in which Caesar played the rôle of Christ; ritual acclamations raised towards the *basileus* crowned by God, the *basileus* on whose behalf they invoked Christ Victorious. All these procedures combined to place the emperor on a superhuman level, where he was seen as an intermediary between the Deity and mankind. In the last analysis, it was because of the very deep significance of the Empire as an institution and because it played a part in sacred matters that it was possible for emperors to intervene so frequently in religious questions between the fourth and eighth centuries.

B. *Confrontation of Empire and Church*

The history of the relationship between the Empire and the Church is that of two institutions which were originally independent but which did not take long to interpenetrate one another. The Empire did indeed exist before the Church and at first the Church was within the Empire from which it drew both the administrative framework and the traditions of its own organisation, while the emperors took it for granted that they should rule over the new religion, as the Caesars had been the heads of the old one: but despite all this it was none the less true that from the fourth century onwards the Church began to impregnate the Empire with its own thinking and to declare that spiritual matters were separate and independent. If harmony between the two authorities was to be achieved, reciprocal recognition of the prerogatives of each was indispensable: control of temporal matters should be the Empire's natural right and own domain, whereas control of spiritual matters fell to the Church. In practice, however, several considerations prevented such an absolute division of their powers from being put into effect: first, the prestige of the anointed monarch, but also – at least in the West – the fact that the old Roman idea of rule by the people had become extinct while spiritual ideas had so penetrated the sphere of the State that the latter was gradually reduced to playing the rôle of a servant at the disposal of the Church and its head, the Pope.

At this point the rising prestige of the papacy must be noted. The movement was slow but, despite occasional interruptions, steady and it was constantly being furthered by one fundamental idea: the primacy within the Church of the successor of the apostle Peter who, according to Leo the Great, had confirmed and revived the notion that Rome had a universal mission. The question then arose as to what was to be the relationship between the Bishop of the Ancient Rome and the Emperor of the New Rome. Two popes, a century apart, gave somewhat divergent replies to this question.

One was Pope Gelasius I (492–6), among whose writings was the famous statement: 'There are two main authorities by which the world is ruled, the sacred authority of the pontiffs and the royal authority of kings. But the authority of the pontiffs is the more weighty in that they will have to be responsible for the kings themselves at the Supreme Court of Judgment.'[10] There can be no doubt that the *auctoritas* so conceived was of the same kind as that enjoyed through 'principate': that is to say a superiority primarily due to the important function of the bishops, and specifically of the Pope, to be the spiritual guides of sovereigns. If in addition it is remembered that, from the end of the fourth century, the Church's tradition was that the apostle Peter was not only the first but the *princeps* of the apostles, the idea that his successor should exercise a veritable spiritual empire is not surprising: nevertheless, this empire wholly respected the proper domain of the other.

A century later Gregory I was Pope and the general atmosphere had changed. In Gelasius's day, the Western Empire was an idea; now it was a reality, and a very solid reality at that: the Caesaropapism of Justinian had greatly harmed the Western Church. In order to counter the confusion between the two realms as outlined by Gelasius, Gregory made it his task to set out afresh and in very precise terms the rights and duties attributed to each, including many extremely fine distinctions. To him the Roman Empire remained the political expression of Christian universality: the Empire was the *christianum Imperium*, the *sancta respublica*, which would continue for as long as the world existed.

---

[10] Jaffé, *Regesta pontificum romanorum*, 2nd ed., No. 632. Text in the *Decretum Gratiani*, ed. Friedberg, *Corpus Juris canonici*, I, col. 340.

He venerated it, he demonstrated that it derived directly from God; he assured it of his devoted zeal behind which no ulterior motive was concealed. But although the Pope sometimes confused Empire and Church in his mind, he nevertheless ascribed two different spheres to them. The latter was the more vast since it comprised populations which did not form part of the Empire; it was entirely spiritual and was to be controlled by the Pope, successor of the Good Shepherd leading his flock, in conformity with the principles enunciated by Gregory in his *Regula pastoralis*. On the other hand, Christianity was to be one of the foremost of the Empire's preoccupations and its essential task was that of maintaining peace within the Church and propagating the Christian faith outside, among the pagans who were the barbarians of former times. Pope and Emperor were therefore two complementary members of one body. However entangled their attributions may be we must nevertheless note that the ultimate aim assigned by Gregory to the Empire was that *terrestre regnum caelesti regno famuletur*:[11] what Monseigneur Arquillière has called 'the ministerial conception of the Christian Empire'[12] could not be more concisely expressed. Beyond the frontiers of the Empire lay the barbarian nations of the West. Because the Pope did not have such scruples about them as a Roman might still feel in relation to an imperial ruler, he could speak with greater firmness, so he dictated the line of conduct which they were to follow: they must aim at complete subjection of the State to the directives of religion. Through Gregory the Great, political Augustinism thus won over the West little by little and ultimately exercised a considerable influence there.

C. *The Pope elevated to equal status with the Emperor: the Donation of Constantine*

Finally, consideration must be given to one last consequence of the shifting of ideas which was taking place at the very heart of the image of the Roman Empire, both Christian and Universal: if the Emperor was to play a rôle in sacred matters, should not the Pope add the prestige of the Empire to the spiritual *auctoritas* which he already held?

The extraordinary document which supplies an answer to that question is known as the 'Donation of Constantine' (*Constitutum Constantini*) and it was produced as supporting evidence for the 'promise of donation' made by Pepin. It is generally admitted that the

---

[11] *Register, Mon. Germ. Epistolae I*, III, 61.
[12] *L'Augustinisme politique*, p. 75.

forged document came into existence between 750 and 760, either because the Donation had been composed in preparation for the voyage of Pope Stephen II or, more probably, because it was written after his return to Italy, perhaps at the moment when the Papal States were taking shape under great difficulties, perhaps immediately after these events. An analytical description of the prerogative is given elsewhere:[13] here one must ask what purpose could have inspired the forger.

The general impression which emerges from his work is that he wanted to delve as far back as possible into the past and produce evidence, from the sayings or actions of the first Christian Emperor, of the rights which the papacy already possessed or was striving to acquire by conquest. It seems, however, that political interest in the strict meaning of the term played only a limited part in the writer's mind. The gift of the West to the Pope is a very vague clause, reflecting a long evolution in the course of which the West had taken on the appearance of a zone reserved, at least in principle, to the spiritual influence of the Roman pontiffs. The case of Rome and Italy is a little more precise; by making Constantine give them back to Sylvester, the forger was in effect stressing the negative scope of his text; the aim was to exclude the Byzantines from the peninsula and to give the Pope grounds to claim that he was their rightful heir.

The main object of the document is to be found at an entirely different level. Indeed, everything suggests that the author's plan was to make the Pope the centre of the concept of empire and to clothe him in the splendour which surrounded the earthly *imperator*.[14] Now, a movement in this direction had already begun: the honours accorded to Popes John I (526) and Constantine I (710–11) on their visits to Byzantium were modelled on the ceremonial which welcomed the *basileus* when he entered a town. The *liber pontificalis*, moreover, assures us also that the Emperor had ordered all his governors in Italy to receive Pope Constantine on his return 'as though it were he [the Emperor] himself whom they saw before them'. Such receptions comprised the display of banners, acclamations, and the service of the bridle and the stirrup – *officium stratoris* – which used to be rendered to the Pope by the most important members of the lay aristocracy. Those are the actual facts which the forger had in mind; he went beyond them, however, when he stated that the entire panoply of an imperial

---

[13] See Documents, III, p. 177.
[14] This argument has been advanced in particular by P. E. Schramm, in his *Sacerdotium und Regnum im Austausch ihrer Vorrechte.*

procession should be accorded to Sylvester and when he showed the Emperor Constantine performing the *officium stratoris* out of respect for St Peter. No ruler ever rendered such a service to any Pope until Pepin who, when he received Pope Stephen II at Ponthion, held his horse by the bridle for a moment, as though he were a groom. Possibly the author was inspired by this incident.

Another innovation is that Constantine is described as offering Sylvester all the insignia of the Empire: the diadem, the *phrygium* (a tall white pointed head-dress derived from the Byzantine *camelaucum*),[15] the *lorum* (consul's scarf worn round the neck), the sceptres, the crimson *chlamys*, the scarlet tunic, the *signa* (eagle and orb), the *banda* (standards) – in a word the entire imperial regalia. Now, to wear or carry the insignia of the Emperor was, as P. E. Schramm has shown, practically to be identified with him. What confirms this impression still further is that Sylvester had taken over as successor of Constantine in Rome, while the latter, out of respect for the holy apostles, had installed himself in another capital; the Emperor had handed over the Lateran Palace to the Pope; and had conferred the privileges and titles of Roman senators on the clergy.

It is worth noting, however, that the forger did not draw all the logical conclusions from his own arguments. In fact he described Sylvester as renouncing the crown (which was an emblem of empire in the political sense of the term), and contenting himself with the *phrygium* (which was the emblem of spiritual sovereignty). Despite this limitation, however, he made it clear that the Pope held the same rank as the Emperor.

Thus, with the Donation of Constantine, the concept of empire had come to be associated with the Roman pontiffs just at the moment when the titular emperor seemed to be getting further and further away from the West. Master of Rome, the imperial city, emperor by reason of the insignia and the emblems, the successor of Peter and of Sylvester henceforth presented the appearance of a ruler in a sector of the former Empire. For centuries the concept of empire in the West was to suffer from the consequences of the *Constitutum Constantini*.

---

[15] It is thought that it was one of the popes of Greek origin who first adopted this head-dress at the beginning of the eighth century: Constantine I wore it in 710–11 during his stay in Constantinople. The wearing of the *phrygium* became general in Rome in the course of the eighth century at the time when the Pope presided over the stational processions.

III. THE ATTITUDE OF THE GERMANS TO THE EMPIRE

The ideas we have so far examined were all products of Roman thought. It is now time to ask what was the attitude of the Germans towards the Empire.

Although before the invasions certain tribes had succeeded in dominating extensive areas, far beyond the confines of their original home, it seems to be well established that they did not at the beginning have any notion of 'empire'. Occasionally a more powerful figure emerged from among the kings of the various tribes, but none, it is clear, ever possessed the attributes essential to the imperial function – its superior status or pre-eminence. The very term used in the German dialects and languages to designate the Emperor is borrowed from the Greek (*Keisar, Kesur, Casere*) – which, more than any other argument, indicates that the notion of empire came to the Germans from outside, in the event, from the Roman Empire.

Their attitudes towards it varied greatly and at this point the names of several individuals must be mentioned – however ephemeral their efforts. First there was Ataulf, who proposed that the Empire should be consolidated by the force of the Goths, and then Theodoric, in whose view the Ostrogoth kingdom was to assume control of all the Germanic peoples—scattered throughout Romania: both of these two seem to have perceived the possibility of reviving the Empire and of themselves taking the road to universality. But in the end the tendency which prevailed was that of the Vandals, Franks and Lombards, conquerors pure and simple, and creators of states to whom the concept of empire was quite foreign. Their chiefs soon considered themselves the equals of the Emperor: Clovis's grandson, the Austrasian Theodebert, opposed the Goth Theodoric and manifested his independence of the Empire in extremely significant fashion.[16]

On the other hand, it is clear that the learned men who lived in the entourage of certain barbarian kings did not hesitate to borrow from the imperial vocabulary such terms as they thought suitable to describe the sovereignty of the kings they served. Thus, although he himself had recognised Byzantine supremacy, Theodoric's chancellery used the words *imperialis* and *imperium* to describe the authority of this King of the Goths, if not the land over which it was exercised. Towards the middle of the sixth century, the historian Jordanes, writing about the pre-Italian past of the Goth people, spoke of the *imperium* when

[16] The striking of gold coins with his own effigy; a letter to Justinian (*Mon. Germ. Epistolae*, III, 133) enumerating the provinces and the peoples over whom he holds sway and rejecting any tie of dependence on the Emperor.

he referred to the union of several different ethnic groups[17] under Theodoric's control. North of the Alps the names of Rome and the Roman Empire were invoked particularly in order to glorify kings and to show them as heirs to the Empire. Thus Clovis was described by Gregory of Tours[18] as a new Constantine, consul and Augustus. In Britain, imperial achievements which had been connected with the island were remembered when any one of the Anglo-Saxon rulers proved capable of exercising hegemony over his colleagues.[19] The first evidence which we have of this development comes from Adamnan of Hy (Iona), biographer of St Columba. According to him (writing about 690), King Oswald of Northumbria, who led several kings in a battle which they won against the Celt Cadwallader in 653, 'was ordained by God to be Emperor of all Britain.' After him a number of different scholars, particularly the historian Bede, used the term *imperium* (*Saxonum* or *Anglorum*) to describe a ruler's authority when it went beyond the confines of his own land and was imposed by him on other princes: thus the image of the Roman Emperor who had power over the *regna* could be said to have been transferred to Anglo-Saxon Britain. Lastly, among the Franks, the legend of their nation's Trojan origins[20] is strong evidence of their intention to proclaim the equality of the two peoples and to assign to the Franks a place in the evolution of universal history. In brief, the ethnic *amour-propre* of the Germans was best expressed by their comparing themselves to, or even identifying themselves with, Rome.

The Germans had not been very sensitive to Roman universalism but seem to have been more interested in the notion of a Christian Empire, in the widest sense of the term, as described above.[21] There were two ways by which they could set about raising themselves to this level. On the one hand each tribe, after conversion to Roman Catholicism, had the absolute conviction that it constituted the chosen people, specially dear to God – among the Franks this tendency is expressed in a particularly striking way in the famous second prologue to the Salic Law.[22] It should also not be forgotten that from the seventh century the anointing of kings was regarded as very important by the

[17] See in the writings of Cassiodorus and Jordanes (*Mon. Germ. Auctores antiquissimi*, vols. XII and V) the word *Imperium* in the index.

[18] *History of the Franks*, Book II, chapters xxxi and xxxviii (*Mon. Germ. Script. Rer. Merov.*, I, pp. 93 and 98).

[19] In the Anglo-Saxon Chronicle of the ninth century (B. Thorpe, Rolls Series, 23, 1861) we find such a ruler called *bretwalda* (= ruler over the Britons or sovereign over vast spaces).

[20] *Chronicle of the Pseudo-Fredegarius*, Book II, chapters iv–vi (*Mon. Germ. Script. Rer. Merov.*, II, pp. 45–6).

[21] See pp. 4–5.   [22] Geffcken (1898), p. 95.

Visigoths of Spain and from the eighth by the Franks and the Anglo-Saxons. For the Franks, the fact that he had been anointed king actually legalised Pepin's usurpation in 751. Indeed the anointing was destined to replace the pre-Christian magical power of the fallen dynasty by a new charism and in particular, it was an expression of the fact that the Lord had chosen a ruler to reign over his people: the king was *a Deo dilectus, a Deo electus*, before being called 'king by the grace of God'. Like the biblical kings whose prestige shed its light on him, the Frankish ruler had, through being anointed, become the Christ of the Lord; the spirit of God had passed into him; the anointing made a new man of him, the adopted son of the Most High. Invested with a sacred function, he became able to exercise in his kingdom a prerogative which the Emperor was competent to exercise in the Roman Empire: he was protector of the faith and defender of the Church. As leaders of Christian nations, able to match the holy tradition of the Roman Emperor with their own charism, these anointed kings thus found themselves encouraged to take part in the government of the Christian Empire.

To sum up, it now looked as though the concept of empire had, between 476 and the period preceding the coronation of Charlemagne, undergone a very definite process of complete dissociation from its ancient heritage. The Roman Empire had, so to speak, been dissolved, yet at the same time expanded into a Christian Empire: this conception at first signified the political body of Christendom, just as that of the Church signified the religious content – and this new kind of empire was governed by all Christian kings together. In Rome, where the city itself acted as a link connecting the two types of universality, Roman and Christian, competition now broke out between the head of the traditional Empire and the head of the œcumenical Church. How far was a synthesis between all the different elements still feasible?

2

The Concept of Empire in the Time of Charlemagne and the Rebirth of the Western Empire

Charlemagne's coronation on 25th December, 800, presents scholars with many problems which are far from being completely solved. In this chapter we shall refer only to the main ones, those which are relevant to our present study. First of all – can a connexion be traced between the rebirth of the empire as an institution and the interpretation given to the expression 'empire' which was accepted in the time of the Frankish kings at the end of the eighth century? Who was it who actually stimulated the revival? And what was the ritual or ceremony by which a man became emperor? After we have dealt with these questions we shall have to try to understand the nature of the new empire and the effect it had on the concept of empire.

I. THE CONCEPTION OF CHARLES, KING OF THE FRANKS, AS AN EMPEROR

During the last years of the eighth century the Frankish state is described for the first time as 'empire' in some documents. Obviously this was, initially at least, a reflection of the strength of the Franks: when Alcuin spoke of the *decus imperialis regni*[1] of his master, he did so because he considered this expression appropriate to describe the royal status of Charlemagne, who, by his splendour and the extent

[1] Correspondence (*Mon. Germ. Epistolae aevi Karolini*, IV, No. 121 (796–7) p. 177).

of his power, appeared to Alcuin to be worthy to bear a still more illustrious title than that of king. As an Anglo-Saxon he was used to the concept of empire which prevailed in Britain at that time and so, quite naturally, described the Frankish state as 'empire' on account of its extent and the fact that it comprised several nations.[2] At the same time, it would have been impossible for Alcuin to consider the King of the Franks as a sort of hegemonial sovereign (i.e. the leader of a group), as was the case in the island of Britain, since in fact Charlemagne's sovereignty was of a very different kind.

It was indeed not only the extent of his kingdom, but the solidity of the position accorded to him on account of his Christianity, which caused Charlemagne to be surrounded by an aura of prestige, of power and of the symbolism attached to the kings of biblical times. He was a new David, simultaneously *rex et sacerdos*, king and priest – this was how the bishops acclaimed him at the Council of Frankfurt in 794, using a formula cast on the Byzantine model – *basileus kai hiereus*,[3] and this evidently inspired the Frankish sovereigns to start imitating the priesthood – a trend which became increasingly strong and ultimately left a deep impression on the Western concept of empire after 800. *Rex christianissimus*, Charlemagne was Christ's representative on earth, the triumphant Emperor, placed under His protection by the wonderful *Laudes*;[4] the *Laudes* were sung to the king on the occasion of the great liturgical festivals and expressed gratitude for the fact that the king's authority was pre-eminent and for the protection which he received from the celestial powers. The King of the Franks was a Patrician of the Romans and, as it were, the protector of the papacy; with these titles it became his duty to take responsibility for defending the interests of Christendom, and this he himself demonstrated – to the outside world by his arms, and at home by assuring the spreading of the faith.[5]

All this explains a certain dualism in the notion of Christendom. *Populus christianus* sometimes meant all Christian people together who regarded Charlemagne as their rector and guide;[6] which had the effect of placing him on a universal plane. On the other hand, although at times it continued to signify the whole of Christendom, in all parts of the world, the concept of *Imperium christianum* did tend more and

[2] Cf. *The Life of Saint Wilbrod*, chapters xiii and xxiii (*Mon. Germ. Script. Rer. Merov.*, VII, pp. 127 and 133).
[3] To be understood as interpreted by Alcuin, 'King because of his power, priest by the authority of education', letters Nos. 178 and 171, *loc. cit.*, pp. 294 and 281.
[4] See Documents, IV, p. 179.
[5] Letter written in 796, addressed to Leo III, *Epistolae*, IV, No. 93, p. 137
[6] See for example Alcuin's correspondence, *loc. cit.*, Nos. 41, 110, 174.

more to be centred on the Frankish monarchy, the domain of the most notable Christian nation. Frequent evidence of this concentration can be found in the liturgy;[7] moreover, a letter written by Alcuin[8] in 798 put the idea into words and from 799 onwards he used the term on several occasions, when writing about the serious crisis which had broken out in Rome.[9]

Having arrived at this representation of a Christian empire (insofar, of course, as it meant more than a mission common to all rulers) one must ask whether it was now possible to move on from there to the notion of an empire over which Charlemagne ruled. There were indications to suggest that this might be so, for example, the fact that the expression recurs insistently in Alcuin's letters during the years 799 and 800, sometimes accompanied by an outline of the link uniting the 'empire' of Charlemagne to that of the Romans, sometimes by the use of titles recalling those given to Caesars.[10] Nevertheless, there is nothing to indicate that the use of terms of this kind had any direct influence on the mind of Charlemagne: the fact that he took such an extraordinarily long time to prepare for his fourth journey south into Italy seems to prove that the contrary was the case. If there was a Christian empire, its head still remained king: surely Alcuin realised this better than anyone – did he not, in his famous letter on the three supreme powers, list first the papacy, then the Roman Empire and after them the *regalis dignitas* of his master?[11]

One should not exaggerate what has been called Alcuin's 'imperial programme', nor the part which he personally played in the re-establishment of the Empire. If the revival was in fact consciously planned by Charlemagne's entourage, it is improbable that Alcuin's point of view was the only one taken into consideration. As a matter of fact, there is an echo of a very different kind in a poem by an anonymous poet to whom we owe the description of the meeting of the King and the Pope at Paderborn.[12] Among the stream of epithets which he poured out on Charlemagne we find phrases which can only be called pure hyperbole; 'Head of the world, summit of Europe . . . placed on the pinnacle of the empire, Charles towers above all the kings of the earth. . . .' On four occasions he calls the King 'Augustus',

---

[7] *Imperium Christianum* or *Francorum* being substituted for *Imperium Romanum*. Not invariably, however: because the Frankish church adopted Roman usage, the old tradition was often maintained.

[8] Letter No. 136.

[9] See Nos. 148, 177, 185, 200, 202, 211, 217, 234.

[10] See for example Nos. 200 and 202.

[11] See Documents, V, p. 180.

[12] *Mon. Germ. Poetae latini*, I: see especially lines 86, 92–4, 98.

once in connexion with Aix-la-Chapelle, which was at that time in the course of construction. As for Aix-la-Chapelle itself, the poet calls it the second Rome, or 'the Rome to come', *Roma ventura*, as if he were talking about the metropolis of a new empire. Nevertheless, we should not make too much of all this: indeed, one striking fact must not be overlooked – in the long list of descriptions attached to the name of Charles, the title of *imperator* does not once occur. Charles was not an emperor; at most he held the rank of one.

So, to sum up: all the written evidence available from before 800 A.D. reveals a vocabulary on matters imperial which is evocative and no more. Was the Empire to be reborn? Let us see what the King of the Franks and the Pope each in turn had to say in answer to this question.

II. CHARLEMAGNE – THE EMPEROR

Charlemagne's own views about the Empire and the concept of empire in general emerge very clearly in the story of his relations with Byzantium. At an early date we find him demanding to be treated as the absolute equal of the *basileus*; this is proved by certain usages of his chancellery, in particular the use of the lead seal to authenticate documents. Yet, despite his imitation of the Byzantine Caesars, Charlemagne demonstrated his antagonism to their pretensions.

In 787, the Empress Irene summoned a meeting of the second Council of Nicaea, in order to settle the question of the Images, and when the Council claimed to lay down the law on behalf of the universal Church, the Franks' reaction was swift; the vehement language of their retort, transmitted to us in the *Libri Karolini* of 792, reflects the indignation roused at the king's court by the Byzantine initiative. Without going into the details of the religious controversy, let us look only at the political idea expressed in this famous document. From the outset it represents Charlemagne as ruler over 'the Gauls, Germania, Italy and the neighbouring provinces',[13] that is to say, the lands to which his double title of King and Patrician were applicable, but whose names evoked those of the provinces of the Roman Empire. He was thus taking advantage of memories of the Empire's past greatness to set himself up as the absolute equal of the ruler of any other part of the Empire, who by tradition had a right to the name

---

[13] *Mon. Germ. Concilia*, II, supplement.

Roman. But he denied the title of emperor to any such ruler; throughout the whole of the document only 'the King residing at Constantinople' is mentioned. Very probably the Frankish chancellery had discovered the precise meaning of the word *basileus* and so the idea of parity between the two rulers was expressed as plainly as possible – it was a denial of any claim by Byzantium to universal domination. In Charlemagne's eyes it was as though the domain of the former Empire had been divided into two great kingdoms; and that of the Franks, being profoundly Christian and orthodox, was inherently universal. 'Here', say the *Libri*, referring to the Cross, 'here is the emblem of our Emperor, [i.e. Christ] Whom our cohorts follow into battle.'

However, nothing actually happened as a result of the enunciation of these principles; Charlemagne did not ever lay claim to the Roman succession in the West; as late as 798 he refused the imperial crown which was offered to him by an embassy from Byzantium.[14] It was enough to him that he spoke in the name of the West and that he ruled there as supreme king. Such was the prestige of his kinghood that the addition of a new title could scarcely augment it.

Yet Charlemagne found himself being borne imperceptibly towards the imperial throne. The initiative for this movement came from the papacy and is to be seen as the last step in its political separation from Byzantium, which had been proceeding by stages – the Italian revolution of 726, the foundation of the Papal State, the conferment of the title of Patrician on the King of the Franks. It was in Rome that the ground was being slowly prepared for Charlemagne's accession to the Empire. Nothing could be more impressive than the account given in P. E. Schramm's book[15] of how one by one the privileges granted in the city to the Byzantine Emperor were accorded to the King of the Franks, the Patrician – a ceremonial reception in accordance with Constantinople customs, prayers for him in the liturgy, the dating of pontifical Acts in accordance with the years of his reign, the presence of statues of him in the churches. The conveyance of these privileges began during the time when Hadrian I was pope and became even more noticeable under Leo III, whose first action was to send Charlemagne an official verbatim record of his election and the keys of the *Confessio* of Saint Peter, the *vexillum Romanae urbis*, as a sign of

[14] Cf. H. Löwe, '*Eine Kölner Notiz zum Kaisertum Karls d.G.*', *Rheinische Vierteljahrsblätter*, xiv, 1949.

[15] *Die Anerkennung Karls des Grossen als Kaiser*, pp. 8–30.

the king's dominion over the city. Five years later, on 25th December, 800, when the king happened to be in Rome in order to re-establish order, which had been seriously upset by the revolt of 799, the Pope took the decisive step.

Leo III certainly did not act on his own and the Romans must have made an approach to the king along with him, but it is difficult to discover just what their rôle was. We cannot completely disregard the evidence of the *Annales Laureshamenses*,[16] in which it is related that a gathering of ecclesiastics and laymen, summoned on 23rd December by the king, to receive Leo III's oath of disculpation, arrived at the decision that the Empire should be re-established under Charlemagne.[17] If such views were in fact expressed, we must nevertheless interpret them less as the election of a king to be an emperor – this was to come later in accordance with the traditional procedures of the Empire – than as a simple wish. The assumption that the question of the Empire was in fact discussed during the weeks preceding Christmas makes it easier to understand how events actually unrolled on that day.

One cannot fail to be struck by the two divergent aspects of the ceremonial which brought about Charlemagne's accession to the imperial throne: it was certainly an adaptation of the liturgy used in Byzantium when an emperor was proclaimed (acclamation, corona-tion, *proscynesis*); but on the other hand it had a peculiar originality, plus a degree of improvisation. Contemporary sources unanimously agree that the first step was the setting of a crown on Charlemagne's head by Leo III immediately after the prayer of the Mass of the day, heard by all present lying prostrated. The Pope's action was the signal for the acclamation by the Romans; the words transmitted to us by the royal *Annales* and the *Liber Pontificalis* correspond exactly to those of the Frankish *Laudes*, except that the titles of King and Patrician are replaced by the imperial appellation. The *Liber Pontificalis* then ascribed constitutional force to this acclamation; later, moreover, it was accepted in Rome as the election of Charlemagne: yet it is important to stress that the essential effect of the acclamation on 25th December, 800, was that Charlemagne was thereby officially recognised as the newly created emperor, or, better still, it was a public proclamation – as in an Epiphany, in the full sense of the word – of the imperial status of the King of the Franks. In addition it was followed by the *Laudes*, properly so called, though it is not really possible to say whether there was a clear distinction between the acclamation and the *Laudes*. Thereafter Leo III 'adored' Charlemagne, that is to say, by the *proscynesis* rendered

---

[16] *Mon. Germ. Script.*, I, p. 37.   [17] See Documents, VI, p. 181.

him the homage which his predecessors (and the patriarch of Byzantium) had customarily rendered to an emperor in acknowledgment of his being invested with a superior eminence.

In the eyes of the Pope and of the Romans the Empire had now been effectively re-established in its former metropolis. It is, however, extremely likely that the new Caesar was not satisfied by the way in which the event had taken place, even if the event itself had pleased him. Einhard's evidence on this point is irrefutable and it is easy to guess the reasons for Charlemagne's dissatisfaction: the important part assumed by the Pope in his accession; the rôle of the Romans, who had been substituted for the Franks; the need to legalise what might be interpreted in Byzantium as a patent usurpation. In a word, a new situation had been created which the Emperor would have to clear up, if not indeed correct.

III. TOWARDS A NEW CONCEPT OF EMPIRE

The question now arises whether Charlemagne's coronation was regarded by the Empire as a whole as being equivalent to the creation of an anti-emperor set up by the *pars Occidentis* in opposition to the *pars Orientis* and whether indeed it actually signified this. In the months which followed, this may well be how it looked to those surrounding Leo III and it was certainly so regarded in Constantinople. Such an interpretation would explain the plan for a marriage between Charlemagne and Irene (mentioned by only one historian, the Byzantine Theophanes), which would have been a way to legalise the proclamation of the Empire. This report, which may well have been founded on no more than a simple rumour, need not be discussed in detail here, but it should be noted as an indication of the initial uncertainty felt at the creation of this new situation.

Charlemagne, however, was not slow to make his own views very plain. He regarded the Empire, which he had perhaps not sought, as based on the principles previously proclaimed by the *Libri Karolini*: absolute equality of the two monarchs. At the same time, between 800 and 814, he directed his Empire internally along two different lines, about which we are remarkably well-informed by the source documents.

Let us look first at the imperial seal with its extremely characteristic inscriptions and engravings.[18] On the right side we find in abbreviated

[18] Reproduced in Schramm, *Kaiserbilder*, II, plate 7.

form the formula 'Our Lord Charles, pious, everlasting and august Emperor', taken from the old titles of the Caesars; on the obverse we see represented the gate of a city, inscribed with the name '*Roma*' and around this the inscription '*Renovatio Romani Imperii*', an expression of the tradition, inherited from antiquity, that the Empire would be 'renewed'.[19] Moreover, in this current of thought, the Roman Empire undoubtedly played a greater rôle than the city of Rome: Charlemagne's imperial title proves this.

It was not until 29th May, 801, that he took the title in its final form; the fact that he took so long to draw this up tells us much about the Emperor's hesitations, and about the trouble he took to make his thoughts clear. The title on which he finally settled was as follows: 'Charles, most serene Augustus, crowned by God, great and pacific Emperor, governing the Roman Empire, and similarly, by the grace of God, King of the Franks and the Lombards.' This formula was a combination of the elements already in use before the year 800 (the royal title, the Caroline Books, the *Laudes*) and the imperial acclamation of the 25th December. '*Augustus, magnus et pacificus imperator*', is a repetition of the ritual formula of the acclamation. '*A Deo coronatus*' puts the emphasis on God's choice and makes the Pope the simple executive agent of the design of Providence: as early as 801 a capitulary bore the superscription '*a divino nutu coronatus*', recalling the '*nutu Dei regis Francorum*' of the Caroline Books. '*Romanum gubernans Imperium*' must similarly be seen alongside the titles which, in consequence of the personal link between Charlemagne and the Franks, had proclaimed the area over which the royal authority was exercised, '*regis Francorum, Gallias, Germaniam Italiamque regentis*'. If we accept that '*gubernans*' has taken the place of '*regentis*', would not the term '*Imperium Romanum*' embrace the three provinces formerly enumerated? In that case it would be evidence that Charlemagne's imperial authority applied to the former Western Empire. But the substitution of '*gubernans*' for '*regens*' is, in turn, evocative. We know now that the expression is not new, as it is found in the *Corpus Juris* and in the formularies used in Italy.[20] Yet it does evoke the task of the captain at the wheel and seems to express very well the responsibility of the Emperor for general control over all Christian people within the scope of the Roman Empire. So it means, 'Emperor in charge of the Roman Empire' not 'Emperor of the Romans'. It is a subtle distinction: Rome conferred the stamp of authenticity on this Empire, born within her walls, but she was not in

[19] See below, pp. 29 *et seq.*
[20] Classen, '*Romanum Gubernans Imperium*', *Zeitschr. für Rechtsgeschichte*, G.A., 1950.

fact its centre. That is the reason why Charlemagne combined the two formulas in his title – '*Romanum gubernans Imperium et rex Francorum et Langobardorum*'; the old personal link uniting these two nations with the king is henceforth set in a framework into which in future other nations may also enter; seen from this angle the Roman tradition was being vigorously restored to life.

On another level too it was re-emerging: in 802, Charlemagne, in his rôle of Emperor, imposed a new oath on his subjects; instructions given to his *missi* on this occasion demonstrate clearly that the inhabitants of the Empire were to be made aware of their responsibilities and that they must be loyal, not only towards their prince in his personal capacity, but to the cause which he incarnated and which was that of the public interest.[21]

In the last years of his reign the direction which Charlemagne had given in this manner to his Empire underwent a vital transformation: it passed from the conception of a Roman Empire to that of a Frankish Empire, and it did so the more easily because from the time of his coronation Charlemagne had not wanted to be Emperor of Rome.

This change must be seen essentially as a concession to Byzantium. A violent anti-Western reaction had set in there, entailing as a consequence the fall of Irene; Nicephorus I, her successor, broke with the Frankish court; from 803 to 810, the two empires fought against each other in Italy. The degree of uncertainty ruling in those years can be measured by the fact that the *Ordinatio* of 806 did not mention the rank of emperor – as though Charlemagne wanted to make reservations about the future. However, in the course of conversations reopened in 810, the Byzantine envoy was able to record that the Frankish ruler nourished no universal ambitions and was not striving to exercise more than a rather superior sort of regal authority in the West. Ultimately they arrived at a compromise: according to Theophanes, Michael Rhangabe, who had succeeded Nicephorus, was resigned to recognising Charlemagne as his spiritual brother and to having him saluted with the titles of *basileus* and *imperator*, Emperor of the Franks. In so doing he was recognising, in the Carolingian Empire, the 'imperial kinghood' which Alcuin had already described before 800. On the other hand, Michael claimed the status of Roman Empire for his own kingdom, giving himself, from 812, the title '*basileus tôn Romaiôn*'.

From then on we note that Charlemagne, though he retained the

[21] See the comments of L. Halphen, '*L'Idée d'État sous les Caroling ens*', in *A travers l'histoire du Moyen-Age*, p. 96.

formula '*Romanum gubernans Imperium*' on his documents, avoided using this title when he corresponded with Byzantium. A letter he addressed in 813 to the Emperor Michael is signed simply: '*Imperator et Augustus idemque rex Francorum et Langobardorum*'.[22] As for the Empire itself, it tended more and more frequently to be described in liturgical manuscripts as '*Imperium christianum*'.

The Franks were the main support of this Empire and Aix was its real capital. The town's status received the full light of day in September, 813, when, the situation on the Eastern side having been clarified, Charlemagne was able to think about his successor. He now made his son Louis his associate, calling him *consors regni*, and enabling him to share his authority, using terms which correct the impressions about the coronation of the year 800 and exclude the papacy from the right to allocate the Empire to the person of its choice. The ceremony took place in the Palatine Chapel of Aix; Charlemagne's youngest son was acclaimed emperor by the Franks; Louis received the diadem from his father or took it himself from the altar. This ritual, although based on that of the association of a Caesar and a Byzantine *basileus*, does indeed throw a light on the Frankish character of the Empire at the end of the great reign. At this stage it corresponds pretty well with the image of which we had a glimpse earlier—the supreme authority *qui praecellit in mundo*, a supremacy which is not tied to Rome. One writer could then say: 'The notion of empire became capable of a geographical and national determination.'[23]

So in the end it was the Christian religion which gave the new Empire its essential stability, that is to say, its fundamental character, regardless of its relations with Rome; as before 800, it remained the *Imperium christianum*. The only noticeable difference by comparison with the first part of the reign was that the imperial status reinforced still more strongly the spiritual and moral dominion of Charlemagne, who was seen to have taken on the responsibility of protecting and preserving God's people to an even greater extent than in the past.[24] We are thus on the road towards the realisation of political Augustinism: the State, conceived as the rule of Wisdom and as preparing the City of God, impregnated by the Spiritual; the Church and the Empire welded together in one Western Christendom.

Thus Charlemagne's concept of empire was first and foremost a religious view of the order of the world.

[22] *Mon. Germ. Epistolae*, IV, p. 546.
[23] F. L. Ganshof, '*La fin du règne de Charlemagne*', in *Zeitschrift für Schweizerische Geschichte*, 1948.
[24] L. Halphen, *Charlemagne et L'Empire carolingien*, pp. 208 *et seq.*

3

Vicissitudes of the Concept of Empire in the Ninth Century

During the century which followed the death of Charlemagne the whole concept of empire, at least as it had been understood between 800 and 814, gradually underwent a process of dissolution. This was primarily due to the fact that the nations living on the different sides of the Alps held different views of the Empire; two images existed side by side, but did not necessarily coincide – indeed, such syntheses as did occur were purely accidental – and in 924 the Empire became extinct.

I. THE CONCEPT OF THE EMPIRE AS A FRANKISH INSTITUTION

Under Louis the Pious, the concept of empire at first retained the form which it had taken towards the end of Charlemagne's reign. Indeed, it became stronger and its influence became deeper. From his first appearance on the scene the new sovereign took the title of *Imperator Augustus*. He thus abandoned at one and the same time the royal titles, which were sacrificed to the Empire in acknowledgment of its status both as a fact and as an institution, and, following his father's example, the connexion with Rome: the new seal, which bore the simple inscription *Renovatio regni Francorum*, was an expression of the same line of thought. At the same time the religious character of the Empire's function was greatly amplified. In the eyes of Louis the Pious and the clerics around him, the Empire, scarcely distinguishable from the Church, was the body of Christ; its essential mission was to ensure

26

the triumph of Christianity: '*christiana religio*', proclaims one of the monetary tokens (incidentally borrowing the phrase from the preceding reign), while in the iconography the Emperor is represented not with the Lance, but with the Cross and the buckler of the faith.[1]

The imperial government toiled methodically to turn this programme into reality. First, they took steps towards a reformation of the Church and thereafter, in 817, started on the constitution of the monarchy. There had to be a monarchy with a constitution in order to facilitate the maintenance of Christian unity and peace. So the former customary divisions were swept aside by the *Ordinatio Imperii* of 817; Lothair, the eldest son of the Emperor Louis the Pious, became his partner and in due course succeeded him as sole ruler. The kingdoms of his brothers Pepin and Louis were made subject to him; the conduct of foreign policy was within the exclusive competence of the Emperor. Thus, politically, the concept of Empire came to mean the preponderance of the *Imperator* over the kings, and the *regna* came, so to speak, under the roof of the *Imperium Francorum*.[2] Under Charlemagne the concept of empire had been linked with the idea of preponderance over the West, but from now on it had an almost exclusively Frankish content.

It was, however, apparently not to maintain this for long. Even before the *Ordinatio* had been promulgated, Pope Stephen IV had hastened to stamp a Roman imprint on the monarchy of Louis the Pious. This he succeeded in doing by means of the anointing ritual, which transformed the imperial function from *nomen* (as it had been until then) into *ordo*. In October, 816, the Pope anointed Louis at Rheims. Furthermore, the poet Ermold the Black, to whom we owe an account of this ceremony, alleges that Stephen IV, in the name of St Peter, placed the diadem of Constantine[3] on the head of Louis, almost certainly an allusion to the right of the ruling pontiff to decide who should wear the imperial crown – a right the popes claimed by virtue of the Donation of the first Christian emperor. This was, of course, a repetition of what Leo had done in 800, and by his action Stephen was seeking to re-institute what Charlemagne had 'corrected' in 813. Simultaneously, he was creating a tradition to which Lothair I, who had been Emperor since 817, had in his turn to submit six years later in Rome. From then on it was accepted that as part of the process of becoming emperor one was obliged to submit to the rite of anointing

---

[1] Reproduced in Schramm, *Kaiserbilder*, II, plates 14 and 15.

[2] H. Mitteis, *Der Vertrag von Verdun*, pp. 71 *et seq.*

[3] Life of Louis the Pious, lines 423–8 (*Mon. Germ. Poetae*, II, p. 36).

and to the coronation ceremony performed in the city of the apostles by the Pope. This was important if only because it had the effect of diminishing the rôle of Aix-la-Chapelle, which thus became no more than the Empire's second metropolis: in addition, it made a breach in the independence of the institution itself by putting it under a peculiarly heavy obligation.

In its new form the concept of empire underwent a serious crisis which began in 829 and was brought to an end by the signature of the Treaty of Verdun in 843, under the terms of which the unitary monarchy was abolished: it was succeeded by three states, to each of which was given a status of absolute equality with the other two. Although the sovereign of one of them, Lothair, had been Emperor since 817, there is no indication that the imperial title gave him any greater juridical rights than his two brothers: the kingdoms which had in 817 been subject to the power of the Emperor were now independent. Moreover, in the years following 843, the expression *Imperium Francorum* suffered a complete eclipse: it is encountered only exceptionally and is then used to describe the Frankish states taken as a group.

Nevertheless, despite these divisions, the unity of the *regnum Francorum* persisted and the concept of empire was thereby preserved: in a letter written to Pope Leo IV, Lothair remarked that the *regnum* was not so much divided as composed of three distinct parts.[4] The sharing of the monarchy, moreover, implied that it was governed in common by the three brothers, and in actual fact a régime which was known as 'the régime of fraternity and concord' made its appearance between 843 and 855, and, in theory at least, took over the functions of the Empire. But this too was swept away by actual events: namely, a re-partitioning after the death of Lothair and the growing ambition of his two surviving brothers, Louis the German and Charles the Bald, to reconstruct the *regnum Francorum* as a single unit for their own benefit.

This policy, which aimed at re-uniting the different territories, revived the concept of empire which, without at first being in any way linked with Rome, became attached to whichever of the Carolingian princes seemed to possess the most power. Thus, when in 869 Charles the Bald was anointed King of Lorraine at Metz, the Annalist of Fulda believed that the reason why he had himself called Emperor and Augustus was 'because from now on he possessed two kingdoms'.[5]

[4] Text in A. Kleinclausz, *L'Empire carolingien*, p. 366, note 1.
[5] *Mon. Germ.*, S.R.G., p. 69.

Similar evidence, with perhaps a more complex background, could be produced for Louis the German: the wide extent of his kingdom and the diversity of the nations over whom he reigned, explain why the monk Notker of St Gall gave him the imperial title.[6]

Even the Empire of Charlemagne itself was affected by this assessment. In Notker's eyes Charles was first and foremost 'emperor over several nations'; and it was this multiple domination which gave him the right, from the angle of apostolic authority, to the title (*nomen*) of Caesar and Augustus.[7] Apparently then, what the Empire was *de facto* took precedence in the eyes of the chronicler over what it was *de jure*: hegemony over numerous peoples was the first step on the ladder leading to the throne of the Caesars. This way of looking at the situation was not unrealistic: it was a reasonable deduction to make from the picture given by those accessions to the imperial throne which the monk of St Gall himself had witnessed. Before studying these, however, we must take a look at another image of the Empire, which existed side by side with the one we have just been describing: this picture is a composite one, made up of the ideas of both the Pope and the Romans.

II. THE ROMANISATION OF THE CONCEPT OF EMPIRE

The coronation of Louis the Pious and Lothair in turn by Stephen IV and Paschal I respectively constituted an affirmation of the connexion between the Frankish Empire and Rome. Although at first extremely artificial, this link became more of a reality when Lothair's eldest son, Louis, came to Pavia and settled there in order to exercise a kind of active and present delegation on behalf of the Emperor. Pope Sergius II consecrated him King of the Lombards in 844; six years later he was anointed emperor by Leo IV, very probably at his father's request, although it must be noted that, unlike Louis the Pious (in 813) and Lothair (in 817), this particular Louis had not previously been elected at Aix-la-Chapelle. This disregard of Aix-la-Chapelle became even more obvious in 855, when, after the death of Lothair, his two younger sons succeeded him, one in Central Francia and the other in Provence, whereas the eldest, holder of the imperial title, found his territory reduced to Italy. As a consequence the Empire, having lost

---

[6] *Deeds of Charlemagne*, Book II, chapter xi, *Mon. Germ. Script.*, II, p. 754.
[7] *Ibid.*, Book I, chapter xxvi, *loc. cit.*, p. 743.

its Frankish foundation, became a sort of Lombard kingdom, recon-
stituted and unified, an Italo-Roman empire;[8] the Emperor became the
Pope's immediate neighbour, in conditions which made co-existence
difficult, particularly during the pontificate of Nicholas I (858–68),
who gave the impression that he himself was the true ruler of the
West; the Empire's rôle developed into being not so much that of
protecting the universal Church as rather that of defending the Church
of Rome against its internal and external enemies. In the second half
of the ninth century, the concept of empire itself took on a Roman
colouring, which it was never again to lose, and was affected by repercussions from various lively influences then current in Rome, which
must now be briefly outlined.

The first of these was an enthusiastic admiration for Rome: one
could almost call it a cult of the city, inherited from the past, but now
imbued with the spirit of Christianity. It was put into words in a
number of expressions, all evocative of splendid pictures: *Aurea Roma*,
Rome gilded by the splendour of her monuments, her past glory, her
present mission; *Roma caput mundi*, capital of the world; *Urbs orbis*,
metropolis of the civilised world which had been converted to Christianity by the city's efforts; Rome, the city of the apostles, 'Oh fortunate Rome,' cried Paulinus of Aquileia in a hymn still used on 29th June,
'crimson with the blood of such great princes, unique in beauty, thou
art more great than all other cities!' Rome, holy city, mother of the
Churches; Rome, residence of the Pope, adorned since the days of
Constantine with the glory of the Empire; Rome, where the Caesars
no longer dwelt but which none the less remained the *Urbs regia*, the
spiritual metropolis of the Empire, likewise the capital of Christendom.
All these images had been familiar to the inhabitants of the city since
the fifth century; at an early date they had been accepted into all
Western literature; the Carolingian renaissance brought them once
more to public notice, all the more so because the city of Rome had
once more become the scene of the Emperor's accession.

This lyrical theme, constantly repeated, encouraged the thoughts of
men to turn towards the possibility of a rebirth, or, as they said in
those days, a Renovation. At the same time, it was not a new idea,
for it was derived from the theme of the eternal nature of the city and
of the Empire, assured by successive resuscitations. Since the moment
when the former Empire had fallen, there had been several occasions
on which a compelling desire for a revival had sprung up and seemed
to be about to be realised – first at the time of Justinian's reconquest;

---

[8] *The Annals of Saint-Bertin* (year 863) describe Louis as *Imperator Italiae.*

then in the first third of the eighth century, when the *sanctae Dei ecclesiae respublica Romanorum* was constituted; lastly, at the time of the proclamation of 25th December, 800, announcing an empire which was the *Renovatio Imperii Romani*: thereafter, hope remained alive in all minds, though one must be careful not to exaggerate the degree to which this affected the Empire; from the period of which we are now speaking the idea of a Renewal seemed to relate not so much to the concept of empire itself as to the groups between which Rome was divided – the papacy and the aristocracy.

The aims of the papacy were apparently the following: to penetrate the Empire with its influence (the Empire was indeed Roman, but this was because it descended from the Rome of St Peter);[9] to bind the Empire to the Kingdom of Italy; to have, in the Emperor, a docile assistant and therefore to be able to intervene in his nomination, if not actually to select him directly; lastly and most important of all, to establish that the rite of anointing was the positive constitutional act by which a man became Augustus. This was in detail the programme of John VIII (872–82). He exploited memories of the past – to remind the emperors of their duties in relation to Rome, to exalt Latinity and the triumphs of the *Romulida gens* and to win over the Roman aristocracy.

The vision of the latter was very much more limited and narrow, scarcely going beyond the horizons of Rome and the state of St Peter. To this feudal society of landowners and warriors, what mattered was to be able to control the papacy as an institution and also the administration of the city and its lands. Any interest which these new 'senators' had in the Empire was restricted to the way it affected their own interests. They recalled that it was they who had acclaimed Charlemagne on 25th December, 800, and therefore asserted that from that date they had the right to participate in the election of every emperor. But what they really cared about was that they should be given a free hand in Rome, whose glorious past they aimed at reviving. They expected that such a return to the Golden Age would be to their benefit, in that it would mean the restoration of old offices and posts: the senate had already been revived, if not exactly as a council at least as a name; governorships and other high posts reappeared in the tenth century. What mattered most to such a *gens togata*, the 'descendants of the Scipios and the Fabii', was to re-establish

[9] A conception which spread also to the Transalpine countries. 'Happy the Empire,' cried the poet Florus, 'had it but known its good fortune, to have Rome for its citadel and, for its founder, Saint Peter, holder of the Keys of Heaven!' (*Poetae*, II, p. 561).

the external trappings of the glory of the old days – 'the *fasces* and the curule chairs, the rings and the triumphal processions, the white tunics and the crimson mantles'[10] – whose reappearance would be the tangible evidence of such a revival. These aristocratic families had a similar image of the Empire: it might sometimes disappear; when it was there the Empire was quite unreal, completely unsubstantial; on the other hand, people liked the picture given by its grandiose setting. For the Romans such a conception of the *Renovatio Imperii* made sense and in consequence they were to play a considerable rôle in enriching the concept of empire in the course of the centuries.

Under Louis II the process was just beginning. Yet, the Roman character of his Empire impressed him sufficiently to stimulate him to write, in 871, his famous letter to the Emperor Basil.[11]

III. ACCESSIONS TO THE IMPERIAL THRONE BETWEEN 875 AND 915

The question of a successor to Louis II in 875 marked the triumph of the conception which both the Romans and the Popes had of the Empire. The papacy took the lead and associated the local aristocracy with its actions. Even before the Emperor died, Pope Hadrian II began to look for a suitable candidate to succeed him and, setting aside Carloman, son of Louis the German, whom Louis II had nominated as his successor, chose Charles the Bald. Writing to him the Pope said: 'We ourselves, all the clergy, the people and the nobility of the whole world and of this city *(totius orbis et urbis)*, desire to have you not only as chief and king, but as patrician, emperor and defender of the Church.'[12]

John VIII continued to implement this programme, being careful to base it on incontestable juridical foundations. He informed Charles that his brothers among the clergy and the illustrious senate of Rome had united at the mention of his name[13] – doubtless the procedure he used was that of a synod, presided over by the Pope, in which laymen participated, and where, acting (according to his own statement) under the inspiration of the Holy Spirit, he caused those present to approve the name of Charles. Some weeks later, on 25th December, 875, the

---

[10] So said Eugenius Vulgarius, contemporary of Pope Sergius III (904–11), in a poem (*Mon. Germ. Poetae latini*, IV, p. 440).

[11] See Documents, VII, p. 181.

[12] *Mon. Germ. Epistolae aevi Karol.*, VI, No. 36 (dated 872), p. 745.

[13] *Epistolae*, VII, No. 59 (written in September 875), p. 311.

King received the imperial unction at Rome, not without first binding himself to be a soldier of the papacy: through being anointed, the King of the Franks was constituted Emperor, as John VIII had himself said.[14] Prompted by the Pope, an assembly of the great and the bishops of the kingdom of Italy, meeting at Pavia in February, 876, gave their approval to what had happened at Rome and in their turn elected Charles, if not King, at least 'Protector, Lord and Defender of us all'. It was the Pope once more who presided at the Council of Ponthion (in the summer of 876), where the Franks received notification of the Emperor's consecration by the Pope and acclaimed their King as Emperor, while on this occasion he wore the *chlamys* of silk and the diadem, and carried the sceptre and gold stick, insignia of his new dignity.[15] The seal he used henceforth bore the inscription *Renovatio Imperii Romani et Francorum*,[16] thus providing a link with the ideas expressed in Louis II's letter. The last act in this long process was John VIII's confirmation of Charles as Emperor, in the presence of a purely ecclesiastical assembly held at Ravenna in August, 877.

Charles's accession to the Empire – *S. Romana Ecclesia religioso utero vos genuit*, wrote John VIII to his spiritual son[17] – had a profound effect on the concept of empire in days to come; the new Emperor found himself compelled immediately to make considerable concessions and had to put himself entirely at the disposal of the pontiff: but as he died in 877 he had in any case no opportunity to undertake anything on his own.

The manner in which Charles the Fat succeeded him had some features in common with the events just related. The candidate was selected by the Pope 'for the benefit and exaltation of the Holy Roman Church',[18] although not without some hesitation, for the imperial throne had been vacant for four years. John VIII anointed Charles the Fat Emperor on 12th February, 881. But the atmosphere was no longer the same as in 875 – Charles did not seem disposed to leave the pontiff a free hand in Rome. What is more, he was interested in neither the defence of the city nor the aspirations of its nobility; the seal he used proclaimed the *Renovatio regni Francorum*, as did that of Louis the Pious.[19] Thus there was nothing Roman about his Empire, and

---

[14] Cf. the records of the proceedings of the Council of Ponthion (*Mon. Germ. Capitularia*, II, No. 279, pp. 348 *et seq.*).

[15] *Annals of Saint-Bertin and of Fulda* (year 876).

[16] Reproduced in Schramm, *Kaiserbilder*, II, Plate 36.

[17] *Epistolae*, VII, No. 56 (written in May, 877), p. 51.

[18] *Epistolae*, VII, No. 224 (written in February or March, 880), p. 199. The first mention of this selection occurs in No. 168 (dated the 3rd April, 879), p. 136.

[19] *Kaiserbilder*, II, Plate 43.

his aim seemed to be the regrouping of the Frankish *regna* under one single sceptre. In fact, beginning in 880 when he had had himself proclaimed King of Italy, Charles the Fat pursued a policy of re-uniting the separate territories, incorporating successively the whole of Germania and then Western Francia under his rule. Charles's ephemeral domination was based on the imperial title (of pontifical origin) and a return to Frankish unity (which was another progenitor of the Empire), but it lacked one essential element – a synthesis of its various components: his Empire was simply a juxtaposition of *regna* under one sceptre.

The two Charleses had taken the imperial title out of Italy: it returned there in 891 only to become confused with the Kingdom of Italy, when it was assumed by Guy of Spoleto and his son Lambert. On that occasion the initiative came from the notables of Italy, who were anxious to acquire an effective protector against external dangers. The Pope had inevitably to follow this movement, but he remained hostile to the two princes, fearing the papacy might be placed under their domination. Ultimately the Pope set up a redoubtable competitor to oppose them – Arnulf, King of Germany, who exercised a *de facto* hegemony over the states which had been created in 887 as a result of the ultimate disintegration of the Carolingian Empire. He was obliged to fight his way to Rome by the sword and to take the city by assault before he was crowned by Formosus in 896. The manner of his accession undoubtedly contributed to the feeling that one could become Roman Emperor by force of conquest, so emphasising once more the military character of the institution: thus the picture of a new type of emperor was built up, which was never to vanish entirely.

The surrender of Italy by Arnulf inaugurated a new period of effacement for the Empire, which persisted up to 962. The institution itself was going steadily downhill. In the cases of Lambert of Spoleto (who died in 898), Louis of Provence (Emperor in 901) and Berengar of Friuli (915–24), it was no more than a title which augmented the prestige of a much fought-over Italian kingdom, and also a means whereby the papacy procured a defender (generally completely ineffective) against the Roman aristocracy which, at the end of the ninth century, had succeeded in bringing down the ecclesiastical administration of Rome and of the Papal States, and in replacing it by its own rule. The Renewal movement bore its first fruits then in the form of Theophylact, master of the wardrobe in the papal palace, master of the militia and senator of all the Romans. Through his daughter Marozia, a 'senatress', his authority was transmitted to his grandson Alberic, who took the title of *princeps* and successfully prevented the transfer of the imperial crown to Hugh of Provence (932–42).

So it was that the Roman aristocracy, in its desire to retain the city for itself, deliberately kept the Western imperial throne unoccupied. Simultaneously, the other universal authority had become totally subject to the masters of the hour: the papacy had never been in such a state of dependency upon a temporal power as it was during the second third of the tenth century in relation to Alberic. No doubt, the aim the latter had in mind was to stimulate the Romans to amalgamate the power of the prince and the power of the Pope: for that reason he thrust his son Octavian (the name alone indicated the kind of programme he had in mind) on to the throne of St. Peter. However, it was under the pontificate of this same Octavian (John XII) that the Empire was to be restored in a manner which the Romans most certainly did not at all expect.

To sum up: two, or even three, images of the Empire can be discerned during the ninth century – the Frankish Empire, Charlemagne's heritage; the Roman Empire, conferred by the papacy either alone or with the support of the city's inhabitants; the Empire which a powerful sovereign acquired by conquest through first making himself master of Rome. The first two of these three conceptions could exist simultaneously without being fused and the imperial coronation could achieve their synthesis. As for the third conception, the seizure of the Empire by conquest (in the style of the Italian expedition undertaken by Arnulf) could also be legalised by an imperial coronation. In each case, whatever the method, the papacy emerged as considerably increased in stature.

BOOK II
Extension and Fragmentation of the Notion of Empire

4

The Diversity of the Tenth Century: the Empire's Second Rebirth (2nd February, 962)

Although, as we have seen, the Empire was reborn and flourished in part of Europe during the ninth century, it requires no more than a brief glance at the reigns of the extremely weak emperors who succeeded one another between 899 and 924 to see that during that period the Empire as an institution ceased to exist in that very same part of Europe. Nevertheless the idea of empire did remain alive in men's minds – it persisted in those states which had constituted the *Regnum Francorum*; it emerged also in Spain and in England. In those countries, however, it had lost all connexion with Rome and, in consequence, was able to inspire only regional empires. The result was that, while its geographical scope was thus expanding, the principal characteristics of the concept were shrinking in value. East of the English Channel, however, and north of the Pyrenees, wherever it was based on the Carolingian tradition, it proved possible to re-establish the connexion with Rome. Although other images may also have contributed, it was this tradition which was to play a preponderant rôle in the rebirth of the Empire in 962. Two main movements can thus be distinguished – the one envisaging an empire quite without links with Rome, the other centred on an empire linked to the memory of Charlemagne's.

I. THE NON-ROMAN CONCEPT OF EMPIRE

This concept, a projection of the purely Frankish picture of the Empire, is encountered in two kingdoms which were never under Carolingian rule and whose rulers, at the end of the ninth century and up to 930 seemed much more powerful than their contemporaries among the *reges Francorum*.

A. *Spain*

In Spain the concept of empire was cradled in the kingdom of León, where several circumstances seem to have contributed to its genesis. First of all the persistence of the custom of ritual anointment of sovereigns assured them of very great prestige – the tradition of the former Visigoth kings came alive again in the monarchy. Another factor was the struggle against Islam, begun in the second half of the ninth century and conducted vigorously by the kings of León: the victories of these kings and the extension of their rule beyond the frontiers of their own states soon attracted the attention of all the Christians in the peninsula. As the kings prospered, so did the Christian Church. The kings of León were the active (though not disinterested) protectors of the worship of St James and in 899 the new church at Compostella was consecrated. Half a century later the idea of setting up an ecclesiastical province was mooted: this would have grouped together all the bishoprics on this side of the Pyrenees, around the former see of Tarragona (not yet won back from the Moors), with a view to preparing the way for political unity.

This background, in which actual facts and high hopes were intermingled, explains how – at first discreetly – the imperial title came to emerge. The many variations on the theme reveal plainly how people felt about it. In one of the title deeds of his son Ordoño II, dated 917, King Alfonso III (866–910) is referred to as Emperor – the first of the rulers to be so called – but he did not himself take the title. Nevertheless a document, preserved in a collection of much later date but very probably authentic,[1] depicts him negotiating with the chapter of St Martin of Tours for the acquisition of a crown which had belonged to the Carolingian treasure. The signature to this letter, *Hispaniae rex*, does not conform to chancellery usage, but it is an expression of the

---

[1] Contrary to Barrau-Dihigo, *Recherches sur le royaume des Asturies* (*Revue hispanique*, 52, 1921), we feel that the authenticity of the text was established convincingly by Erdmann, *Forschungen*, pp. 32–3.

fact that, as a consequence of his victories over the infidel, Alfonso III's rule extended to the interior of the peninsula.

During the tenth century, several of his successors were called 'emperor', generally in the chronicles and in the preambles to various charters, though the title does not ever appear in a personal form or in official documents issued by the chancelleries. The most characteristic expressions are to be found in a letter written in 954 by Ordoño III to Sisnand, the Bishop of Compostella, where the King's title, *Servorum Domini servus*, echoes pretty closely the title of the Pope; and in a chronicle telling of Ramiro III (967–84), where the epithets *Flavius princeps et magnus basileus* evoke both the last Visigoth kings, who were thought to have belonged to the *gens Flavia*, and the title of the Byzantine emperors.

In brief, here is a resurgence of the imperial title, used regionally; an appellation which conferred prestige and reinforced a king's status; an honorific with no pretension to external supremacy and for internal use only. It had its counterpart in the title of *apostolicus*, taken by the bishops of Compostella, and its justification in the victories gained by the Christian kings of Spain over Islam. In this connexion, it is significant that it disappeared whenever military defeats occurred, for instance at the end of the tenth century when the Caliph Al-Mansour attacked and took possession of Compostella in 997: on the other hand, when the caliphate disintegrated, the hopes to which that event gave rise caused the imperial title to re-emerge from the shadows. The essential factor is that it remained tied to the kingdom of León, thus representing the tradition of the unity of the peninsula. Sancho the Great, King of Navarre, who, in 1033, became master of León and Astorga, was called emperor, at least on some coins, and the title later passed to his son Ferdinand I (1037–65) under whom León was united with Castile. Ruler over two kingdoms, one of which bore the name of empire, Ferdinand seemed, by virtue of his military successes, to justify his status of emperor, which was indeed recognised by his own states and some beyond. It became the custom, eventually firmly established, for his successors to bear the imperial title.

B. *Britain*

When Anglo-Saxon rulers in the tenth century started to use the imperial title, they did so as a consequence of an accumulation of ideas, to which we have already drawn attention. First, people recalled occasions when emperors had been proclaimed by the Roman legions stationed in the island, and they also had in mind the notion of an *orbis britannicus*, distinct from the *orbis romanus*.[2] Superimposed on this ancient tradition was the actual fact of regionalism: the authority of the former *bretwalda* assimilated to that of the Empire and the notion of *Imperium Anglorum*, which Bede emphasised in relation to the policy of hegemony practised by certain Anglo-Saxon kings. Lastly, the need to defend the island against the Norse invaders favoured territorial concentration: an Anglo-Saxon state gradually evolved around Wessex with Alfred the Great as its centre, and his successors played a fairly important rôle in the tenth century.

It was during the reign of Athelstan (924–40) that the concept of empire was born. By occupying the kingdom of Northumbria in 926 Athelstan had gained control of all the territory of modern England. He had considerable prestige, which can be measured by recalling the matrimonial alliances of his sisters, who married Charles the Simple, Hugh the Great and Otto I of Germany. This background explains why, in the text of an official document drawn up in 930, the title *Imperator* appears associated with the idea of the personal supremacy which the King seemed to exercise, even outside the island. This is, incidentally, the only occasion on which it is encountered in an authentic document – more frequently the appellation used is *basileus*, which is also evidence of the superior rank held by the King.

What gave these titles reality, however, was the fact that the King actually dominated the whole of Britain, having taken over and continued the hegemony hitherto exercised temporarily by the *bretwalda*. This makes intelligible the very varied terms which the chancellery from then on attached to the expressions *totius Britanniae* or *Britannici orbis*: thus, for example, *rector, rex, agonista, monarchia, ierarchia, primicerius, curagulus*,[3] all words which described the authority exercised by the sovereign over the whole of the island. All were equivalents of the title *bretwalda* – they are by themselves sufficient proof that this Anglo-Saxon 'empire' was far more a scholarly conception than a positive doctrine of public law.[4]

The usages adopted under Athelstan continued to prevail under his successors, whose titles conveyed as much the scope of their territorial domination as the hegemony exercised by them over various peoples (Angles, Northumbrians, Picts, Britons). Here and there the appellation *Imperator* or *casere* (*Kaiser*) appears. Thus in some documents King Edred was called *cyning* and *casere totius Britanniae*. A few inno-

---

[2] See above, p. 6.   [3] An amalgamation of the words *curator* and *regulus*.
[4] Erdmann, *op. cit.*, p. 41.

vations made their appearance under King Edgar: the first document
in which he was described as emperor (one dated 28th December, 964)
attempted to justify the title by declaring that, unlike his predecessors
who failed to extend the Empire beyond the boundaries to which
Athelstan had increased it, the King 'has been able, by the grace of
Divine Providence, to bring under the rule of the Empire of the Angles
all the kingdoms and islands of the ocean, together with their extremely
savage kings, as far as Norway and the greater part of Hibernia; he
has compelled all of them to bow the head *omnibus meis imperiis*'.[5] These
were strange statements, contradicted by the real facts: perhaps the
King's intention was to use the concept of empire as a means of
affirming loudly the independence of his territories, vis-à-vis the
Empire, which had just been reborn on the continent under Otto I.
However that may be, Edgar showed a noticeable tendency to hold on
to the title – this king was almost the only ruler in the island who used
it in a personal form. 'I, Edgar', says the document quoted above,
'*basileus* of the Angles and of all the kings of the islands which surround
Britain, Emperor and Lord of all the nations contained within its
borders,' a formula which conveys very well the notion of the *orbis
Britannicus*. In 970 we find a simplified version: 'I, Edgar, by the grace
of God, august emperor of all Albion'.[6] Yet he was not able ever to
enforce the use of the title with complete success: the expressions
'emperor' and 'king' are used side by side in documents.

Despite the great crisis created in England by the death of Edgar,
King Ethelred is sometimes referred to by the title of *Imperator*. The
last example of its use is to be found in a document issued by the
conqueror of the Anglo-Saxons: 'I, Canute, Emperor, who by the
favour of Christ have taken possession of the kingdom of the Angles,
in the island'.[7] His biographer defined the implications of this title by
recalling the plurality of the realms dominated by Canute: 'all five
kingdoms – Denmark, Anglia, Britain, Scotland, Norway – having
been defeated by him, he became emperor.'[8]

So, just when the Empire had ceased to exist on the continent, the
title of emperor appeared in England, only to become extinct when
a Roman Empire was re-established. Yet it never had more than a
semi-official status in the island. The Anglo-Saxon 'empire' was from
every point of view a national empire, expression of the supreme
authority exercised by the ruler over the different elements which made

[5] Gray-Birch, *Cartularium saxonicum*, London, 1865, III, No. 1135.
[6] *Op. et loc. cit.*, No. 1259.
[7] Kemble, *Cartularium saxonicum*, IV, No. 727.
[8] *Mon. Germ. Scriptores*, XIX, p. 520.

up the population of England. Unlike the position in Germany where, as we shall see, the evolution of a similar authority, successfully imposed by a king on different ethnic groups, was the preliminary step towards the throne of the Roman Empire, the Anglo-Saxon Empire found its fulfilment in the strong kingdom which William the Conqueror and his successors were able to establish in England.

II. THE CONCEPT OF A FRANKISH EMPIRE NORTH OF THE ALPS IN THE TENTH CENTURY

The Frankish tradition persisted in the kingdom of the Western Franks and it was resurrected by a foreign dynasty in the neighbouring kingdom in the East, so that the comparative history of the two states in the tenth century presents a diptych. In France the Carolingian dynasty continued to exist, despite some interruptions, up to 987, thus surviving the Germanic line by more than half a century. Conrad of Franconia, successor of Louis the Child (who died in 911), was still related to the old dynasty, but at his death in 919 the kingdom of the Eastern Franks passed to Henry of Saxony.

It seems probable that on the death of Louis the Child, Charles the Simple considered he was the lawful heir to the old Carolingian empire. It is certainly significant that he took the title of '*Rex Francorum*' in 911, thus breaking with the accepted usage of chancelleries in the ninth century, according to which rulers who did not wear the imperial crown were simply entitled '*Rex*'. It looked as though he were anxious to affirm thereby his rights to the entire succession of Charlemagne. In the same year, in fact, we find him establishing himself in Lorraine, where the aristocracy quickly rallied round him. From Lorraine he tried to validate his claims on Germany, but, defeated by Henry of Saxony, he had to recognise that the latter was King of Germany when he signed the Agreement of Bonn in 921. Four years later he was dethroned by the Robertian party and at that point the Lorrainers, who were attached by no ties to the new dynasty, crossed over to Henry I. Charles the Simple's successors none the less maintained their claim to the country, which had been the heart of the Frankish monarchy, and resurrected it again during the reign of Lothair, in particular in 978 when the King pressed on as far as Aix-la-Chapelle. In 987, after the Capetians were substituted for the Carolingians, as the result of a plot of which the court of Saxony seems not to have been unaware, France's dreams of empire were abandoned, temporarily at least. So far as the concept of empire is concerned, however, the important thing is that the efforts made by Charles the Simple and Lothair to regroup the former territories of the Empire under their sceptre caught people's imaginations sufficiently for Richer of Rheims, a historian writing at the end of the tenth century, to describe the relationship between the two Frankish kingdoms as though both still formed parts of one and the same monarchy: reading his story, we realise that the notion of the *Regnum Francorum* was still very much alive and that many links still existed between the old dynasty and the neighbouring kingdom.[9]

The reign of Otto I in turn reveals that he too was inclined to take his direction from the same traditions. Only the essential facts can be recalled here. Otto I was the second Saxon king and was anointed at Aix-la-Chapelle, thus recreating the connexion with the Charlemagne tradition. His kingdom was Frankish and remained so in its structure – it was the memory of Charlemagne which inspired the conquest and Christianisation of the Eastern borderlands of Saxony. Like Arnulf in his time, Otto played a leading rôle in the former Empire of the Franks: in France we find him arbitrating in disputes between Carolingians and Robertians; in Burgundy he exercised a real protectorate by following deliberately in the footsteps of the *reges Francorum* to whom he refers in a document dated 959.[10] Then, again like Arnulf and like some princes of Southern Germany nearer to him, he descended into Italy. Immediately after his expedition in 951 the title of *Rex Francorum et Langobardorum* (or *Italicorum*) appeared on documents, modelled on the title used by Charlemagne. The logical outcome of this policy was not reached for a decade – when Otto I was crowned Emperor.

The considerable contribution made by Frankish tradition to the persistence of the concept of empire can be appreciated by reading the text of a little treatise on the Antichrist, composed towards 950 by the monk Adso of Montiérender for Queen Gerberga, wife of Louis IV and sister of Otto I.[11]

This work is a study of a subject which had incessantly occupied men's minds since the beginning of the Christian era, i.e. speculation about the end of the world. There was, of course, already a belief that

[9] Richer, *Histoire de France*, ed. Latouche (*Classiques de l'Histoire de France au Moyen-Age*), two volumes, Paris, 1930–7. The following passages are particularly relevant: Book I, chapters iv and xii; Book II, chapters xvi, xviii, xxx and xlix; Book III, chapters xliv and lxvii.

[10] Charter (No. 199 of the *Mon. Germ. Diplomata*) for the Abbey of Lure, *ut sub mundiburdio deinceps maneat regum Francorum*.

[11] Sackur, *Sibyllinische Texte*, pp. 104–13.

the Roman Empire was the fourth and last of the universal monarchies predicted by Daniel.[12] From the fourth century onwards, new features were constantly being added to this tradition, the most important of which was that the last emperor would come to Jerusalem where, on Golgotha or on the Mount of Olives, he would make an offering of his realms to God; this act would precede the coming of the Antichrist, whose reign would end on the Day of the Lord. Details of the evolution of this complex theme cannot be given here but it must be noted that, in those circles in the West where people were contemplating the possible end of time, the rebirth of the Empire in 800 gave rise to a positive current of optimism. This event was regarded without hesitation as the re-emergence of the Roman Empire – an interpretation which allowed the coming of the Antichrist to be postponed into an even more distant future.[13] Adso allied himself with this stream of thought, but he went much further. Living at a time when the Empire had ceased to be a reality, he did not allow himself to be troubled about these speculations. He explained to Queen Gerberga that the Antichrist would not make his entry into the world until all the nations which had formerly been subject to the Empire had seceded from it[14] and he declared that that time had not yet come. 'We do indeed see,' he wrote, 'that the larger part of the Roman Empire is destroyed, but so long as there are Frankish kings whose duty it is to uphold it, its prestige will not entirely disappear, because it will be supported by those kings.' Thus he saw the Frankish kingdoms as the supporters of the Roman Empire, the survival of which was the essential condition of the world's salvation. But there was more to come: whereas up to then the rôle of the last Emperor had always been assigned by the prophets to a Byzantine ruler – the mysterious Emperor Constans – Adso announced that one of the Frankish kings would be the sovereign in power at the end of the time, and would be the last person to hold sway over the Roman Empire as an integral unit; he would surrender his insignia in Jerusalem and this would mark 'the end and consummation of the Empire of the Romans and Christians'. Nothing could be more impressive than this dual appellation: it shows that Adso, just like the contemporaries of Leo the Great, assimilated the two universal authorities with one another: Roman Empire and Christian Empire were both one.

The perspectives opened up by this treatise are indeed immense, but

[12] See above, p. 4.
[13] See, for example, the commentary on the end of the world made by Bishop Haimo of Halberstadt, P. L. 117, 779.
[14] The starting point for Western eschatology is the idea of *discessio*: II Thess. ii, 3.

they could be realised only in the remote future. It would therefore be a mistake to think that the little work had an immediate far-reaching effect. There is nothing to indicate that it ever came to Otto's notice or that it stimulated him to restore the Empire. But, quite independently of the fact that the theories propounded were later to dominate eschatological speculation, it is necessary to mention the treatise at this point because it was an element in the survival of the concept of empire in the tenth century and was also evidence of the continuity established in people's minds between the Roman Empire and the Frankish Empire.

III. OTTO I's ACCESSION TO THE IMPERIAL THRONE

When in the last months of 961 Otto I set out on the road to Rome, it was at the request of the Pope, John XII. The full import of this papal initiative can best be appreciated if one remembers that at that moment the city was in danger of falling under the domination of the former King of Italy, Berengar of Ivrea. Preferring the guardianship of a distant prince to the tyranny, as he feared, of an Italian emperor, John XII followed the example of his predecessor Formosus, who had invited Arnulf into Italy to counter the Spoleto dynasty. On 2nd February, 962, he crowned Otto emperor in St Peter's; as on 25th December, 800, the status of emperor had thus been given to the ruler of the most considerable kingdom of the age.

How did contemporaries regard this empire? The first interpretation given was that of the Pope himself. On 12th February, he caused a 'privilege' to be written in which it was stated that in consequence of his victory over the Hungarians and many other heathen peoples, the King of Germany had come to pay a visit to the apostolic see in order that he might receive the triumphal crown of the Empire from St Peter, as a reward for his defence of the Church.[15] John XII apparently intended by his action to make quite clear the distinction between the cause and the effect of the Emperor's promotion: military successes were of less interest to Rome than to Germany, but these had been victories over the enemies of Christendom; the title of Emperor was a reward granted to Otto by the head of the Roman Church, who expected still other services from him. Since the end of the ninth century this had been the Court of Rome's classic interpretation of the Empire's significance.

[15] Jaffe, *Regesta pontificum romanorum*, 2nd edn., No. 3690. See, for example, the text in the chronicle of the Saxon annalist, *Mon. Germ. Script.*, VI, p. 616.

However, Otto I did not understand it thus, as his policy towards John XII at once made very plain. His entourage conceived no little antipathy towards an empire which ran the risk of becoming the tool of the Pope – the chronicler Widukind of Corvey,[16] by his interpretation and even more by his silences, proves this and at the same time shows that in the eyes of the Germans all that really mattered was the manner in which their sovereign first acceded to the imperial throne. The chronicler's line of thought must now be studied.

It is apparent that the only way to obtain a clear idea of what he was thinking is to consider all the passages in his chronicle in which the important words *Imperium* and *imperator* occur. To Widukind, Charlemagne and Arnulf appear to be emperors quite naturally, and without any reference to a Roman coronation, by virtue of the mere fact that they ruled over several nations: the monk of Corvey had been brought up on Bede and was not unaware that the Anglo-Saxon kings bore the imperial title. But in his writings he presented Henry I and Otto I equally as emperors: both alike had been saluted with an imperial acclamation by their warriors after victories which they had won over the Hungarians at an interval of twenty-two years, the one at Riade in 933 and the other at the Lechfeld in 955.[17] This point becomes even clearer when one realises that Widukind was transposing into the present the designation of emperors by the victorious legions of the past, about which he had read in his history books. Doubtless it is possible that he was also confusing the shouts of victory with the imperial acclamation proper – this seems all the more probable when one notes that he attributed the title of King to Henry I immediately after his triumph in 933, thus giving the impression that he was simply describing the spontaneous homage of the victorious army to its leader. The real difficulty arises from the fact that, unlike Henry I, Otto is always referred to as Emperor after 955 – apparently implying the constitutional validity of the Lechfeld proclamation – and that Widukind maintains a complete silence about the events which took place at Rome in 962. The affair becomes all the more perplexing if one agrees with certain historians that the greater part of the chronicle was written not before, but five years after, the Emperor's coronation.[18] Does this mean that the writer had his reservations about the Pope's initiative and about an honour which might drag Otto into Italian complications? Perhaps so, but we can say no more than 'perhaps'.

[16] *Rerum gestarum saxonicarum libri*, III (*Mon Germ.*, S.R.G., 1935).
[17] Book I, chapter xxxviii and Book III, chapters xlviii and xlix.
[18] For a recent account see E. Stengel, *Die Entstehungszeit der Res gestae*, in *Festgabe für K. Strecker*, 1941, pp. 136–58.

We should doubtless be better informed if we could be sure that we understood exactly what meaning the monk gave to the expression *imperium*. It is, for example, a striking fact that the word is used very often in connexion with the rise of the House of Saxony, seeming thus to be an argument in favour of its legality, or better still of its fitness to be the successor of the Frankish dynasty. The *summum Imperium*, the *de facto* hegemony exercised under King Conrad by Duke Otto of Saxony, would thus create the original foundation for a claim to the succession to the throne. Henry I, who succeeded in imposing himself on different ethnic groups in Germany, is called *imperator multorum populorum* and he leaves to his son, Otto, a *magnum latumque Imperium*.[19] Then came the victory at the Lechfeld, an obviously decisive success: the warriors who acclaimed Otto were recognising it was with the aid of God that he had been able to triumph. Widukind, projecting into the present a custom of the Late Empire, was at the same time transposing into a Christian setting the very ancient notion of the *felicitas* or *Koenigsheil*, which enabled kings, on whose shoulders the safety of their people rested, to win their victories. To him this acclamation appeared actually to create the empire, an empire directly instituted by God: after that a further religious consecration was unnecessary, particularly as Otto had already been anointed at Aix-la-Chapelle at the beginning of his reign.

The Empire was, then, in Widukind's eyes, first and foremost an authority of exceptional character, practically charismatic. Yet when he attempted to define its historical significance and to place it in its setting of continuity there was only one empire of which he could possibly take account, namely the Empire of the Franks, whose tradition, as we have seen, had survived uninterrupted during the tenth century. The state bequeathed by Henry I in 936 to his son was *omne Francorum Imperium*. At Aix-la-Chapelle Otto received from his consecrator the sword, 'as a symbol of the power which is conferred on him over the Empire of the Franks'; the death of Liudolf inflicted a serious wound on the Empire of the Franks. In 972, because Otto was staying in Italy at the time, the Archbishop of Mainz exercised a regency over *totum Imperium Francorum*.[20]

The feeling about this Frankish tradition was so strong that Otto himself was inspired by it in his government of the Empire. Faithful to the example of Charlemagne in 812 and to that of Louis the Pious,

---

[19] References for these three quotations: Book I, chapters xvi, xxv and xl. See also the studies of Beumann, mentioned in the bibliography.
[20] See respectively Book I, chapter xli, Book II, chapter i, Book III, chapters lvii and lxxiii.

he generally used the title of *Imperator Augustus* without mentioning any connexion with Rome. Yet, on some documents dated 966, the title *Imperator Romanorum et Francorum*[21] is used, which seems to be evidence that Rome indeed formed part of this Frankish Empire.

And so we come to the third image to be found at the cradle of the restored Empire. What right had this Empire to be accepted as the successor of the Roman Empire? On this point there are many different and contradictory opinions. How did Widukind regard the Romans? To him they were no more than one of the nations composing the Empire, a nation under the rule of the Saxons, who had been the bearers of the concept of empire ever since their union with the Franks in the time of Charlemagne. No ties of sentiment bound Otto I and his warriors to Rome: the famous diatribe of Bishop Liutprand of Cremona[22] proves this emphatically. In the political field people found it difficult to grasp that a continuity might be established between one empire and the next. On the other hand, the necessity to stress the Roman character of the new empire, if only to confront Byzantium, was soon plain to all. At this point a conflict broke out between the Emperor and some of his supporters. Whereas Otto, faithful to the Frankish tradition, seems not to have thought of anything but a status of parity between the two monarchies (as his title *Imperator Augustus* proves) we can see, by contrast, the idea of a Roman empire taking shape around him, Rome conferring on the Ottonian rulers the double distinction of authenticity and pre-eminence.

Such thoughts were, to some extent at least, provoked by the opposition which Otto I encountered on the part of Byzantium as he made his way to Southern Italy, and by the refusal of Nicephorus Phocas to recognise his imperial status. The view taken by the Romans is forcibly expressed in the description given by Liutprand of Cremona of his embassy to Constantinople in 968, in which he makes a point of recalling the letter written by Louis II to Basil, and directs a veritable stream of propaganda simultaneously against Byzantium and in favour of the seizure by Otto I of the title of Emperor of the Romans. It did not make sense, he declared, for Nicephorus to claim the title of the Caesars; at most he was 'Emperor of the Greeks', whose language and customs he, like his predecessors, adopted when he quitted Rome.[23] By contrast, look at Otto I: he hastened to the aid of the city of the apostles; he rescued the papacy; he gave Rome back the laws of Valen-

---

[21] In 966. Cf. *Mon. Germ. Diplomata Ottonis*, Nos. 322–6 and 329.
[22] See Documents, VIII, p. 184.
[23] *Relatio de legatione* [*Mon. Germ.*, S.R.G., 1915, chapter vii].

tinian, Theodosius and Justinian; surely it was indeed he and he alone who was the true *Imperator Romanorum*.[24] This is the point at which Liutprand's view differed most from that of Louis II. In the eyes of the Carolingian, the source of his power lay in Rome: he had become emperor by being anointed. For Liutprand this event was only the ultimate consequence of the services rendered by Otto: the victory referred to by Widukind was evidence of the creative power which, for the Lombard bishop, was the foundation on which the Empire rested and the basis of his master's hold over Rome. Similarly it is odd to observe that Liutprand was not afraid to mention the prerogatives which Constantine had granted to the Church through his Donations, in East and West alike.[25] The papacy had received from Otto everything in his own lands which was due to St Peter – this being without any doubt an allusion to the restitution which Otto agreed to make to John XII and to his successors, but which was made as part of a *pactum* and not as a result of the Donation – whereas no one had ever seen a *basileus* take action of that kind. Liutprand thus brought once more into the light of day the original scope of the famous forgery which was aimed first and foremost against Byzantium.

And so the theme of the succession of the Roman Empire had now been formally set out for the first time. When Otto I's reign ended, it became the subject of new developments – in two fields: that of universality and also that of the part played by the Pope in deciding who was to accede to the *Imperium Romanorum*. When it is remembered that the nun Roswitha included Otto in her list of the Caesars, recording also that his rule extended to the *orbis romanus*;[26] and that Widukind included in his chronicle the letter in which Otto announced that his son had received the imperial crown from the Pope,[27] we realise that the new empire, while remaining in substance profoundly Frankish, was in process of adopting the dual tradition, Roman and pontifical. In 982, less than ten years after the death of his father, Otto II began to use the title *Imperator Romanorum*, which thereafter became established in chancellery usage.

In the first half of the century the concept of empire was diffuse, but later it tended to become centred on the Ottonian rulers. On its fringes, the imperial title used by the Anglo-Saxon kings had scarcely

---

[24] *Relatio*, chapter v. [25] *Relatio*, chapter xvii.
[26] *Gesta Ottonis*, Winterfeld, S.R.G., 1902. See particularly Preface I, V, 30–4.
[27] Book III, chapter lxx.

any significance and that of the kings of León was valid only within the Iberian peninsula. The Roman Empire was about to be reborn, but the various interpretations to which it gave rise were to be responsible for the future complexity and uncertainties of the concept of empire.

5

The Concept of Empire in the Iberian States

Between 1065 and 1157 the concept of empire spread fairly widely south of the Pyrenees. Radiating from León where, as we have seen, it was already rooted, it made a particular impression on the kings of Castile, who had been almost continuously masters of this kingdom. The essential element in its programme was still Iberian unity, which on several occasions seemed to be very close to realisation.

For example – when Alfonso VI, son of Ferdinand I, was king (1065–1109) he brought about the most considerable concentration of territory that had ever been seen in the peninsula since the time of the Visigoths. Confined at first to the restricted area of León and Asturias, he was by 1072 master of Galicia, Portugal, the whole of Castile and half of Navarre. He carried on an unceasing war against Islam which resulted in some brilliant successes, such as the capture of Toledo in 1085, but also some setbacks, such as his defeat at Sagrayos in 1086. There is no doubt that his finest claim to glory is that he was able to maintain the independence of his territories against the Almoravides. His prestige was considerable: for example he played the part of arbitrator between other Christian princes, who contributed contingents to his armies and recognised his pre-eminence. The Muslims regarded Alfonso VI as the King of Kings; within his own territories he was emperor and his neighbours in Aragon and Navarre accorded him recognition under this title.

Yet it would be wrong to speak at this stage of a clearly defined

or an exclusive title, since it did not entirely take the place of that of
rex. It was, moreover, neither precise nor unique, since it had a number
of variant forms and some of these seem to have been affected by the
events of history in general.

In 1072,[1] on the occasion of his being anointed king, Alfonso gave a
'privilege' to the church of Compostella in favour of the apostle 'under
whose sovereignty all Spain lies',[2] while he himself took the title of
princeps et rex Hispaniae. It is possible that in his own mind he regarded
these expressions as having an imperial connotation, but it was in 1077
– the year of the drama of Canossa – that the actual word 'emperor'
appeared for the first time on documents.[3] Followed by the determin-
ing words *totius Hispaniae*, it was the expression of supreme authority
over the whole of an area or over the nations residing in it. Thus we
find sometimes *Dei gratia totius Hispaniae imperator*, sometimes *imperator
constitutus super omnes Ispaniae nationes*. It is perhaps possible to throw
light on either or both of these formulas by examining the relations
which the King maintained with Gregory VII and his successors. The
first form of title was used in 1077–81, then on several occasions
between 1085 and 1103: it might be regarded – if not at the time
when it was originally used, then at least when it recurred – as a way
of affirming independence against the claims which Gregory VII was
liable to deduce from the Donation of Constantine.[4] As for the second
version, it is very possible that it was suggested to Alfonso by a message
in which the Pope greeted him with the title of King of all the Spains.[5]

It is incidentally appropriate to note that the notion of 'all the
nations of Spain', over whom the imperial authority of the King of
León extended, included Muslims, as is proved by various private
charters in which the inscription of the date contains the expression
*Adefonso imperante tam christianorum quam paganorum omnia Hispaniae
regna*; doubtless this is as much a reflection of the old concept of the
supremacy of the Emperor over several kingdoms as of the title which,
according to Arab historians, Alfonso used in his correspondence with
the princes of Andalusia: Emperor of the two religions.

---

[1] The murder of his brother Sancho enabled him to unite León and Castile in that year.
[2] Text in *España Sagrada*, vol. XXXVI, app. 26, p. liv.
[3] C. Erdmann, *Forschungen*, p. 36, considers that we can see here cause and effect: the
humiliation of Henry IV encouraging Alfonso VI, just as the fact that the imperial throne
was unoccupied at the beginning of the tenth century encouraged the heirs of Alfonso III
to use the imperial title.
[4] *Register of Gregory VII*, I, 7, and IV, 28 (E. Caspar, I, pp. 11 and 375). See below,
p. 84 and note 23.
[5] *Reg.*, VII, 6, *op. cit.*, II, p. 465, Cf. also, in 1088, the ordinance of Urban II concerning
the see of Toledo which became the religious metropolis *totis Hispaniorum regnis* (Jaffe,
Regesta Pont. Rom., 2nd edn., No. 5366).

In addition to those two main forms we find the imperial title of the King of León especially associated with Toledo. Not, be it noted, that this link was created immediately after the capture of the former Visigoth capital; it was only after he had victoriously defended his conquest throughout seven years against the Almoravides that Alfonso VI is described as *Toletanus imperator* or as *Toletani imperii magnificus triumphator*, two formulas which were sometimes substituted during the first years of the twelfth century for those which were an expression of the desire to achieve Iberian unity under Castilian hegemony.

There was a moment, after the death of Alfonso VI, when Iberian unity almost came about as a result of the second marriage of his daughter Urraca to Alfonso the Battler, King of Navarre and Aragon, who thus became ruler over the country of Castile, excepting only Galicia which had been left to the young Alfonso VII, Urraca's son by an earlier marriage. The Battler, following the example of his great-grandfather Sancho, resuscitated the imperial title for his own use, so long as he was lord of León – fresh evidence of the fact that the concept of empire was well rooted in that kingdom. It is very significant that in one document at least his wife called him 'Emperor of León and King of all Spain'. He himself, imitating Alfonso VI, described himself as 'by the grace of God, Emperor of Spain' on the majority of his official documents between 1110 and 1117, sometimes enumerating the kingdoms over which he held sway.[6]

Later he began to use the imperial appellation less frequently, as Alfonso VII, aided by his mother's divorce and also what has been called Calixtus II's Burgundian policy,[7] furthered his own cause with increasing success. Urraca's young son was crowned at Compostella in 1111, acclaimed king at Toledo in 1118 and made a knight in 1124; two years later he inherited the kingdom of León. From then on began to appear the imperial title, which had already featured on certain of his documents, with increasing frequenty on official acts.

In 1127 Alfonso VII and the Battler came to an agreement whereby the Battler surrendered Castile to his rival and 'forbade people henceforth to call him emperor'.[8] If this really was the decision of the powerful King of Aragon, who thus effaced himself before his stepson, it could be thought to illustrate with extreme clarity the concept then

[6] Examples in Menendez-Pidal, *El Imperio hispan co*, pp. 32–9.
[7] P. Kehr, *Das Papsttum und die Königreiche Navarra und Aragon*, Abhandl. der preuss. Akad. der Wiss. Phil. Hist. Kl., Berlin, 1928, No. 4, p. 42.
[8] '*Chronicle of Saint John of la Peña*', in Menendez-Pidal, *op. cit.*, p. 38.

existing in Spain of the territorial substratum to the imperial title. Alfonso VII's good fortune did not stop at this point: when in 1134 the kingdom of Aragon was broken up, he, as King of León and Castile, became also the sovereign of the Christian states south of the Pyrenees; he imposed his rule on the King of Navarre; Ramiro II of Aragon surrendered Saragossa to him temporarily and paid him homage; and his influence was extended by bonds of vassalage over the county of Barcelona and even beyond the mountains, over the county of Toulouse and the lordship of Montpellier.

This was the background against which the imperial title has to be seen and against which Alfonso used it increasingly from 1126. Throughout the next ten years the same uncertainty as to its precise terms can be observed as in the time of his grandfather: examination of the documents[9] affords evidence that the chancellery of Castile generally regarded the sovereign as king, but that he himself, when speaking in the personal form, took the title of *Imperator totius Hispaniae*, thereby affirming that he had regained hegemony over Spain, lately usurped by Alfonso the Battler. But whereas the 'empire' of the latter had been lawful by the mere fact of his power alone, Alfonso VII deemed it necessary to base his own empire on legal action: on Whit Sunday 1135 he had himself crowned emperor.[10]

Henceforth and until the end of his reign, the title *Hispaniae Imperator* was inscribed on all chancellery documents. Furthermore, from 1135 to 1139 all documents and from 1139 to 1145 a certain number of them, were dated by the years of the Empire. After 1136, the formula of sovereignty which followed the date normally enumerated all the different territories over which the Emperor's authority extended: *Adefonso imperatore, imperante in Toleto, Legione, Caesaraugusta Nagera et Castella*;[11] from 1147 Cordova, Baecia and Almeria were also incorporated in the list. The first of these soon disappeared – the town was retaken almost immediately by the Almohades – but the other two continued to be included in the enumeration. In some documents even the bonds of vassalage established between the Emperor and other rulers were evoked – all so many pieces of evidence of the concept that a plurality of dominions under one and the same sceptre gave a ruler the right to the title of emperor. The Emperor's titles were enriched too, particularly towards the end of the reign, by epithets modelled on those borne by the Roman emperors: *Ego Adefonsus, pius, felix, inclitus,*

---

[9] Cf. the study by P. Rassow, *Die Urkunden Kaiser Alfonso VII.*
[10] See Documents, XIII, p. 191.
[11] In Hueffer, *Das spanische Kaisertum*, p. 45.

*triumphator ac semper invictus, tocius Hispaniae divina clementia famosis-
simus imperator.* The aim of all these titles was to increase the prestige
of Alfonso VII's person at a time when he was acquiring kinship with
certain European dynasties through marriage: in 1152 he married as
his second wife Richilda, cousin of Frederick Barbarossa; two years
later Louis VII of France became his son-in-law. The exaltation of the
imperial title was at that time pushed to such extremes that some documents mention, alongside the Emperor, his two sons and his two
daughters, one of whom was Queen of Navarre and the other Queen
of France. As for the scope of the honorific titles, essentially it involved
the claim to control the Christian rulers in the peninsula. With the
exception of Portugal (established in 1143, the last to be created) which
preserved its independence, all the kingdoms gave Alfonso VII recognition in his rôle as supreme head of the war against Islam. Two facts
illustrate this very well – first the expedition to Almeria in 1147, which
was a joint undertaking under the direction of the Emperor, 'walking
in the steps of Charlemagne', as the poet to whom we owe our description of the conquest was pleased to recognise.[12] Four years later, moreover, we find Alfonso, by the treaty of Tudela, disposing of lands still
held by the Muslims in favour of his vassal, Raymond-Berengar IV
of Aragon: all Spain seemed to belong to the Emperor.[13]

It is clear from several pieces of evidence that the imperial title of the
King of Castile was acknowledged north of the Pyrenees. In the eyes
of St Bernard and of the Annalist of Cambrai, the Spanish Empire
appeared in a kind of way to be the Third Empire. It is, however,
certain that the imperial status of Alfonso the King was not officially
admitted by either the papacy or the Germanic Roman emperors.
Conrad III and Frederick I always referred to the 'kingdom' of Spain,[14]
no doubt in deference to Roman law, under which only one empire
existed – that of Rome. This was the principal reason why the title of
emperor was dropped after Alfonso's death in 1157, although the
partition of the Castilian domains among the ruler's heirs was another
important contributory factor.[15]

If we look at those two facts side by side it seems possible to arrive

[12] Poem inserted in the imperial chronicle (*España Sagrada*, vol. XXI, p. 400).
[13] Analysis of the treaty in Menendez-Pidal, *op. cit.*, pp. 50-2.
[14] Cf. the letters of Conrad III to Manuel Comnenus and of Frederick I to the Bishop
of Brixen, inserted in the *Gesta Frederici* of Otto of Freising, Book I, chapter xxv, and
Book IV, chapter lxvi.
[15] For a comment on the brief reappearance of the title under Ferdinand III, in 1248,
after the capture of Seville, cf. P. E. Schramm, *Das Kastilische Königtum*.

at the following conclusions: (1) At the time when the Iberian peninsula formed a world on its own, isolated from the remainder of Christendom, a Hispanic empire was feasible, but it became extinct at the moment when, on account of the play of Alfonso VII's foreign policy, it was tending towards integration in the West as a whole: in this respect it was following, at a distance of half a century, the evolution of the Spanish Church, which Gregory VII and his successors had contrived to bind more strongly to the see of Rome. (2) In Spain itself, the idea of one supreme imperial control was replaced from the second half of the twelfth century by that of complete equality between the different kingdoms – the *cinco reinos* each having their own individuality while together they represented an indissoluble moral unit, forerunner of Spain's future national unity. But at the same time it is in the last analysis undeniable that the way was paved for this unity by the fact that the Iberian states had passed through a period during which they had accepted the idea of being an empire.

BOOK III
Attempts at a Synthesis: the Empire between Theory and Reality

6

The Ottonian and Salian Era
(Second half of the tenth and whole of the eleventh centuries)

Three powers, three types of influence, three trends of thought surrounded the new Empire, at its birth on 2nd February, 962 – the
Byzantine Empire, which enjoyed the continuity of ancient tradition,
the Papacy, which, despite occasional setbacks, aimed at control over
Christendom, and certain Western states which were showing signs
of imperial aspirations at various levels – and it had to establish and
define its own doctrine. What indeed was the Empire exactly? And
how did people feel about it? How far was the old concept of empire
suited to reality? And, on the other hand, how did reality affect the
evolution of the image of the Empire? In the end, after a slow process
of development, a concept of empire did emerge from the institution
and its activities, and slowly too it achieved a certain cohesion: for
a long time several different ideas existed simultaneously, supporting
the Empire in ways which varied according to the epoch and the
temperament of those on the throne at the time. Little by little a
synthesis was reached, though even then some gaps remained. We
must now try to follow this evolution, tracing the themes most easily
studied, that is to say, those we can find in written texts and
iconography.

I. THE RELIGIOUS MISSION OF THE EMPIRE
ADVOCACY OF THE ROMAN CHURCH

From Frankish times it had always been the chief task of every emperor to act as the champion of the Roman Church and this principle was immediately reinstated. Before reaching Rome, Otto I made a vow to John XII that he would aid him; by the terms of this vow he engaged himself to work for the exaltation of the Church of Rome and to restore to the Pope the whole of the patrimony of St Peter which had already come under the authority of the Empire or might do so in future. Similarly, in the course of the ceremony of anointing, Otto promised the Pope to be his protector and his defender. In practice, relations between the two powers were regulated from 962 onwards by a *pactum*, which confirmed the right of the papacy to its possessions and guaranteed the continuation of various Carolingian privileges;[1] in addition, Otto reinstated the *Constitutio romana* of 824, while the Romans swore an oath to him that they would elect no pontiff without his agreement.[2] These measures, inspired by Frankish tradition interpreted in an authoritarian sense, and based above all on the divine character of the Emperor's authority, ensured that for a century the emperors had control over the institution of the papacy.

Admittedly the methods by which control was exercised varied in the course of this period. There was indeed nothing in common between the direct domination of the papacy by the Emperor, which existed under Otto I, and the protectorate exercised during the first half of the eleventh century by the emperors through their representatives – in effect the counts of Tusculum. On the other hand, actual collaboration between the two powers was exceptional and hardly ever took place save in the case of Otto III and Sylvester II. That was the only occasion on which the Pope was represented in the iconography: normally the Emperor was depicted alone, because it was he alone whose duty it was to supervise the happy concord between the *Imperium* and the *Sacerdotium*. The question we must ask ourselves is how far the fact that he was the Church's champion enabled the Emperor to exercise his authority over the entire Christian Church of the West. We cannot answer the question, but we know that the problem was bound up with that of the position then accorded to the Roman Church within the bosom of the Universal Church and any light thrown on that point would at the same time help to elucidate the prerogatives of the imperial advocate. However that may be, it

[1] *Mon. Germ. Diplomata*, vol. I, No. 235.
[2] Text in Liutprand, *Liber de rebus gestis Ottonis* (*Mon. Germ.*, S.R.G., p. 174).

should be noted that no opposition was ever displayed towards those popes who were – directly or indirectly – appointed by emperors. In fact, as late as 1046 Henry III had the necessary prestige and authority to depose three pontiffs and nominate others in their place, who were then accorded recognition by the whole of Christendom.

II. THE EXTENT OF THE CONCEPT OF EMPIRE

The term 'Roman Empire' had always contained within it the notion of universality and we must now ask whether the Ottonian monarchy was about to follow a path which would result in its being actually involved in universal domination. It is easy to be misled by the pens of contemporary scholars. They did indeed extol Otto towards the end of his reign as emperor of the world, but this was no more than a classic theme; since the fall of the Roman Empire, universality had been merely an idea and Charlemagne's Empire was universal only in so far as it coincided, in the West (excepting certain sectors), with the framework of the œcumenical Church. In the second half of the tenth century the practical scope of the concept was apparently still further reduced. Otto I was faithful to Charlemagne's example and never in any way claimed *dominium mundi*: neither he nor any of his successors ever raised any claims to Byzantium or France. Yet the Ottonian Empire certainly did enjoy a genuine pre-eminence in the world at that time, as much because of its connexion with the papacy as by its territorial scope. Outside of Germany and Lombard Italy, the Kingdom of Burgundy was tied to it by bonds of dependence; in the East the Germanic *regnum* was in process of achieving the annexation of important sectors of Slavia. The reign of the Emperor culminated in an apotheosis in 973 through the Diet of Quedlinburg where Slav delegates, Hungarians and even Bulgarians were among those present. It was only natural in such conditions that the idea of pure universality should be replaced by one which discerned that the essential feature of the Empire lay in the plurality of the areas over which the Emperor exercised effective sway and in his hegemony, in theory or in fact, over various nations. This conception demonstrated a genuine effort to adapt the old theory to the realities of the contemporary world, but these facts also made it possible for the idea of universality to be resuscitated – as was proved by the startling vitality of Otto III's concept of empire.

*   *   *

This can be seen as the first attempt to create a synthesis out of several images. First there was the very detailed memory of Charlemagne around which the young Emperor built up a real cult and by means of which he aimed at reviving the Empire in the form of a Christian Empire or Imperial Christendom, under the sole control of the Emperor: in relation to Otto III the popes were to be no more than high priests charged with the ministry of prayer.[3]

. But this Empire was to take the political form of the Roman Empire and here we see what a difference there was between Otto III and his grandfather: the latter regarded the Empire as superficially Roman, particularly when it came to the question of succession, but in Otto III's eyes it was to be actually so. The son of a Byzantine princess, he was brought up in the most authentic imperial tradition – which similarly inspired his great rival Basil II. Moreover, since 997, he had been deeply influenced by his teacher, Gerbert. The latter's political thinking had gone through some instructive hesitations: he had scarcely known the Roman Empire except in its decline; deeply conscious of the universality of Christianity he had disputed that of the Roman Church; he was a supporter of the Ottonian monarchy and could not at first imagine the possibility of its ever being assimilated to the Roman Empire. From the moment when he reached the Germanic court, however, all his uncertainties vanished. As early as 997 his famous manifesto: 'Ours,ours is the Roman Empire . . .'[4] went booming forth; Otto, Greek by birth, was *Imperio romanus*, Roman by virtue of the Empire he held.[5] He was therefore cast for the rôle of the true emperor and his was the task of restoring the Empire to its original glory.

In order to implement this programme the first thing to be done was to place the city of Rome once more under the authority of the Emperor, for it had seceded from the Empire for the second time since the death of Otto II, under the patrician John Crescentius. When, in 998, the city had been finally reconquered, Otto III could be observed taking up once more the task of implementing the idea of 'renewal'; *Renovatio Imperii Romanorum* was inscribed on the seal of that year, accompanied by significant images: on the one side was Charlemagne's head, on the reverse a female figure carrying the lance and the buckler: *Aurea Roma*.[6] Partly because it suited his personal

[3] See Documents, IX, p. 184.
[4] *Liber de rationale*, addressed to Otto III (P.L., 139, 287).
[5] Letter No. 107, in the edition of Gerbert's correspondence, edited by J. Havet, Paris, 1898.
[6] Reproduced in Schramm, *Kaiserbilder*, II, plate 69a.

taste, but partly also to accustom the inhabitants to the presence of the Emperor, Otto took up residence in Rome. He demonstrated thereby that he was not afraid to upset the tradition, established by the Donation of Constantine, that the city had been handed over to the holy apostles as a gift. The imperial palace was situated on the Aventine; the court was sumptuous; the Emperor lavished titles and honours on his supporters, the most important of which seems to have been, in all probability, that of patrician, or of 'lieutenant' for the whole Empire.

This double tradition, Carolingian and Roman, put Otto III on the road leading to universality. At the beginning of his reign the Empire was pictured as a grouping of various peoples; the iconography shows us Rome (or Italy), Germany, Gaul (Moso-Rhenania), Slavia – all offering their gifts to the Emperor enthroned in his majesty.[7] But this setting was destroyed in the year 1000. Gerbert had become Pope Sylvester II; under his influence, the notion of *Imperium christianum* appeared persistently on the agenda. Otto I's grandson, with a wonderfully sure eye, realised that the pattern of pure and simple annexation of lands to the *regnum* of Germany could no longer possibly be preserved; the Empire should form a framework within which different nations could live their own lives. This was the deep significance underlying Otto III's actions in Poland and Hungary. Both these countries were taken into the Empire and their leaders were invested by the Emperor – in the year 1000 Boleslav of Poland received the title of Co-adjutor of the Empire, and Stephen of Hungary was given a royal crown. The difference in the titles accorded to these two clarifies their personal positions in relation to Otto III: in respect of part of his lands Boleslav was a vassal of the Emperor, whereas Stephen was not bound to him by any ties of dependence. This integration of new states into the Empire produced an intermingling of several different images – the Byzantine prototype of a hierarchy of rulers surrounding the *basileus*, the imperial prerogative of creating kings, the concept put into words by Otto III's title of *servus Jesu Christi*, which St Paul had borne: he was the emperor-apostle, charged with the duty of assuring the spread of Christianity. In fact, the entry of Poland and Hungary into the Empire was accompanied by the creation of two metropolitan churches, Gnesen and Gran, while Latin missionaries were sent out as far as the Russian lands, as though the *Imperium Christianum* of the West aimed at penetrating into the Byzantine sphere of influence.

Thus, as the Empire increased in extent, so did the domain of St

[7] Reproduced in Schramm, *Kaiserbilder*, II, plate 75, and in Marc Bloch, *Société féodale*, II.

Peter, on the understanding that the latter was always to remain under the sway of the Emperor. This was the fundamental significance of the title *servus apostolorum*, used by Otto for the first time at the beginning of 1001, between the two events which took place in Poland and Hungary, when he intervened in the affairs of the Papal State, categorically rejected the Donation of Constantine[8] and reduced the Pope's temporal rôle to that of a 'lieutenant' charged with the administration of properties which remained the possession of the Empire, while he, the Emperor, on the other hand absorbed the papal prerogative of being the superior representative of the apostle, the tutelary genius of Christian Rome.[9] So, when Stephen of Hungary had done homage for his lands to St Peter, the *servus apostolorum*, who was at the same time, as the latest documents of his reign demonstrate, the *Romanorum Imperator Augustus* or the *orbis Imperator Augustus*, the latter was able to incorporate this new domain into the Empire. The service of St Peter, the administration of his earthly patrimony, were, in Otto III's eyes, so many means of achieving universality; the objectives of the Empire were identical with those of Christianity.

The successors of Otto III did not pursue this universalist trend. Henry II returned to more restricted objectives and was content to proclaim the renewal of the *Regnum Francorum*. The Empire could therefore no longer be identified with the Christian world, though it continued to cast its radiance over it; in return, the whole of Christendom had an interest in the Empire's destiny. This is the impression which emerges from a letter written by Abbot Odilo of Cluny, inviting Henry II to gather around him counsellors drawn from the whole world, so that he might, with their advice, 'maintain order in the Roman Empire'. There can be no doubt that the counsellors he referred to were ecclesiastics: so, by keeping in touch with the Church, the Empire could be maintained 'in universalism'. At the same time, in the political field, the Emperor enjoyed pre-eminence in the world: he was, as the same text informs us, the cynosure of all other peoples.[10]

And so he remained throughout the whole of the first half of the eleventh century. In 1032, under Conrad II, when the Kingdom of Burgundy was acquired, the Empire took its final shape. The first

---

[8] See Documents, X, p. 186.

[9] In the relevant iconography certain items show Otto III in the immediate proximity of the apostle – there is even a representation of the Emperor being crowned by Peter and Paul: see *Kaiserbilder*, II, plates 76 and 78.

[10] See Documents, XI, p. 188.

Salian ruler and his son Henry III were, furthermore, successful in extending their suzerainty over Bohemia and Hungary.

Thus universality reverted to a weakened form – hegemony of the Emperor – though it continued to be preserved as a concept, the central basis for which was its Roman past.

III. THE PERSON OF THE EMPEROR

A. *Emperor of the Romans*

Otto III's *Renovatio Imperii Romanorum* may indeed have been ephemeral – the Romans revolted against it in 1001 – but it was none the less an attempt to implement some of the hopes which were current in Rome and, by extending them beyond the exclusively municipal framework, to direct them towards higher ends. Far from dying out with Otto, the idea of restoring the past continued to haunt men's minds. What survived of the Roman Empire may have been no more than an idea, but by contrast the image of its ruler became more precise. It is depicted in flattering colours in a treatise written in Rome about 1030 – the Handbook of Ceremonial at the Imperial Court (*Libellus de Caerimoniis*).[11]

This is an odd work. The author was indubitably a layman and he started out from the Donation of Constantine, where he found a list of a certain number of honours, ceremonial vestments and symbols, ceded by the Emperor to Sylvester I. Gathering all these together he invested Caesar with them, thus re-creating the picture of imperial magnificence. For the remainder of his documentation the anonymous author used the writers of the Late Empire, the *Etymologies* of Isidore and doubtless also the Byzantine court etiquette about which he was able to obtain oral information. He was also not afraid to project the Roman customs and institutions of his own time into the distant past. The result of his laborious efforts is a curious essay in political archaeology, some aspects of which are worth outlining briefly.

In accordance with the purist Roman tradition he shows us the Emperor as the *praecelsus monocrator*. First he is seen ascending to the Capitol, *imitator Julii Caesaris*, in solemn procession, and giving thanks to the God Saturn who has placed him at the head of the world; then the crowd acclaims him in three languages and hails him by bowing down to the earth. The Emperor's raiment is minutely described. It is the costume of the rulers of Byzantium, mingled with sacerdotal

[11] Schramm, *Kaiser, Rom und Renovatio*, II, pp. 90-104.

elements borrowed in part from the dress of a high priest of the Ancient Law (a mantle representing the celestial vault and decorated with little bells) and in part from the apparel of bishops (a ring, and gloves of fine linen). The most characteristic passage describes the Emperor's different head-dresses – crowns of leaves, a crown of peacock feathers, a mitre[12] and a *phrygium* (the latter a memory of the Trojans who founded the Roman Empire), and lastly a golden diadem around which runs the inscription: 'Rome, capital of the world, holds the reins of the earthly globe.' Surrounding the prince are some of his supporters and helpers: the Count of the palace; the consuls in charge of the provinces; some judges charged with uttering the Law 'in Rome, in the Leonine City and in the whole world'; the man who held the title of Patrician, lieutenant-general of the Emperor, whose particular responsibility was to be the guardian of the churches and of the poor, an image clearly influenced by the memory of the title of patrician instituted by Otto III. There is even provision for the manner in which these different officials were to be invested and the manner in which the Emperor would create citizens in order that 'the number of Romans may be increased'.

The *Libellus*, with its extraordinary profusion of colour and cere-monial, and its lack of political substance, is the perfect expression of a mentality which clung to the past. It was written to flatter the imagination of the Romans, yet it was not in fact completely alien to the spirit of the Salian rulers, as is testified by a variety of indications which, cumulatively, gave a progressively Roman tinge to their vision of the Empire.

Externally this already existed. Ever since the time of Otto III the official garb of the Emperor had been that of the *basileus*. Its essential elements can be studied in the iconography: a tunic reaching to the knees and gathered at the waist by a belt, footwear of red leather, a crimson *chlamys*, open at the right side, and held in place by a *fibula* on the shoulder. In the treasure chambers of Bamberg cathedral Henry II's mantle is preserved, embroidered with the constellations and the signs of the Zodiac: it is not difficult to guess the symbolic meaning of this item, which was intended to represent the firmament, just as the golden orb which the Emperor held in his hand, the *pallea aurea*, was a sign of his universal rule. Here too is the seal used by Conrad II after his coronation: its reverse depicts the plan of a town –

[12] This head-dress also was derived from the Byzantine *camelaucum*. In the first half of the eleventh century it tended to become the liturgical head-dress of the Pope, and then of the bishops, to whom the Pope had conceded it. But at that moment it could equally well be worn by the Emperor.

the *Aurea Roma* – around which is written the inscription quoted in the *Libellus*.[13] Similarly, Conrad's sceptre has an eagle mounted on it, the emblem of Roman victory. Lastly, when Henry III in 1046 revived the title of patrician for his own use, so as to enable him to make nominations to the apostolic see, he insisted on clothing himself with its insignia – a white mitre with a golden circlet ornamenting its base, a green *chlamys* and a ring.

So much for the external equipment: we must now look at the field of politics. It is clear that from the time of Conrad II, the expression *Imperium Romanorum* tended to embrace all three kingdoms – Germany, Italy, Burgundy – and this had the effect of welding them into a union which held together for more than two centuries. But it must not be assumed that the concept of the Roman Empire was centred exclusively on one group of territories: in fact it still persisted vaguely outside this framework, in the form of an appeal to universality. Within the Empire itself, certain Roman and Byzantine principles tended from as early as 962 to have a strong influence on the imperial succession. In 967 Otto I had had his son crowned Emperor at his side, either because he was following the example of Louis the Pious and Lothair, or because he wanted to imitate the Byzantine custom of associating a *basileus* and his future successor in partnership. At the same time, the title of Augustus was extended to all members of the Saxon dynasty. Half a century later the young Henry III, son of Conrad II, was decorated with the very Roman title of *Spes Imperii*, which was reinforced by being turned into *rex* the day after he was anointed at Aix. Wipo, the official biographer of the first two Salians, called him *Caesar futurus*. We find Henry III calling himself *Rex Romanorum* immediately his father died, as though he were anxious to declare himself the ruler of the Roman Empire from the moment of his accession to the throne in Germany, even before his head was encircled by the diadem of the Caesars. This title, which guaranteed the succession of the royal line to the Empire, can be seen in the last analysis as the expression of an ever closer assimilation between the *regnum* and the *Imperium*, and at the same time the increasing Romanisation of the Salians' image of the Empire.

B. *The sacred character of the Emperor*

This fundamental aspect of the concept of empire was a heritage from antiquity which Byzantium had successfully preserved for itself. In

[13] Reproduced in Schramm, *Kaiserbilder*, II, plate 95a, cf. that of Henry IV, plate 108.

the West, the Empire was given the prestige of holy things by the Church. From 816 onwards, accession 'to the pinnacle of monarchy' had included the anointing of the Emperor, as was already the practice in the case of kings. This ceremony was combined with the coronation of the ruler, which was of Byzantine origin and was used in the West for the first time in 800. Coronation in turn then became part of the anointing of kings. The person who consecrated the Emperor was always the Pope, just as it had always – at least since the fifth century – been the right of the Patriarch of Byzantium to crown the new *basileus*. It must be stressed that from the ninth century onwards many different opinions on the significance of the rite had been aired. Some believed that heredity regulated the transmission of the Empire and that the anointing rite played a rôle only in so far as it was the expression of confirmation by God of the new prince. Side by side with this belief, however, a view began to be expressed, particularly among those around John VIII, that the rite dispensed by the supreme pontiff to the Emperor, whom he had designated, possessed a constituent value in itself.[14] Such thinking did not disappear entirely but it did drift into the background in the times of the Saxons and Salians, when the hereditary right to the Empire was reasserted, at least in so far as it was able to win acceptance in Germany.

At this point it is necessary to take a quick look at the signs and symbols which were an expression of the sacred status of the Emperor and which reinforced the status he had already acquired from his anointing as king in Aix-la-Chapelle.

Information about the actual procedure of the anointing rites for this particular period is somewhat meagre. There is a very little in the chronicles and an extremely sketchy *ordo* known as *Cencius I*,[15] which is thought to date from the first third of the tenth century. Very probably it was filled out in practice by texts borrowed from other *ordines*. It may also be assumed that new elements were progressively added to enrich it such as are extensively described in the very erudite work compiled at the end of the twelfth century (*Cencius II*), which records the ritual constituting the Emperor's consecration. As the sequence in which these accretions appeared is as yet unknown, reference must first be made to the indications given by *Cencius I* and, in order to interpret certain insignia, these must be complemented from the

---

[14] See above, pp. 31 and 33.
[15] From the name of the cardinal-chancellor of the Roman Church at the end of the twelfth century, who incorporated it in his *Liber censuum*: now called *Ordo B*. Text published in Eichmann, *Kaiserkrönung*, I, and Andrieu, *Pontifical romain*, I, No. 35a, p. 251.

German *ordo* for the anointing of a king – the formulas used for that ceremony are full of Carolingian tradition and more vigorous than those of the imperial ritual in the form in which we know it.

The main information available about the latter is that the Emperor was anointed by three bishops, those of Albano, Porto and Ostia, whereas the coronation proper was the prerogative of the Pope. Bearing in mind that a bishop is anointed by three consecrators, it is easy to see that in external form at least the Emperor was anointed in the same way as a pope. It must be noted, however, that whereas the Frankish kings of the ninth century were anointed, as were bishops, with the holy *chrism* and on their heads, the Emperor, according to *Cencius I*, received the unction on his right forearm and between his shoulders, and it was oil of the catechumens which was used for this purpose. It is important not to draw hasty conclusions from this difference in ritual, dating from the tenth century, or to deduce therefrom that emperors ranked as inferior to bishops. It should not be forgotten that the *ordo* had been drawn up in Rome at a time when consecration of bishops was still unknown: it would seem, therefore, that for the anointing of the Emperor the authorities had confined themselves to reproducing the practices of the ritual baptism.[16] It is not until the end of the eleventh century and the beginning of the twelfth that signs can be perceived of the introduction of a qualitative differentiation between the anointing of bishops and that of the Emperor. What is relevant here for the moment is that the Emperor, through the anointing, became the Christ of the Lord, the adopted son of God and responsible, in the words of one of the prayers said at the ceremony, for the government of the Church.

The anointing was followed by the coronation, which was performed by the Pope. It is possible that in the eleventh century the scene of this rite was moved from the *Confessio* of St Peter towards the altar of St Maurice, supreme patron of the Empire from the time of Otto I. The laying on of the diadem was performed 'in the name of the Father, of the Son and of the Holy Spirit', which shows better than any learned treatise can, that it was God who crowned the prince, the Pope being only the human intermediary. Like Charlemagne and like the *basileus*, the Saxon and Salian Emperor was *a Deo coronatus*. He was so acclaimed in the *Laudes*[17] and so represented in the iconography of the tenth and eleventh centuries.[18]

[16] Erdmann, *Forschungen*, p. 71.   [17] See Documents, IV, p. 179.
[18] See, for example, in Schramm, *Kaiserbilder*, II, plates 64 and 65 (Otto II), 81 and 85 (Henry II); very clear persistence of a Frankish representation, cf. plate 29 (Charles the Bald).

The design and form of the imperial crown is full of profound symbolism, which can help to illuminate and complete this basic description of the ritual. The crown in the treasure chambers of Vienna clearly reveals Byzantine influence, but its design is none the less original. It is difficult to assign a precise date to it: the inscription on the arc names Conrad II, but it is also possible that it had already been worn by Otto I. The diadem is outlined by eight little plaques of gold inset in it; four of these are decorated with pictures in enamel, the others are empty, but glittering with gold and jewels. Eight small semi-circular fields form the arc which runs from front to back, recalling the casque of the Caesars. As the figure 8 was the symbol of eternal life, the crown can be recognised as a representation of the holy city, the new Jerusalem, which is built on the plan of a square or an octagon and the walls of which are covered in gold and jewels: the Palatine Chapel of Aix was also built on an octagonal plan. Thus the Empire was the forerunner and herald of the universal and eternal reign of Christ. Every one of the components of the 'sign of glory' – it is thus that the *ordo* describes the crown – brings fresh variations on this theme. For example, a cross can be seen on the little gold plaque in front, sign of the victory of the *christianissimus princeps*; below it there is a white opal, the only one of its kind, the *orphanus*, *der Waise* or *der Weisse* of the German poets, shining with a brilliant fire and assuring the Emperor of pre-eminence over all the kings, to whom it shows the way they should follow. One of the four enamel images represents Christ, the Emperor of the world, the others show David, the symbol of Justice, Solomon – wisdom, Hezekiah – long life (even as the *Laudes* pray that their emperor may enjoy *Vita et Victoria*).[19]

In addition to the crown there were other insignia which represented the majesty and the mission of the Emperor. The sword he received at his anointing made him defender of the faith and of Christendom. The sceptre, emblem of sovereignty, has already been mentioned, but, in addition to the short sceptre, the iconography also illustrates the long baton or staff (the *virga*), scarcely distinguishable from the pastoral crosier, an indication that the authority of the Emperor had an almost episcopal quality.[20] The same was true of the ring which he wore on his finger, symbol of the union which had been concluded between the

---

[19] These details have been taken from the admirable analysis by Eichmann, *Kaiserkrönung*, II.

[20] See, in Schramm, *Kaiserbilder*, II, plates 68, 73, 74, 75, 78 (Otto III), and 104b and c (Henry III). The *Virga* was also carried by the Frankish rulers; cf. plate 9 (Charlemagne), plates 17, 18 and 19 (Lothair), plate 26 (Charles the Bald).

prince and the community of believers. After the Investiture Contest *virga* and ring ceased to be insignia of emperors (or kings).

Finally, no sketch of these representations would be complete without mention of one particular emblem belonging to the Emperors which, however, was not handed to them either when they were consecrated as kings, or in Rome. This was the venerated Holy Lance or Lance of St Maurice,[21] which had an obscure history and which originally had the significance of a holy relic, since it contained (though no one knew since what date) a nail from the Cross of Our Lord fixed in a small cavity, worked into the central part of the Lance. Political concepts were superimposed on its religious significance when in 926 the Holy Lance passed from the Kingdom of Burgundy into the possession of the House of Saxony. At that moment the relic became not only the emblem of German kingship, but also the means by which to validate claims on Italy. The Holy Lance was mounted on a block of wood and borne in front of the Emperor like a standard. In the course of the eleventh century, it found a place in the Cross of Empire, an authentic reliquary, dating from the reign of Conrad II. Both of these objects were new symbols of the sacred nature of the Emperor's functions.

Thus the century which followed the rebirth of the Empire in the West presented a concept of empire which was in a constant state of change – advancing and deepening. This concept emanated from a period which found it impossible to produce a rational theory of sovereignty. It was created by delving largely into Frankish tradition and it then took on a tinge of Roman colouring. Centred on the supremacy of the Emperors, it bore within itself the aspiration towards universality. It oscillated to some extent between the power of the Germanic rulers and the theme of the Renovation of the Roman Empire. It was expressed in images, in actions and in symbols and drew its greatest strength from the vision of divine authority wielded on earth by the representative of Christ-Caesar. It was in his capacity as *typum gerens Christi* that the Emperor controlled the papacy and appeared as the true head of the Church of the Empire – the two institutions were fused in him. The synthesis of all these elements can best be left to Bishop Benzo of Alba in whom the concept of empire in the eleventh century found its most brilliant herald;[22] but at the

---

[21] The latter name was the more usual in the eleventh century. Cf. Folz, *Souvenir et légende*, pp. 457 et seq.

[22] See Documents, XII, p. 188.

same time it should be noted that his call to Henry IV was a genuine cry of alarm, for, as he had observed, radically different tendencies had already appeared which presented a profound challenge to the very essence of the concept of empire.

7

The Concept of Empire and the Papacy

For more than two centuries the papacy and the Empire were in conflict. The fundamental and deep-seated reason for their disagreement was the fact that the ideas and ambitions cherished by each interpenetrated those of the other. It is, of course, well known that the emperors had always claimed that they ruled the Church in the dual tradition of Rome and the Carolingians, but it is less generally appreciated that the popes extended the conception of themselves as rulers of the Church to include the idea of an empire over which they also reigned. There is no doubt that this idea was far from being the sole inspiration of their actions and that it appeared indeed only intermittently; but it was latent and had been so, as we have already seen, since the first centuries of Christendom. It re-emerged at the point in time when the Church once more became fully aware of itself, that is to say from about the middle of the eleventh century, and it persisted during some of the most illustrious pontificates up to the time of Boniface VIII. To obtain a clear grasp of this concept of empire is not easy, because it was found at one time in the spiritual, at another in the temporal sphere and sometimes even simultaneously in both. It must therefore be analysed by examining it at several levels: its external setting, the internal transformation of the pontifical *auctoritas*, and lastly the new interpretation given to the term 'empire' itself.

I. THE SETTING: THE PAPACY, HEIR OF THE
ROMAN EMPIRE

As a logical consequence of its emancipation, which had been the subject of the Investiture Contest, the Church was submitted in the course of the second half of the eleventh century to a re-organisation in depth, the result of which was to incline it towards ever-increasing centralisation. From 1054, by which time the break with Byzantium was complete, the Western Church had taken on a Catholic and Roman appearance. Side by side with these developments awareness of its ancient heritage was re-awakened and it was as though the idea of *Renovatio* became centred on the papacy. The papacy seemed to seize for itself the tradition of the Christian Roman Empire, using the expression 'Empire' in its most spiritualised sense to signify the universal Empire which Leo I had envisaged for the successors of Peter. Cardinal Humbert of Moyenmoutier, one of the greatest protagonists of the Reform, drew a parallel between ancient Rome and pontifical Rome, painting the former in dark colours. At the same time he recognised that it was the Empire of ancient Rome which had paved the way for the Empire of the Roman Church whose 'power extends as far as the Kingdom of the heavens; at its summit the apostolic see, invested with all authority, both divine and human, holding the reins of heaven and earth, is situated immediately beneath Christ'.[1] Had not the moment come to assert the continuity of the Empire, the fact that the one Empire was a continuation of the other? Indeed, certain images now began to emerge which could be used to illustrate this principle and at the same time greatly enhance the prestige of the Roman Church and that of its head. In the last resort these all had their inspiration in the Donation of Constantine which was now, after a long period of oblivion, brought out and incorporated in the principal canonical compilations of the eleventh century, thereby becoming part of the great collections of the following era.

A. *The Roman* Curia, *senate of the Church*

It will be remembered that Constantine was alleged to have granted senatorial honours to the Lateran clergy. The same idea now re-emerged in expanded form in the writings of Peter Damian, who compared the rôle of the Roman clergy to that of the former senate. 'In the same way', he wrote, 'as the senate of ancient times aimed at

---

[1] Schramm, *Kaiser, Rom und Renovatio*, II, pp. 128–33.

making all nations subjects of the Roman Empire, so the spiritual senators of the universal Church have a duty to work for the submission of all mankind to Christ, the true Emperor.'[2] That this analogy became reality we learn from the progressive organisation of the Roman *Curia*.

And so this expression, which first appeared only incidentally towards 1060, in the time of Nicholas II, became common usage under Urban II. It completely ousted the term *palatium*, just as that had been substituted for *patriarchium*. The new word was evocative of the two ideas at once – a court in the feudal sense of the word, equipped with various offices (treasury, chancellery, chapel), and the senate of ancient Rome. The essential factor was the fusion of the three categories of cardinals in one single college, which was started under Leo IX, was strengthened by Nicholas II and completed its development about 1100. Abandoning their original functions, these dignitaries as a body became henceforth the Pope's counsellors in his government of the Church; moreover, after 1059 they enjoyed the privilege of electing the Pope. They formed, as the Code of Canon Law states to this day, the senate of the Roman Pontiff. We may well see, in the assimilation of the *Curia* to a medieval court, what looks like an adaptation of Roman institutions to feudal times, but in fact the new presentation, which resuscitated the former senate in the College of Cardinals, was far more important in its consequences – if only because it became permanent. Times were changing and the pontifical administration was adapting itself to the changes. By having recourse to the remote past, it was able to restore imperial absolutism for ever, thus establishing this principle as the essential feature of the government of the Church from the time of the Investiture Contest.

B. *The Pope, bearer of the imperial insignia*

Here we have another image, complementary to the first, but even more likely to stir the imagination. It had its origin in the *Dictatus papae* of Gregory VII, in which he claimed that the Roman pontiff alone had the right to wear the insignia of the Empire.[3] Of these insignia two in particular must be examined: the crown and the red cope.

Once again reference to the Donation is necessary, for by it Constantine gave Sylvester the imperial diadem and the *phrygium*: Sylvester

---

[2] *Opusc.* 30, chapter VII, P.L., 145, 540.

[3] *Register*, II, 55a, eighth proposition (apparently directed against similar claims advanced by the Byzantine Patriarch) ed. Caspar, I, p. 204.

refused to use the former but agreed to allow the Emperor to place the latter on his head. Very soon, however, this emblem began to evolve into a crown: it is extremely significant that in a Roman *ordo* of the ninth century the tall white cap was already being called a *regnum* – doubtless because its base was in the form of a circle. In the same text too, it is stated that on the day of his ordination at St Peter's the Pope made the master of the stables place the *regnum* on his head outside the church before he mounted his horse.[4] After that there is a break in the evidence and when next mentioned about the middle of the eleventh century, the former *phrygium* had changed in both shape and meaning. For one thing, it had given birth to the mitre – Leo IX was wearing it, and permitting certain bishops to use it, before it became something which the entire episcopate could use. From then on it seems that there was no particular head-dress reserved for the Pope, which was somewhat embarrassing for him, all the more so as at the end of the eleventh century onwards and during a good part of the twelfth century Peter's successors found it necessary to travel a good deal throughout Christendom. In the light of these circumstances it is easy to understand how the former *phrygium* came to undergo a further transformation, described by H. W. Klewitz.[5] At its base there was a circle which became a jewelled diadem, such as is represented in certain frescoes of the church of St Clement, which date from the end of the ninth century. So the tiara was born: in the twelfth century the first diadem was replaced by a crown with florets; to this were added two others, one during the thirteenth century, the other almost certainly in the Avignon period; and this gave rise to the term *Triregnum*,[6] as the papal head-dress was henceforth designated. But it was not the object alone which was changed – its significance underwent a profound transformation at the same time: what had been a purely spiritual emblem in the Donation, was henceforth regarded as a symbol of sovereignty. No one has put this better than Innocent III, who remarked that the Roman pontiff wore both the mitre, *in signum pontificii* and the *regnum*, *in signum Imperii*.[7]

The tiara, emblem of temporal government, could not be used by a pope as a head-dress when he was performing his religious functions. On the other hand, from the middle of the eleventh century, pontiffs

---

[4] P.L., 78, 1007. For a discussion of the date of this text, cf. Andrieu, *Ordines romani*, I, 487.

[5] *Die Krönung des Papstes* – see bibliography.

[6] At that time perhaps expressing the Pope's dominion over the three parts of the world.

[7] Sermon for the feast of St Sylvester, P.L., 217, 481; cf. the third sermon *in consecratione pontificis*, col. 665.

were depicted wearing the *regnum* at the celebration of the most solemn masses[8] – e.g. Gregory VII at Christmas 1075 – following the example of the Emperor and of the kings of France and England, who wore their crowns at all great religious festivals. Paschal II, third in succession after Gregory VII, was the first pope to be crowned on the day of his assuming office (in 1099): during the twelfth century this became a regular custom.

The *cappa rubea*, which Sylvester is similarly alleged to have received from Constantine, seems to have been even more important than the crown. Because it was the imperial cloak, it was an additional sign of sovereignty, but it was also a sign of investiture. From the time of the Investiture Contest, the 'enmantling' of a pope had been, along with his enthroning in the Lateran, the most essential rite of his accession to the supreme pontificate. Moreover, if an election were disputed, the fact of having been able to take immediate possession of the red cloak was considered as a criterion of legitimacy: Victor IV, for example, was elected in 1159 by a minority only, but over Alexander III he had the advantage of holding the cloak.

And so the process which began during the Investiture Contest reached its culminating point in the thirteenth century, when all the symbols of empire became attached to the papacy. Popes such as Gregory IX and Boniface VIII are seen to be in every respect successors of Constantine – the description of the enthronement of the former and the actions and attitudes of the latter are ample evidence of this.[9] We must now investigate the extent of the special powers which these emblems symbolised.

II. THE INTERNAL EVOLUTION OF THE PONTIFICAL *AUCTORITAS*

In the middle of the tenth century the ground had already been prepared for a reform of the Church. The reforming movement was first directed towards the moral and religious regeneration of the clergy, but after 1050 its original aims were extended and the effective establishment of Roman primacy became its ultimate objective. It was bathed in political Augustinism of which it was surely the most complete expression, for, in the eyes of the reformers, the State existed only as a servant

---

[8] The restoration of the stational liturgy is the work of Leo IX. Eighteen stations were described as 'crowned'.

[9] See Documents, XIX, p. 201 and XXII, p. 207.

or organ of the Church and its fundamental purpose, its duty, was to
cooperate in saving souls. The supreme responsibility for their salvation
lay, however, with the head of the Church: such was the theory propounded continually by Gregory VII. His *magisterium* was founded on
the power to bind and to loose; it was essentially religious, and, moreover, moral. The Pope was the arbiter of consciences, the judge of the
deeds of all men, including rulers. When any rulers showed themselves
to be unworthy of their function it was the duty of the Pope to inflict
sanctions on them. All this was inspired by tradition pure and simple.
What was new was, first, that Gregory took up his position at a point
beyond the view previously expressed by Gelasius, in that he recognised
but one reality, the Church;[10] and, secondly, that he applied his
principles with harsh rigour. There is no doubt that his double deposition of Henry IV and the intransigence with which he imposed the
Reform must have seemed to his contemporaries – not without reason
– to be patently revolutionary.

This was the first conception of the relations between the papacy
and the empire but, in the twelfth and thirteenth centuries, a new
doctrine began to evolve side by side with it. According to this theory
Peter and his successors inherited all the powers of Christ, who was
both the Priest above all others and the King of the universe. The
Pope was thus entitled on two grounds to rule the world. Princes –
and an emperor was in no way an exception to the general rule – were
but his mandatories. Starting out from the notion of moral *magisterium*,
of *ratio peccati*, the idea that the Bishop of Rome had direct authority
super reges et regna gradually emerged. Let us now try to distinguish
the stages of this development.

A. *Some of the arguments used in the debate: allegories*
Like the insignia of authority, allegories served the two supreme
authorities of Christendom either in turn or simultaneously.

For example, there was the image of the Two Luminaries. In the
mystique of the Roman Empire the Emperor was held to be the
incarnation of the *Sol invictus*, the *Sol iustitiae*, and in the thirteenth
century this image, with the same significance, was revived in connexion with Frederick II. During the Investiture Contest it had

---

[10] When Gregory quoted the famous text in his second letter to Hermann of Metz
(*Reg.*, VIII, 21, in Caspar, II, p. 553), he left out the passages which affirmed the independence of each of the two powers in this world. Cf. also his letter to Rudolf of Rheinfelden (*Reg.*, I, 19, I, pp. 31–2). For a study of all these ideas, see the two works of
Mgr. Arquillière.

been replaced by a comparison of the two luminaries (taken from Genesis), which served as an argument in the debate on the relationship between the Spiritual and the Temporal. Gregory VII made use of it in a relatively moderate sense: writing to William the Conqueror, the only deduction which he drew from the co-existence of the two luminaries was that the rôle of guardian of spiritual matters fell to the popes; he did, however, demand that the King obey any precepts which he should think fit to give to him.[11] One century later the allegory was given a clearly political interpretation as is testified by the letter which Innocent III wrote to the rectors of Tuscia,[12] in which spiritual power is represented as the source of all light, while the moon only reflects the light it borrows from the sun: the firmament – the higher unity which presides over these relationships – corresponds to the Church which embraces the universal community of men, and therefore also all nations.

The symbol of the Two Swords underwent an analogous evolution. For a long time it was only a simple metaphor, and, from the time of the Patristics, had represented spiritual power and temporal power. Charlemagne's dual status as *rex et sacerdos* led Alcuin to demonstrate, in a famous letter to his master, that he possessed the two swords to defend the Church *foris et intus*.[13] During the Investiture Contest, the image was transformed into an argument, based on Matthew xxvi, 51 and Luke xxii, 35–8, and was employed by both sides, sometimes with the object of co-ordinating the two powers, sometimes in order to affirm the preponderance of the one over the other. The papacy in particular made use of it in this last sense, without however, immediately proceeding to act on the consequences which might flow from it. For example, towards the middle of the twelfth century, St Bernard formulated the argument thus:[14] Peter was holder of the two swords; the spiritual sword was to be wielded by the Church, the other on behalf of the Church; the one by the priest, the other by the knight, but only on a sign being given (*nutu*) by the priest and on the orders of the Emperor. In setting down this theory, St Bernard did not perhaps go quite so far as to suggest that the papacy possessed direct power over the temporal world. Nevertheless, the argument he formulated implied an obligation on rulers to obey, even in matters temporal, the orders

[11] *Reg.*, VII, 25 (Caspar, II, pp. 505–7).
[12] P.L., 214, 327.
[13] *Mon. Germ. Epistolae*, IV, No. 171, p. 281. The image was preserved in the collective memory. In the middle of the twelfth century, the argument in favour of the holiness of the Emperor celebrates the *inclitus ventilator utriusque gladii*.
[14] *De Consideratione*, Book IV, chapter iii (P.L. 182, 776).

of Peter's successor. On occasion Innocent did indeed have recourse to the symbol of the swords to ensure a programme of understanding and cooperation between the papacy and the Empire,[15] but his successors no longer observed the slightest restraint. The Canonists offered them important arguments with which to debate, for in their eyes the unity of the body of Christendom demanded that the head of the Church alone should be ruler: from Rufin to Hostiensis and to William Durand of Mende the Decretalists were unanimous in declaring that the two swords both belonged to the sovereign pontiff.

At this meeting-point of Allegory and Law, we must try to obtain a clear idea of Innocent III's concept of empire.

B. *Innocent III's conception of imperial authority and the papacy*

This conception stands out in brilliant colours, so rich that they frequently conceal the outline of its contours. The first feature which strikes one is that the Pope took up a position outside time and that he aimed at controlling what was eternal in man. This explains why he searched in the remotest past for the sign of Revelation on the government of the human race, regarded as a unit. It seemed to him that the great figure of Melchizedek, forerunner of Christ, simultaneously priest and king, was such a one, in view of the fact that of the two functions which were fused in him the priesthood was regarded as both senior and of superior status to his authority as king. In his capacity as vicar of Christ, which placed him on an exceptional plane – 'less than God but greater than man'[16] – Innocent claimed that both authorities were in their entirety united in him.

This vision, projected outside time, found historical justification in the person of Pope Sylvester. When he received from Constantine the power and the insignia of the Empire he became outwardly the representation of the dual position held by Melchizedek.[17] Yet it must not be forgotten that by that time the Donation had already taken on a significance quite different from what it had possessed in the past: it was now no more than the recognition by Constantine of the dual authority of the Bishop of Rome.[18]

Lastly, it was important to Innocent that this universal empire should be seen to be the successor and heir of the Roman Empire. So he revived Leo I's line of thought to remind people that 'God had estab-

---

[15] See, for example, his message to Otto IV in 1209 (P.L. 216, 1162).
[16] Second sermon *in consecratione pontificis* (P.L., 217, 657–8).
[17] Sermon for the feast of St Sylvester, *Ibid.*, 481. [18] See below, p. 83.

lished the principate of the Church in the place where the imperial monarchy had established its residence'.[19] When he acceded to the pontificate, the Pope became united in mystical matrimony to the Church of Rome which here took the place of the divine entity, *Roma*; she brought him as a dowry 'the fullness of spiritual power and wide extent of temporal possessions',[20] this last expression signifying the Empire in the most idealised sense of the word. But in Innocent's eyes Rome was also the new Jerusalem – it was so defined in the legend which gave a new form to the little church of *Quo Vadis* – the city where the holder of the highest authority of the priesthood was to be found, installed there by God, an authority which might in certain special cases be used to exercise jurisdiction in affairs of state.

The Decretal[21] which defines this competency is, however, very cautious in tone and very subtle. The only grounds it gives for the intervention of the pontiff in the government of a state is the old *ratio peccati*, i.e. the *magisterium* of consciences. When he had to explain his ideas to monarchs, Innocent III knew that he must keep within the traditional limits. It was when he confronted the Emperors, his most dangerous rivals, that the Pope advanced his views on the superiority of his own authority.

III. THE PAPACY AND THE EMPIRE

The most illustrious victim of this important increase of pontifical authority was to be the Empire, which, let it be said, did not go down without putting up strong resistance to the Pope's claims; there will be an opportunity to revert to this later and to assess its effect. At this point we must draw attention to the fact that it was arguments based on the Donation of Constantine and the *Translatio* of the Empire which permitted the papacy to contest the independence of the institution and which also gave grounds for changes to be made in the ritual of anointing, beginning in 1208 – changes which had the effect of diminishing the status of the Emperor's person.

It was on the eve of the Investiture Contest that the Donation of Constantine assumed the significance of a political argument, thanks

---

[19] Letter to the Patriarch of Constantinople in 1199 (P.L., 214, 761).
[20] Third sermon *in consecratione* (P.L., 217, 661).
[21] *Per Venerabilem* (P.L., 214, 1133) or Decretals of Gregory IX, X, *Qui filii sint legitimi*, Book IV, tit. XVII, C. 13 (Friedberg, II, pp. 714-16).

to the pens of the controversialists and also of the pontiffs themselves. This did not happen until it had been suitably revised, for it would have been impossible to reconcile the papal claims to universal government, based on spiritual *magisterium*, with those imperial powers which the papacy owed to the kindness of an emperor. Just when the reform of the Church was starting, Leo IX made the first attempt to resolve this difficulty. He explained that Constantine, convinced in his heart of the high dignity which clothed the successors of Peter, bearers of an authority which had existed prior to his own, had given back to Sylvester the imperial honours, etc. which he had received from God Himself.[22] The expression *reddere* was thus substituted for *donare*: the Pope was no longer under an obligation to the Emperor and could therefore freely enjoy his rights to temporal sovereignty. All the same, it is remarkable that Gregory VII's only use of the famous forgery was on a symbolical level; all his other references to it are merely allusions.[23] On the other hand, the disputants in the two camps made great use of the Donation in their debates. The most tendentious interpretation given to it by the pontifical polemists appeared in a treatise by Honorius Augustodunensis in the first third of the twelfth century. According to this author, Sylvester received from Constantine not only the imperial crown, but also the assurance that no emperor would ever accede to supreme power without the consent of the Pope, who saw in this gesture the return to him of the right to dispose of the *dominium mundi*. Sylvester, aware that he needed a helper for the defence of the Church, immediately exercised this right and at once made Constantine responsible for the Church's defence by handing over the sword and the crown to him.[24] The original legend was thus completely reversed; the Emperor was now under an obligation to the Pope and, although this was not said in so many words, had become his vassal. Sylvester's action could scarcely be interpreted otherwise than as an investiture conferred by him. Numerous fairly clear pieces of evidence exist to prove that the Roman court allowed itself to be won over little by little by representations of this type. One need only recall the fresco painted on the walls of the Lateran Palace in the time of Innocent II, with the object of illustrating how Lothair of Supplinburg had become emperor; or the word *beneficium* applied to the Empire by Hadrian IV,

[22] Letter to Michael Caerularius, Patriarch of Constantinople, P.L., 143, 752.
[23] Thus, for example, with regard to Spain: the *regnum* of Spain belonged since ancient times directly to St Peter (*Reg.*, I, 7 [1073] and IV, 28 [1077], in Caspar, I, pp. 11 and 345). Cf. also *Reg.*, IX, 3.
[24] *Summa gloria de Apostolico et Augusto*, chapter xvii (*Mon. Germ. Libelli de lite*, III, p. 71).

which unleashed the indignation of Frederick I at the Diet of Besançon in 1157.[25]

In the course of the second half of the twelfth century, the papacy withdrew temporarily from this position, and in consequence the thesis of pontifical sovereignty over the Empire faded into the background for a time; but subsequently Innocent gave an interpretation of Charlemagne's coronation as emperor which enabled him ultimately to make a clear pronouncement, affirming the rights of the Roman pontiffs in relation to the imperial accession.

In fact the events which took place on 25th December, 800, had been the subject of much discussion ever since the ninth century: had not Charlemagne become emperor as a result of the initiative and actions of Pope Leo III? The Emperor's publicists minimised the rôle of the Pope, maintaining that he had acted only in agreement with the Romans and with a mandate from them; or they suggested that Charlemagne had become ruler over the Empire as a result of his conquests. The opposite camp insisted that the initiative had been Leo III's and pointed out that the imperial crown was a symbol of the supreme temporal honour which the Pope had decided to confer on the King of the Franks. But there was more to it than that – both parties alike regarded the coronation of Charlemagne as a sign of the *Translatio* of the Empire. In the most general meaning of the term, *Translatio* indicated the passage of an institution or of an honour from one place to another. It was regularly used to describe the rebirth of the Western Empire, without implying that the transfer had caused the imperial authority in Byzantium to come to an end. It seems more probable that people saw the *Translatio* as putting an end to the domination still exercised by the *basileus* over certain territories in the West. First employed in the ninth century, the expression had been used, since the Investiture Contest, to cover the controversy concerning the accession of Charlemagne to the Empire,[26] up to the moment when Pope Innocent III conferred an official validity on it by making his famous intervention in the political schism which divided Germany on the death of Henry VI.

Innocent III – who had, incidentally, been implored by the electors of one of the kings (Otto of Brunswick) to intervene in the debate – declared that regulation of the matter was by right a function of the

---

[25] See these two facts placed side by side in the *Gesta Frederici* of Otto of Freising, III, 10, in Simson, S. R. G., 1912, pp. 176-7.

[26] Evolution of the controversy and the main texts in Folz, *Souvenir et légende*; see the index.

papacy because it was the papacy which had transferred the Empire from the East to the West, in the person of Charlemagne, and because it had thus become the supreme authority which could decide who was to rule the Empire.[27] These two principles became decisive in settling the conditions of accession to the Empire, which the Pope compared with those of accession to ecclesiastical positions. The foundation on which his arguments rested was the election of the future emperor – *Romanorum rex in imperatorem postmodum promovendus*. Frederick I and Henry VI had sought to ensure that the principle of hereditary succession to the Empire should prevail, but Innocent III reacted vigorously against their attempts. He formally recognised the right of the German princes to elect their king, stressing incidentally – in order to bind them more closely to the Holy See – that they had received this privilege from the papacy at the time when the *Translatio* of the Empire was carried out by the Pope. But this election, contrary to the principles which German public law aimed at imposing, did not automatically confer all the authority of an emperor on the King of the Romans – it only made him a candidate for the imperial throne. It was the Pope who was the judge of his worthiness and fitness to be entrusted with this function. In fact, Innocent was reserving to himself the right to examine the King and to approve him, as though he were an ordinand. Only with this approval could the King be permitted to rise to the status of emperor. He would in the last resort become emperor only by the laying on of hands conferred by the Pope – 'a gesture of benediction, of coronation and of investiture'.[28] Although the Pope still did not say so in so many words, the position of the Emperor could be compared to that of a vassal. The conclusions drawn by Innocent III from the *Translatio* thus coincided with those which some people thought flowed from the Donation of Constantine. All that remained was to fuse the two arguments into a synthesis from which the final consequences could be drawn – that was the work of Innocent III's immediate successors.

First there was Gregory IX, expressing his views vigorously in a letter addressed in 1236 to Frederick II.[29] The imperial polemists had denounced the Donation as an arbitrary decision of Constantine's and, as such, a nullity, but Gregory denied this, saying that it had received the approbation of the senate of the whole Empire and that the first

[27] Among other documents, see the *Deliberatio super facto Imperii* (P.L., 216, 1025–1029).
[28] *Deliberatio*. For the theory concerning accession to the Empire the reader should refer particularly to the decretal *Venerabilem*, dated 1202; P.L., 216, 1065, or *Mon. Germ. Constitutiones*, II, No. 398.
[29] *Mon. Germ. Epistolae saec. XIII*, p. 604.

Christian prince was on this occasion handing over to Sylvester not only the imperial insignia but indeed the whole Empire and particularly Italy – the importance of such an affirmation is studied below.[30] Pursuing his line of thought, the Pope saw in the *Translatio* of the Empire to Charlemagne a delegation to a suitable person of the monarchy of which the sovereign pontiff was the repository, without the substance of the Pope's authority being thereby affected in any way whatsoever. Each imperial coronation renewed the first grant of the temporal sword to the Emperor by the Pope. The former was therefore dependent on an authority superior to his own.

Towards the middle of the century, under Innocent IV, who deposed Frederick II at the Council of Lyons in 1245, the doctrine of papal omnipotence reached its apogee and remained there until the drama of Anagni. To provide a basis for this authority the Pope used every argument at once – starting with the *ratio peccati* and the authority of the keys, then the Donation of Constantine, which, in Innocent's eyes, no longer signified anything more than the renunciation by the Emperor of the tyrannical power which he had hitherto exercised. It was from Sylvester that he had received the imperial power within the Church, in order that he might use it in the interests of the papacy. As for the *Translatio*, it was the perfect illustration of the Pope's superior right to dispose of the Empire.[31] The Emperor was no more than the vassal and vicar of the Roman pontiff – the latter stood between him and God and was his creator. What is more, as is confirmed by certain sources, the Pope had become the 'real emperor.'[32]

All these ideas led to a considerable diminution of the prestige of the Empire, as is plain from the last *ordo* of the anointing ceremony, which dates from the pontificate of Innocent III and was first used on the occasion of Otto IV's coronation. Scarcely any changes were made in it after that date and it was used for the last time at the anointing of Charles V in 1530.

This *ordo* was plainly intended to establish that the ceremony had ceased to be the expression and sign of confirmation of the Emperor

---

[30] See p. 125 and note 8.

[31] Among the numerous texts the reader is advised to refer here to the one which is most typical by reason of the diversity of thought expressed therein, viz. the indictment directed by the Pope, at the end of 1245, against Frederick II, (Winkelmann, *Acta Imperii inedita*, II, p. 697).

[32] See, for example, the annotations to the Decretals, made by Henry of Susa (*Hostiensis*), *Commentarii in V libros Decretalium*, Book III, tit. 34, chapter viii, Nos. 26, 27, pub. in Venice in 1581, vol. III, p. 128. See also Documents, XVIII, p. 199, II.

by God. Henceforth the Pope alone was the source of the Emperor's authority and the anointing and the crowning were acts of constituent value. In this *ordo*, Innocent III was recalling and confirming John VIII's line of thought:[33] it was from the Pope that the Emperor held not only his title but also his authority. Nothing indicated this change better than the new form of the *Laudes* from which the important clause *a Deo coronatus* was eradicated.[34]

The significance of the anointing had also been diminished. Since the second half of the eleventh century the papacy had been trying to reduce its importance, in order to contest the right which the Emperor claimed it gave him to participate in the government of the Church. In his second letter to Hermann of Metz, Gregory VII had observed that a layman could not be given a power equivalent to that attributed to an exorcist: 'spiritual emperor to chase out demons'.[35] This juxta-position of the imperial title and that of a minor order is striking: the Emperor was to descend from the quasi-episcopal level to which the consecration had hitherto elevated him, to a much lower status. In the course of the twelfth century the works of the canonists and the symbolists made a clear-cut distinction between the anointing of an emperor and the anointing of a bishop. From the tenth century the use of the oil of the catechumens for the emperors had put them in a position inferior to that of the bishops, for whom the holy *chrism* was used. Innocent III was a great jurist and by denying a sacramental character to the ceremony he put the finishing touch to its evolution.[36] So, in the *ordo* drawn up by him for the ceremonial anointing of the emperors, the actual anointing is performed separately from the mass, although until that time it had taken place during the mass, following the procedure used for bishops and priests. Henceforth it took place before the *Introit* at the side altar of St Maurice.[37]

By contrast, the main act of the rites was now the handing over of the insignia of empire, performed before the *Confessio* of St Peter, thus illustrating clearly the rôle of the Pope. Nothing conveys this better than the formula for the *traditio* of the sword: 'Receive', says the Pope, 'this sword taken by our hands from the body of the blessèd Peter and conceded imperially to thee for the defence of the Holy

---

[33] See above, pp. 31 and 33.

[34] See Documents, XVIII, p. 199, I. Text of the *Ordo* of the anointing by Eichmann, *Kaiserkrönung*, I, p. 259, or in Andrieu, *Pontifical romain*, II, p. 385.

[35] *Reg.*, VIII, 21 (Caspar, II, p. 555).

[36] It retained this character into the middle of the twelfth century, being strongly rooted in men's minds. See below, p. 102 and Documents, XV, p. 195.

[37] Here, in the middle of the eleventh century, the insignia used to be handed over. See above, p. 71.

Church of God.' The Emperor was thus represented as no more than the battle arm of the papacy, which was the holder of the two swords, and which delegated one of them to the *invictissimus imperator Romanorum*.

8

The Concept of the Empire as a Roman Institution

I. GENERAL CHARACTERISTICS

If we except England and Spain, where the concept of empire took on a special form, it can be said that from the time of its restoration in the West the Empire never ceased to have some connexion with Rome. At times this was very superficial – for example, as already mentioned, in the Frankish countries between 814 and 875, or about the date when Otto I acceded to the throne – but it became steadily more solid under the influence of the movement towards the *Renovatio Imperii Romanorum*, which first appeared in the middle of the ninth century and derived its strength from a belief in the continuity of the Empire. Beyond this very general principle, however, no precise formula emerged. The perpetuity of the Empire was a fiction; so too was its universality; the Emperor, as depicted by the *Libellus de caerimoniis*, was a brilliant ornament.[1] In turn, the attitude of the Romans towards an empire which had borrowed its name from them, but which in reality never ceased to be profoundly Frank and Germanic, had been extremely variable, ranging from a claim to the right of participation in the accession of the prince to an affirmation of the Romans' independence of any foreign ruler and their right to live entirely turned in on themselves – as demonstrated by the history of the city in the tenth century. Even when brought back within the fold of the Germanic monarchy, Rome still would not renounce her hopes of becoming once more the true capital of an emperor in whose selection she would have played a preponderant rôle.

[1] See above, pp. 67 *et seq.*

To a certain extent such hopes were stimulated at the beginning of the second half of the eleventh century by the renascence of Roman law, one of the most noteworthy events in the intellectual history of the West, comparable in its effect to the revival of philosophy which began about the same time in the Transalpine countries.

Roman law had, of course, never ceased to be known and applied in the territory of Rome and of the former exarchate of Ravenna. In 1032, disregarding for the first time the principle of the personality of laws, the Emperor Conrad II issued a *constitutio* which prescribed that all disputes between Romans and Lombards in Rome and in the district around it were to be judged exclusively in accordance with Roman law.² It continued to be studied if not in Rome itself at least in the cities of Northern Italy, notably at Pavia and Ravenna. It was taught in the schools as part of the *Trivium* by masters of rhetoric aided by experts, the *legisperiti* or *iurisconsulti*. Those two centres were eclipsed at the beginning of the twelfth century by the school of Bologna, headed by the illustrious Irnerius, who directed studies of the great Justinian compilations. From then on knowledge of the *Corpus Iuris* developed and spread widely. It contained, in particular, a doctrine of the Roman Empire on which the glossators made it their task to comment. At this point, a summary analysis of their thinking is necessary for a proper understanding of the reason why the only attempt made in the twelfth century to put into practice a doctrine which seemed to be commendable for its simplicity and vigour resulted in failure.

II. THE JURIDICAL FOUNDATIONS OF THE EMPIRE

The doctrine just mentioned was based entirely on the law of investiture or *Lex Regia*, which is enunciated in the preamble to Justinian's *Institutes*: 'Whatever has seemed good to the prince is to have the force of law, in view of the fact that, by the *Lex Regia*, the people have granted to him the whole of their empire and their power'³ – the Empire thus originated in a delegation by the Roman people. How then was this fundamental reality to be reconciled with the evolution which the Empire had undergone since classical times – an empire territorially very different from the former one – over which foreigners ruled, and which was bowed down under the weight of a heavy obligation to the papacy? An empire of which the Romans were no longer masters but subjects? A radical attitude of mind ought to have led the Romans to

---

² *Mon. Germ. Constitutiones*, I, p. 82.   ³ *Institutes* ,I, 2, 5–6.

deny the legality of the institution, but in fact they came to terms with it.

Indeed, they can be seen struggling, though not entirely successfully, to restore the independence of the Empire's government in relation to the ecclesiastical authorities. In addition, while admitting that the Roman Empire was no longer what it had been in the past, they affirmed that it remained universal because it still stood for that part of mankind which was superior to all the rest by its dignity and its unity, and that its laws thus had a general significance. One last problem remained to be solved – that of the origin of the emperors and of their accession to the Empire. The Romanists did not pose the problem: they adapted themselves to the facts. Their notion of the enduring nature of the institution so dominated them that their chief aim was to appropriate the emperors for Rome so that they might become the restorers of Roman laws in the world and thus appear as 'the imitators of those whose successors they claimed to be'.[4] The earliest signs of this point of view appeared during the first third of the eleventh century, in the *Libellus de caerimoniis*: when investing a judge with his functions, the Emperor handed over the Justinian Code to him, and invited him to make use of this compilation when he dispensed justice 'to the City, the Leonine City and the whole world'.[5]

If, then, it was natural for the jurists to turn for practical purposes towards the emperors, it is equally certain that the emperors quickly realised the fact that Roman Law was capable of providing them with an instrument of authority and absolutism: an alliance was soon formed between Roman Law and imperial authority. In this connexion it is interesting to note that one of the manuscripts of the *Institutes*, written in Italy in the second half of the tenth century, was found at the court of Henry II. Certain laws, such as the Law of Majesty (*Lex Digna*), were utilised to the full under Otto III and, later, under Henry III.[6]

The *Lex Regia* on the other hand proved more difficult to manipulate. It might possibly have liberated the Empire from the papacy, but there was a risk that it would also have made accession to the imperial throne dependent on election by the Romans, and the Germanic emperors were anxious not to be under the tutelage of either the popes or the Romans. Nevertheless, it appears that, at the height of the Investiture Contest, at least one attempt was made to exploit Roman public law in favour of Henry IV. Three forged 'privileges' drawn up

[4] *Quaestiones de juris subtilitatibus*, probably by Irnerius (ed. Fitting, Berlin, 1894), 1, 16.
[5] In Schramm, *op. cit.*, II, pp. 123–4.
[6] *Mon. Germ. Diplomata*, II: dipl. of Otto III, No. 339, dated 999; *Constitutiones*, I, p. 102: constit. of Henry III, dated 1052.

between 1080 and 1084 by members of the circle surrounding Peter Crassus, the Ravenna jurist, and intended for diffusion in Rome, showed the people of the city, 'who made the law according to custom', delegating their entire power and sovereignty first to Charlemagne and then to Otto I. Thus these texts legalised the Germanic Empire and at the same time explicitly recognised the right of the Romans to dispose of the supreme authority.

Though potentially important, these documents[7] were nevertheless only of an occasional character and the ultimate conclusions were never drawn from them. A striking fact about them is that the author of the forged 'privileges' laid great emphasis in his writings on the point that the Roman people, when they voted the *Lex Regia*, actually divested themselves of their powers, once and for all. The law of investiture therefore was valid only for the past and there could be no question whatsoever of the Romans profiting from the famous text in the present or in the future: henceforth Caesar alone had the right to determine who should succeed to the Empire. It should be noted, likewise, that the person who inspired these forgeries was the same Peter Crassus who later, in his apologia for Henry IV, defended the doctrine of imperial heredity, basing his arguments on those Roman laws which controlled the transmission of private property.[8]

The only possible conclusion appears to be that at the beginning of the twelfth century the doctrine of the delegation of the Empire by the Roman people to a supreme sovereign was still no more than pure theory – and at that a theory about which the specialists in Roman Law were themselves not in agreement. Some, such as Azo and Hugolin, held that the law of investiture had not been an effective transfer of rights but a mere concession – which could always be revoked – to the Emperor, who remained the procurator of the people. The great majority, however – Irnerius, Placentin, Roger, Accorso – adhered to Peter Crassus's point of view and considered the *Lex Regia* to be a purely historical notion. In practical terms this might have proved dangerous for those emperors who adopted it only partially in order to use it as an argument against the papacy. The Romans, however, remembered it when they attempted to start a revolution in 1143.

---

[7] Moreover, these same texts record the right to invest the bishops, which the papacy was alleged to have conceded to the two emperors; hence they are known as the 'false investiture privileges'. Detailed analysis in Folz, *Souvenir et légende*, pp. 126–31.

[8] *Defensio Heinrici regis* (Mon. Germ. Libelli de lite, I, pp. 432 et seq.).

III. AN ATTEMPT TO APPLY THE DOCTRINE: THE ROMAN COMMUNE AND ARNOLD OF BRESCIA

The Roman revolution was born of a state of mind which can be glimpsed in the pages of the *Mirabilia Urbis Romae*. This work was compiled about 1140 by Benedict, Canon of St Peter's. He prefaced it by a treatise on the early history of Rome, intended to integrate the foundation of the city in the scheme of universal history as set down by the great chroniclers of the eleventh century. It is a description of the monuments of Rome and at the same time a collection of all the legends which were loosely attached to its famous ruins. It is recognised as the oldest example of scholarly topography. About 1154 the *Mirabilia* were combined with the *Libellus de caerimoniis* and together they constituted the *Graphia aureae urbis Romae*[9] – an authentic account of imperial splendour set in the framework of Rome. Nevertheless, the original inspiration for these books was concerned much less with the interests of the Empire than with those of the republican era of the city. It is true that the Palatine and the residences of the emperors figure in them, but it is the Capitol which constitutes the main centre of interest in the first of these compilations. The Capitol, cradle of the city, head of the world, residence of the senate and of the consuls who governed the universe from the top of the hill. . . . In the immediate neighbourhood of the palace, in the temple of Jupiter, stood statues hung with little bells, each of which represented a province. If a rebellion broke out in any territory then the appropriate bells rang to give the alarm: the Capitol was thus a kind of magic mirror of the Empire. It was on this hill too, that the Emperor Augustus saw the famous vision which appeared before him to announce the Redemption of the world. The Capitol was thus glorified as the soul of the city, witness of its greatness in both pre-Christian and pre-imperial eras. It was, as it were, a symbol of the third Rome, which belonged neither to the Pope nor to the Emperor, but which would have liked to be an entity in itself and mistress of its own destiny.

In 1143 the Capitol became the residence of the Council of the Roman Commune, established as a result of the movement which carried the Italian towns towards emancipation from their lords. More than half a century later Rome followed the example of the cities of Northern Italy, but in Rome the venture was peculiarly perilous because of the exceptional importance of the city's landlord – the Pope – who was

---

[9] Readers should consult the version with critical commentary given by Schramm, in *Kaiser, Rom und Renovatio*, II, pp. 68–111.

94

able to exploit venerated texts for his own use, and capable also of mobilising powerful alliances against the city. In addition, in an atmosphere where the past was the object of such an infatuation as existed at the time in Rome, it was essential that every attempt to create something new should take on the appearance of a restoration of the past – the Council of the Commune was called the senate, the senatorial era was used in dating legal instruments, while the SPQR sign also reappeared. Everything was thus done to give the impression of a return to the tradition of republican Rome. Yet the concept of empire had become inseparable from the Roman city – the complex symbolism of the Capitol proves that this was so. This also explains why the Romans had to take up a position vis-à-vis the Empire almost immediately: the attitude they adopted was suggested by a cleric who already had a loaded past, Arnold of Brescia.[10]

It is difficult to discover the precise rôle played by Arnold in the evolution of the Commune. Probably, however, his main contribution was that he gave the Romans a political doctrine: one which was an original link in the chain of mediaeval doctrines and comprised two main features. One was a campaign directed against ownership of property by the Church and the temporal power of the clergy. Arnold wanted the Church to be poor, completely detached from contemporary secular things and restored to evangelical purity. The spirit of the Milanese *Pataria* lived again in him; and his second theme was to pave the way for the Emperor Frederick II. The essential fact to note here is the part played by Roman Law in his arguments. According to the reports of the chronicler Otto of Freising, he had already been maintaining at Brescia that everything (royal prerogatives, land and other property and possessions) belonged to the prince and that the prince could not grant concessions to any but laymen.[11] In Rome, where the people had just formed themselves into a Commune against the Pope, he hastened to assure them that the latter had no right to interfere in the administration of the city, that the Donation of Constantine was an apocryphal fable and that they must get rid of those clerics who were trying to reduce Rome to servitude – Rome, 'seat of the Empire and source of freedom'.

The association of those two expressions shows clearly that Arnold

---

[10] Pupil of Abelard in Paris; after his return to his native land, Brescia, he preached against the temporal power of the clergy. Convicted by a Roman synod, he returned to France, accompanied Abelard to the Council of Sens, went into exile in Zürich, then made his peace in 1145 with Eugenius III, who, strangely ill-inspired, assigned him to Rome to reside.

[11] *Gesta Friderici*, II, 28 (Simson, S.R.G., 1912, p. 133).

was as much a republican by inclination as an imperialist by sentiment. The Empire he envisaged was one which would have Rome as its true centre and which would be absolutely free from the pontifical grasp. Like all the other Romanists, however, he came to terms with the Empire as it already existed, on condition that it was willing to be led back to its real sources. By conviction as much as for tactical reasons, he advised the Romans to seek contact with the King (Conrad III) and to ally themselves with him against the Pope. On his initiative three letters were in fact addressed to the King of the Romans, inviting him to repair as quickly as possible to Rome in order to receive the Empire there and to instal himself in the capital of the world.[12]

The King, who had similarly been begged by Eugenius III to come and re-establish order in Rome, swung back and forth between the senate and the papacy. When his nephew Frederick took over from him in 1152, the pace quickened. A message went off almost immediately to the second of the Hohenstaufens, written in a much bolder tone than the earlier letters: Frederick is congratulated on his election but is reminded that he ought to have requested confirmation of it from Rome, 'creator and mother of all emperors'; let him make haste then to send his representatives and legal advisers to negotiate his right to the Empire. The new Sovereign declined this invitation. Hidebound by tradition and very authoritarian, bound to the papacy by the Concordat of Constance (1153), under which he had pledged himself to work with all his strength to make the rebels submit to their master, he arrived in Rome in 1155 to be crowned. For him there was no question of submitting to the conditions laid down by the Senate – the town which had been conquered by Charlemagne and Otto I must be induced by force to obey its Emperor once more.[13]

So it seemed that the Roman doctrine of the Empire could not be imposed unless the Emperor was of a mind to adopt it as his own. Frederick's refusal entailed the temporary check of Arnold of Brescia's ideas. Meanwhile, the old idea persisted – that the Romans had the right to decide who should rule over the Empire – and this conception was supported by the studies of the legal experts. It is true that in Rome itself at the end of the twelfth century this image died out completely, largely because of the radical changes made in the Commune's system

---

[12] See Documents, XIV, p. 192.
[13] See the account given in the *Gesta Friderici*, II, 29–33, *op. cit.*, pp. 135–41.

of government,[14] but it re-emerged later as one of the main arguments used by Frederick II in the course of his dispute with the papacy.

[14] This transformation, which began under Clement III (1187-91) and was continued by Innocent III, consisted fundamentally of the reduction of the number of senators, from fifty-six to two or one, appointed annually and selected from among the local aristocracy. When one remembers that, in the first half of the thirteenth century, the popes were recruited almost exclusively from this class, it is easy to imagine the community of interests established between the papacy and the nobility regarding the governing of Rome.

9

The Doctrine and Mystique of the Empire in the Time of the Hohenstaufens

Save for one very brief interruption the Hohenstaufen dynasty ruled the Empire from 1137 to 1250 and during this period the concept of empire came to fruition in the West. It had matured in earlier centuries; since the Investiture Contest it had been involved in struggling against the doctrine of a pontifical empire, and this conflict had actually strengthened it, enabling it to gain in internal cohesion. Henceforth it was a whole, embracing at one and the same time the past, the present and the future.

I. THE PRESTIGE OF THE PAST

A. *The continuity of the Empire*
A very definite awareness of this continuity is the first fact which it is important to underline: it had never before emerged with such clarity. At the beginning of the twelfth century, the Empire rested on a dual tradition, the two components of which had not yet reached a point of fusion. The Frankish tradition was bound up with various aspects of the actions of the rulers and many intellectual conceptions – but to what degree can it be said to have been a living force? It is surely significant that the expressions 'empire of the Franks' and 'kingdom of the Franks' ceased to be used after the eleventh century for either the Empire or Germany. As the Frankish tradition faded, the memory of the Roman

Empire gained by contrast in intensity, particularly from the time of Otto III and the Salian dynasty. More than any other fact the title *Rex Romanorum* adopted by each future emperor from the moment of his accession to the royal throne of Germany, testifies to this. Thus we can perceive the juxtaposition of several ideas: the Roman Empire, the Franks who had arrived later on the scene, and lastly the Germans (*Teutonici*), who were through their rulers holders in turn of the illustrious succession. Nevertheless, no effort had ever been made to form a logical link between the successive transfers of sovereignty – the first chronicles of universal scope were restricted to a mere listing of the sequence of the rulers.

However, a theory of continuity can be observed emerging little by little. For example, Ekkehard, Abbot of Aura, in his chronicle, emphasises strongly the importance of Charlemagne, on the ground that he made it possible for the Germans to take over the succession of Rome. See also the *Kaiserchronik*,[1] written about 1150 in Bavarian dialect, which relates the history of the emperors from Augustus to Conrad III without a break in continuity. In the eyes of the author it was the Romans themselves who decided no longer to choose a prince from among themselves but to turn to kings from outside. This somewhat brief but undoubtedly convenient transition enabled the poet to introduce the history of Charlemagne and the rulers who succeeded him. It remained only to explain this continuity, to eliminate the rôle of chance (thus showing that it was the will of God), in a word, to fit the Empire, in the form in which it then existed, into Providence's own designs. This was what Otto of Freising aimed to do in his chronicle.[2] The author wrote it at the time during Conrad III's reign when the Empire had ceased to exist, and presented it to his nephew Frederick I, with the object of stimulating him to restore the prestige and glory of the institution.

Otto of Freising's thoughts followed the Augustinian line but he projected it into the political sphere. The great scholar had had a purely religious vision of the Two Cities, quite unrelated to any national setting – the mystical Body of Christ contrasted with the empire of Evil – seeing them as intermingled until they were finally separated at the Last Judgment. Frederick Barbarossa's uncle, Otto, however, abandoned this transcendent plane and saw the Two Cities as distinct – the earthly city and the city of God, celestial and eternal. The earthly

---

[1] This work and the preceding one are discussed in Folz, *Souvenir et légende*, pp. 146–7 and 159–70.
[2] *Historia de duabus civitatibus*; Hofmeister, S.R.G., 1912.

city was not necessarily the city of the devil, but it could be identified with the great empires which had followed one another since the creation of man, and its task was to prepare the celestial Jerusalem.

In Otto's interpretation, the Roman Empire took its place in the succession of *regna* which constituted the history of the earthly city. Coming after the Empires of Babylon, the Medo-Persians and the Graeco-Macedonians, it was the last stage. The most important event in the fourth universal monarchy was the conversion of Constantine – which assured the triumph of Christianity. By this event the Empire became amalgamated with the Church – *una civitas, id est Ecclesia, sed permixta*[3] – and became in a kind of way its earthly body. Actual events soon made this identification of the two institutions impossible and the Bishop of Freising was facing realities when he contrasted the growth of the one with the progressive dissolution of the other. Nevertheless it persisted as an underlying idea in his chronicle and its survival was aided by the fact that the Emperor exercised his power in the Church side by side with the Pope. Otto repeatedly emphasised that God had ordained two powers to rule over His Church – his attitude was frankly Gelasian.

In spite of growing old, as did the world itself, the Roman Empire continued to survive. Admittedly the authority of the Emperor, whose seat had been transferred to Byzantium, had become weaker in Rome itself, but the name 'Roman' persisted and responsibility for the Empire was taken over by Charlemagne and the Franks, whose close kinship with the Romans predestined them to carry out this function: they were the last to hold the illustrious monarchy 'to which pagans used to attribute eternity and which we ourselves regard as almost divine'.[4]

But whether the Franks were to control the Empire until the end of time or not, it is evident that their rule did extend into the era in which Otto of Freising was writing. He was firmly convinced of this; for him the *Teutonici* were a branch of the Frankish people, their kingdom was a part of the *regnum Francorum* and the accession of Otto I and his successors in no way interrupted the continuity of Frankish control of the institution. On the contrary they actually achieved its complete restoration, for, after the extinction of the Carolingians, the Empire had been temporarily usurped by the Lombards.[5]

And so the concept of empire became quite clear: the Empire had not ceased to be the former *Imperium Romanorum*; its mission was

---

[3] Prologue to Book VII, p. 309 *op. cit.*
[4] Prologue to Book V, p. 236.
[5] Book VI, chapter xvii, pp. 276–7. These Lombards were the Italian emperors at the end of the ninth century and the beginning of the tenth.

universal by virtue of the rôle its head played in the government of the Church; but the controllers of the monarchy were Frankish and Franco-Germanic.

B. *The Frankish heritage*

Thus the concept of empire was the means of re-establishing the Frankish tradition, which was accepted all the more inevitably because it appeared at that very moment to be the vital force animating the kingdom of France.[6] The Hohenstaufen era was that of Louis VII, but also that of Philip Augustus and of St Louis, and in the course of this period some obscure hopes very gradually became realities. It now looked as though a positive rivalry had broken out between the Empire (which had once more become aware of its Frankish past) and the neighbouring *regnum Francorum* (where the idea had always remained firmly rooted). It could even be said that there was a Frankish restoration in the twelfth century under Frederick I, which culminated in the canonisation of Charlemagne on 29th December, 1165,[7] and the splendour of which caused a temporary eclipse of the other kingdom. Incidentally, this restoration was able to enhance the concept of empire by making a number of contributions to it, among which the following should be noted:

1. *The possibility of assuring the predominance of the Transalpine kingdom within the monarchy as a whole.* This objective was an important preoccupation throughout the reign of Frederick I. The concept of empire was to radiate from Aix-la-Chapelle – the throne, tomb, and sanctuary of Charlemagne. The political literature of the time moreover shows with considerable skill how swiftly men's minds could pass from the notion of Franks to that of Germans. Aix-la-Chapelle was the *sedes regni Teutonici*. At least once during Frederick I's reign the expression *Imperium Teutonicorum* was used to describe the monarchy as a whole – a kind of manifestation of ethnic *amour-propre* capable of being transformed later into national sentiment, and, as will be seen later, able also to evolve a new form for the Empire.

2. *The theme of the emperors' control over Rome and Italy.* This was given expression by Frederick I's attitude when he faced the Roman Commune and when he recovered the royal prerogatives which he represented as

---

[6] See below, p. 134.
[7] On this point, see Folz, *Culte liturgique*, with texts revealing the concept of empire.

rights exercised by Charlemagne and Otto I in the towns of Lombardy.[8]

3. *Finally, the means of resuscitating the concept of divine monarchy.* Strongly contested by the Gregorians and their successors, but maintained in its entirety by the imperialist party, this theme underwent a genuine revival towards the middle of the century. Several different conceptions converged at this point – and the first of these was a belief in the sacramental value of the anointing, despite developments aimed at eliminating it from the list of sacraments. Like his predecessors, especially Charlemagne, Frederick loudly claimed the status of the Christ (the anointed) of the Lord.[9] This was the principle which governed the Emperor's ecclesiastical policy when he intervened in the pontifical schism in 1160 and attempted to impose a pope of his choice on Christendom. As an anointed ruler Frederick did indeed take, on earth, the place of the King of Kings and this vicarate conferred on him the right and power to 'rule over all men and in particular to rule over the clergy'.[10] No one has put this better than the *Archipoeta*, prince of the poets of his reign: 'No rational being disputes that thou art, by the will of God, constituted king over the other kings and thou hast deservedly acquired the sword of vengeance and the buckler of guardianship over all Christian people.'[11] It is unnecessary therefore to have recourse to the idea of a connexion with Rome in order to understand the universality which Frederick I claimed – it was derived to a great extent from the Frankish tradition of divine monarchy. In a word, this universality was not political but religious. And, in accordance with the tradition of Charlemagne, it included the duty to protect all Christian people.

C. *The contribution of Roman Law*
But the Empire was essentially Roman and as such it derived advantage from the rediscovery of the idea of public sovereignty, in the light of the *Corpus Iuris*. In turn, this affected the thinking of Frederick, who extracted from Roman Law everything which could serve his authority. Nurtured on the vision of history which Otto of Freising had revealed to him, he was, from 1154 onwards, influenced also by the School of

---

[8] Cf. Otto of Freising, *Gesta Friderici*, Book II, chapters xxx and xxxiii, xxxix and xlvi, *op. cit.*, pp. 136–8, 141, 203–4, 220.

[9] See Documents, XV, p. 195.

[10] *Mon. Germ. Const.*, I, No. 240, p. 235.

[11] Third verse of the imperial ode, *Salve mundi domine*, Manitius, *Die Gedichte des Archipoeta*, Munich, 1929, p. 38.

Bologna. His project, restated on many occasions, of restoring the Empire to its ancient splendour, bears the imprint of the thinking of both.

It is difficult to classify the various essential elements contributed by Roman Law to the concept of empire, but it does seem possible to indicate a few principles which helped to strengthen the conception during the reign of Frederick I and, later, flourished in the time of his grandson.

The Empire is unique – one God, one Pope, one Emperor, one Church – this characteristic, strongly affirmed in the twelfth century, was what condemned the Hispanic Empire. Next there was the continuity of the Empire – strongly supporting this theory the glossators attributed equal validity to all supplementary legislation, capitularies and imperial *Constitutiones*. For his part, Frederick proclaimed that he 'was following the example of his divine (*divi*) predecessors, Constantine, Justinian and Theodosius and likewise Charlemagne and Louis the Pious, and that he venerated their holy laws as if they were divine oracles'.[12] Following those who went before him, he had his *Constitutiones*, such as the famous 'privilege' for the students of Bologna, inserted in the *Corpus Iuris*.[13]

Then again there was the universality of the Empire – on this point too the glossators were explicit: because the Roman Empire continued to exist, its ancient laws preserved all their validity and were applicable, as were the new laws, to all nations who were or ought in law to be under the Empire.[14] In theory at least Frederick extended the same principles to imperial authority,[15] but their practical application involved subtleties which are a credit to the prince's political realism.

Lastly, as an institution, the Empire derived directly from God and as such it possessed the prestige of sacred things: *sacrum Imperium* became the classical term employed to describe it. Everything which affected the Empire, or the Emperor, was sacred. The Emperor's authority, guaranteed by the Law of Majesty, was absolute. The prince was the living law on earth and the supreme legislator who created or annulled the law.

This brief sketch of the themes built up around the concept of the Empire as a Roman institution reveals a picture closely complementary to that painted by Otto of Freising. And yet, a great difference can be noted between the latter's point of view and that of the glossators:

---

[12] *Mon. Germ. Const.*, I, No. 227, pp. 321–2.
[13] *Ibid*, No. 178, p. 249.
[14] See, for example, Huguccio of Pisa, Commentary on the *Decretum Gratiani*, c. 12, D.I.
[15] *Orbis et Urbis gubernacula tenemus, Mon. Germ. Const.*, I, No. 161, p. 224.

the bishop could not refrain from thinking of Church and Empire as identical, whereas the Roman Renewal stamped the Empire with a more secular imprint without in any way detracting from the sacred character it possessed by virtue of its divine origin. The imperialism of the Hohenstaufens oscillated continually between these two poles.

In brief, the imperial doctrine of the Hohenstaufens was built up on two main bases – that the Empire was a Frankish heritage and a Roman institution. It is true to say that under Frederick I the two components were successfully reconciled with some degree of harmony, but by the end of the twelfth century the position was completely reversed. For various reasons the Frankish tradition suffered an eclipse[16] and henceforth, at least as a political programme, it became centred on the kingdom of France. On the other hand, the concept of empire, abandoning the Frankish intermediary, became more definitely stamped with a Germanic character and above all with the vision of Rome which finally triumphed under Frederick II.

II. THE PRESENT: THE DUAL ASPECTS OF THE EMPIRE

The political history of the twelfth century in Western Europe is marked by the re-establishment of the monarchical state, based on the feudal system. The Empire did not remain entirely untouched by this evolution. Some features of the restoration, which in the last analysis had the effect of giving more depth to the concept of the state, must be noted here, although by reason of the structure of the Empire they were less visible and had less effect in the imperial monarchy than in the kingdom of Sicily, in England and later in France. For example, there was the reinforcement of the prestige of the ruler as a result of the interplay of the dual tradition described above. Then there were the efforts devoted by the Hohenstaufens to assuring the independence of the Empire as an institution. It was, incidentally, not easy to achieve such independence entirely, because the accession of the ruler to the universal and Roman monarchy was necessarily dependent on the Pope's intervention. Although they came to terms with this necessity, the emperors did try to neutralise its effects by stressing the imperial character of their sovereignty even before the ceremony at Rome. So the Empire had now two aspects: the Empire restricted to lands grouped within the three *regna*; and the universal Empire.

[16] On the fate of Frankish tradition at the time of the Hohenstaufens, cf. Folz, *Souvenir et légende*.

A. *The restricted Empire*

The attention of the Hohenstaufens was attracted to the idea of the Empire as a state standing on foundations which existed outside the Church as much by a study of the principles of Roman Law as by the example of Byzantium, with which contacts were multiplied in the course of the twelfth century. How could the emperors of the West have failed to be influenced by the notion of an empire reflecting the structure of a state where all authority was concentrated in the hands of the *basileus*, and where nevertheless there was no conflict of authority between the spiritual and temporal powers?

The first signs that the Western Empire might imitate the Eastern made their appearance in the reign of the extremely weak Conrad III. After his first contact with the Byzantine ambassadors in 1139, this King of the Romans took the thoroughly imperial title of Augustus, which from then on was always attached to the King's name in official documents. Three years later Conrad called himself 'august emperor of the Romans' in a letter to John Comnenus, to whom he accorded only the title 'Emperor of Constantinople'. What could this mean but that the King of the Romans regarded himself as emperor even before he had received the diadem from the hands of the Pope? In fact Conrad never wore the diadem; none the less he retained the custom of calling himself emperor in his correspondence with the Byzantine court, if only to affirm his own right against redoubtable competitors.[17]

Frederick I followed this example. Although he was crowned emperor on 18th June, 1155, he adopted the title before that date: for example, in his edict of 1152 for the regulation of public peace, as though he wished to show that the principal mission of the Emperor in his states was to be the making of legislation; and again in correspondence with Manuel Comnenus and even in the official documents ratifying the Concordat of Constance, which he concluded in 1153 with Eugenius III.[18] The fact that the *Curia* recognised the imperial title can be explained only by a desire to avoid a dispute and by the goodwill of the Pope who interpreted the unusual appellation in the same spirit as Conrad had justified his use of it – emperor in anticipation.

The trend thus started was never halted. Throughout his reign

---

[17] On this subject see W. Ohnsorge, *'Kaiser' Konrad III*; examples of letters in Jaffe, *Bibl. rerum Germanicarum*, I, Nos. 237, 243, 244, 245, 343. The title was, moreover, given to Conrad by Wibald, Abbot of Stavelot (same collection, Nos. 180, 201, 258, 279) and by two princes who were quarrelling over the throne of Denmark (Nos. 338 and 343).

[18] References: *Mon. Germ. Const.*, I, No. 140, p. 195; Jaffe, *Bibl.*, No. 410, p. 548; *Mon. Germ. Const.*, I, No. 145, p. 202.

Frederick proclaimed again and again that he held the Empire from God alone, through his election by the princes. We must now examine the significance of this principle, which was accepted into and became part of German public law. It resulted in a diminution in the importance of the part played by the Pope in the Emperor's accession when he exercised the pontifical prerogative of anointing and it had the effect of an affirmation that the principal source of the Emperor's authority was his being chosen by the princes – described in a contemporary text as 'co-adjutors in the glory of the Emperor and of the Empire'.[19] Because of this, Frederick's pronouncement can be regarded as originating the formation of the electoral college. It was directly responsible for the failure of Henry VI's attempt to assure for his dynasty a hereditary right to the Empire. In 1198 Frederick's doctrine triumphed, for in that year a group of princes did in fact elect, as successor to Henry VI, his brother Philip of Swabia *in imperaturam Romani solii*.[20]

In recent expository studies of this phrase it has been conjectured that it described all the sovereign powers over a particular territory – the Empire of the three kingdoms, the Empire of which the *regnum Teutonicorum* was the most powerful part. In any event, Innocent III interpreted it thus when he noted that Philip had, by the election of the princes, become the ruler of the *regnum Teutonicum, et quantum in eo est, Imperium*. This is the same Empire as the one which had earlier been called *Imperium Teutonicorum*[21] in one of Frederick I's edicts. Between that Empire and the Empire proper – the Roman and universal Empire – there was no friction, but there was interpenetration. In a way, possession of the first was the necessary condition, the indispensable legal title, for acquisition of the second. From the second half of the twelfth century a 'privilege' set out under the name of Charlemagne declared that the rulers of Germany, enthroned at Aix-la-Chapelle, were qualified to receive the imperial coronation in Rome, by right (*iure*).[22]

So the princes had become the electors of the emperor. *In des Kyseres core*, in the election of the Emperor: these are the opening words of that chapter of the *Mirror of the Saxons*, which describes the election of the King (*Kuning*) of Germany.[23] Nothing could be more revealing

---

[19] Forged charter of Charlemagne (No. 295), incorporated in a title-deed by the imperial chancellery.

[20] And not *in imperatorem Romani solii*, as printed in *Mon. Germ. Const.*, II, No. 3, p. 3.

[21] References: *Deliberatio* of the Pope, P.L., 216, 1025-9; imperial constitution of 1167, *Mon. Germ. Const.*, I, p. 325.

[22] See Note 19.

[23] *Sachsenspiegel, Landrecht*, ed. K. A. Eckhardt (1933), vol. I, part III, paragraph 57, p. 141 and paragraph 52, p. 137.

than this confusion (or perhaps equivalence) of expressions in the mind of Eike of Repkow. The concept of empire penetrated the *regnum*, accompanied by memories of emperors elected by the people of Rome. The first revival of this practice – admittedly for very different reasons – took place at Rome itself in 1212 when, on the initiative of Innocent III, Frederick II was acclaimed emperor by the population of the city.[24] Much more important was the question of succession to the senate, which the German princes officially claimed when in 1237 they elected Conrad IV, son of Frederick, King of the Romans and emperor-to-be. Their decree was not directed merely against the doctrine set out in Innocent III's bull *Venerabilem*. They based the right of the princes on historical facts which permitted no admission of the idea that Rome could transfer her sovereign rights to Germany. During the troubled time when the Romans lost their power and their juridical prerogatives, the Empire at first experienced some fluctuations and uncertainties, then settled permanently with the princes of Germany, who thus became the source of the Emperor's authority, just as they were already the defenders of the institution of empire. As 'fathers and lights of the Empire' they then took the place of the senate.[25] Certain source-documents reveal the real reason for these events (only implied in this text) – the conquest of Rome, an episode in which the Frankish element played the rôle of a link connecting past and present, as it had done in other fields. The author of the re-written version of the German *Roland* reported that when Charlemagne had become master of the Roman Empire by conquest, he granted the Germanic warriors, an-cestors of the princes, the privilege of disposing of the imperial crown in future in favour of such person of their choice as they might elect.[26] Even after the fall of Frederick II the idea that emperors should be elected was still firmly entrenched and, despite the doctrine of the papacy (which distinguished the election of the King of Germany from accession to the Empire – reserving the latter to itself), the congress of electors, meeting in Brunswick in 1252, formulated the celebrated principle of public law that the election of a man as King of the Romans conferred on him the full exercise of the imperial rights in the Empire (this meant the restricted Empire) and that the anointing at Rome

---

[24] Chronicle of Ursperg (*Mon. Germ. Script.*, XXIII, p. 373).
[25] *Mon. Germ. Const.*, II, No. 239, p. 439. The importance of this text can best be appreciated by seeing it alongside the advances being made about the same time by Frederick II to the Romans, evoking the *Lex Regia*; see below, p. 113 and Documents, XX, p. 203.
[26] Stricker, *Karl der Grosse*, ed. Bartsch (1859), lines 450–76 (first third of the thirteenth century).

added nothing to this sovereignty, *nisi nomen*, except a title, the classic title of the holder of the universal monarchy.[27]

So, during the Hohenstaufen epoch, under the influence of the dual (Roman and Frankish) tradition, the foundations for a national empire were laid. In the last analysis this was evidence from Germany of the way the whole idea of nationhood, which first emerged in the twelfth century, was gaining in depth. The essential thing was to know whether this restricted empire was always distinguishable from the universal empire. When in 1199 the poet-knight, Walter von der Vogelweide, invited 'his emperor', Philip of Swabia, to place on his head the diadem adorned with the famous white opal, guiding star of all princes, it is almost certain that he was thinking of the universal Empire just as much as of the restricted Empire. Such confusion was simply exacerbated by the growing influence of national sentiment. And despite the fact that when the Hohenstaufens had died out its character became more and more artificial, the universal Empire did in fact hinder the consolidation of the other, the national Empire.

B. *The universal Empire*

The vision of a universal empire occupied the foreground of the Hohenstaufens' dreams. This was reflected in the literature of the time and in official documents with an increasing intensity which inevitably provoked some vigorous national reactions. Attempts to realise the concept of universality, however, went much further than the phrases used by poets and politicians: and in addition they gave expression to an interpretation of the Empire and its functions which varied greatly from one ruler to another. So it is possible to envisage three different methods of accomplishing their aims, each put forward by one emperor of the Swabian dynasty.

In the minds of Frederick I and his contemporaries, universality had a twofold basis – the Roman character of the Empire and the rôle of the Emperor in the Church. The latter has already been analysed above

---

[27] On this text cf. K. Zeumer in *Neues Archiv*, vol. XXX, pp. 405 *et seq.* It is interesting to note that almost half a century before this pronouncement, John Zemeke (*Johannes Teutonicus*), the distinguished annotator of the *Decretum Gratiani* had noted that it was the election by the princes which created the authentic emperor (*Glossa ordinaria*, pub. Basle, 1512, chapter xxiv, dist. 93). His master, the canonist Huguccio of Pisa, also thought that it was the election by the people and the princes which created the emperor although he did not indeed bear the title until he had received the crown from the hand of the Pope. *Ante enim fuit imperator quam papa, ante imperium quam papatus.*

and there is no need now to do more than recall the function of the Emperor in the earthly City, the *regnum transitorium* or the *temporale Imperium*, as some documents of the reign call it, Christendom governed by the Two Swords.[28] But alongside and mingled with this religious notion there was also a political aspect. Numerous pieces of evidence, which, admittedly, differ somewhat from one another, give us some idea of how this was conceived. Official documents and edicts refer to the government of the City and of the world, as being the responsibility of the Emperor alone, whose authority extended *super gentes et regna*. The Italian chronicler Otto Morena[29] asserts that Frederick received from a Doctor of Bologna the assurance that the *dominium mundi* belonged to him. And 'the world' was, over and above the Empire proper, the sum total of those countries which gravitated about him and whose heads, the *provinciarum reges* or *reguli*, as the chancellor Rainald of Dassel put it at the Diet of Dole in 1162, had a duty to bring their policies into line with those of the Emperor.[30]

These expressions do not constitute an absolute innovation. The idea of *provincia* may well have been communicated to the chancellor by the glossators of the *Corpus Iuris*. The word *regulus* had been used quite frequently by others before Rainald – in the ninth century it was applied in the *Annales* of Fulda to the kings of the countries which were created by the dismembering of the Empire of Charles the Fat. Contemporaries of Henry III and of Henry IV, such as Benzo of Alba, used it to describe the various sovereigns who were to be found on the fringes of the Empire. The real novelty of the word in 1162 lay in the official use made of it by that ardent imperialist, the chancellor, and in the protestations which it aroused on the part of certain national publicists[31] – it must not be forgotten that this was a time when the different countries had suddenly become more strongly conscious of their own existence.

It seems likely, however, that Rainald's words went further than his master's ideas. Frederick never disputed the absolute sovereignty of France and England. If he did actually lean towards universal dominion he probably envisaged it in the classic form of *auctoritas*, i.e. a certain pre-eminence in the Christian community. This was a kind of authority which could, moreover, be recognised by other rulers without their

[28] For examples, see in Stumpf-Brentano, *Reichskanzler*, III, Nos. 169, 341, 379, and in *Mon. Germ. Const.*, I, No. 182, p. 253.
[29] *Mon. Germ. Scriptores*, XVIII, p. 607.
[30] For an account of this see the chronicle of *Saxo Grammaticus* (Holder-Egger, S.R.G., Book XIV, chapter xxviii).
[31] Such as *John of Salisbury, Letters* (ed. Giles, Oxford, 1848), I, Nos. 59 and 189.

independence suffering the slightest diminution thereby, as is proved by the letter which Henry II, King of England,[32] addressed to the Emperor in 1157, inviting him to enter into an alliance with him. It was a moral authority, which included a kind of patronage of rulers and their countries and which, if exercised by the Roman Emperor, could not but be universal. No one has put this better than Otto of Freising: *auctoritas ad quam totius orbis spectat patrocinium.*[33]

Within this general mission it is worth recording the relations which Frederick maintained with those countries over which the Empire had traditionally extended its influence – Denmark, Poland and Bohemia continued to gravitate round him, while towards the end of his reign Hungary, the pawn of Germano-Byzantine rivalry, was persuaded to recognise the superior influence of the Emperor of the West. In the face of facts the formulas used by chancelleries diminished in absolute value, but the essence of the ideas which they expressed was not thereby lost: the political primacy which Frederick I exercised in Europe was sometimes disputed, but, taken as a whole, it was real.

Was it possible to go beyond the stage of 'superior status' and transform it into a sort of domination? The very short reign of Henry VI (1190–1197) left the impression that the concept of empire had reached its apogee. At the beginning of the thirteenth century Caesarius, Abbot of Heisterbach, wrote as follows: 'As the sun exceeds in power and in brilliance all the constellations of the firmament, so the Roman Empire shines with a more brilliant splendour than all the kingdoms in the world. The monarchy resides in it; as the stars receive their light from the sun, so the kings hold their sovereignty from the Emperor.'[34] This statement is not pure hyperbole. It revives the use of an allegory dear to the doctrinarians of papal authority. Brought up by his tutor, Godfrey of Viterbo, on the theme of universal monarchy, the son of Frederick I tried to make it a reality by employing such means as the feudal system offered him. He acted as though he wanted to extend the network of his dependencies (which had until then consisted of the small kingdoms on the Empire's borders which had attached themselves to him) in such a way as to include all the states of Europe. Thus he made Richard Cœur-de-Lion his vassal; the intention to do something of the same kind with Philip Augustus is also attributed to him. Just at this

[32] See Documents, XVI, p. 196.
[33] Chronicle, Book VII, chapter xxxiv, p. 367; cf. *Gesta Friderici*, Book III, chapter xiii, p. 181, *Romanum Imperium totius orbis asylum.*
[34] *Dialogus Miraculorum*, II, 235 (ed. J. Strange, Cologne, 1851).

time a plan was being sketched out to transfer the axis of the Empire to the Mediterranean – a region where the concept of empire was fortified by Norman tradition. Henry VI was King of Sicily and he looked towards Castile and Aragon; he received tribute from the Saracens of Africa and from the Balearic Islands. But above all he was aiming at the Byzantine Empire. Although the idea of conquering the other empire may well have originated at the end of Frederick's reign it was now being taken really seriously. After the fall of Isaac Angelus, Henry VI announced that he was the defender of the rights of his sister-in-law Irene, who had married Philip of Swabia. Alexius, the usurper, was compelled to pay tribute, which was material evidence of his dependence in relation to the Western Empire. In 1195 Henry VI organised a crusade which appears to have been in fact a kind of rehearsal for the one which was to capture Constantinople in 1204. Feudal ties had already been extended to certain countries of the Latin East – Leo of Armenia, whom Henry VI elevated to the rank of king, and Amalric of Lusignan, King of Cyprus, both became the Emperor's vassals. The time seemed to be approaching when the two empires would be reunited in one single one and when the unity which existed before Theodosius would be re-established.

But all this power, which dazzled contemporaries, lacked a solid basis. In achieving universality the Empire had been transformed into a 'complex of states, of rights of suzerainty, of feudal relationships and zones of influence'.[35] Had he succeeded in establishing the hereditary right of the House of the Hohenstaufens to rule over the Empire, Henry VI would have been able to implement his policy fully, but he failed to achieve this. His premature death brought the immediate loosening of all the bonds which had been woven about the Empire and gave rise to a crisis from which the Emperor's authority was never again to recover.

During the great crisis of 1198 to 1215 the concept of empire was shaken to its depths by Innocent III, but it was destined to cast a brilliant light on the world once more (for the last time) at a later date, under Frederick II. This Roman Emperor, who reigned also over the kingdoms of Sicily and Jerusalem, gave the concept universal scope and it was also affected, more deeply than in the past, by the ascendancy of Roman Law and of its interpretation, a reflection of several currents of

---

[35] H. Mitteis, *Der Staat des hohen Mittelalters*, p. 309.

thought which intermingled at the Court of Palermo. The main aspects are described in the following paragraphs.

(*a*) First there was the fact that the concept of empire had for the first time found a country in which it could take root. Germany was out of the question because it was developing towards a structure which prevented the Emperor from exercising in any part of the country the authority which Roman Law reserved to him. On the other hand Frederick had control over Sicily, which had for more than a century been accustomed to Norman absolutism: so in a way Sicily was to supply the concept of empire with the raw material which would enable it to flourish.

Indeed, in order to appreciate the extent of the concept of empire we must turn to the *Liber Augustalis*, a great work of codification. This collection was intended for application to a kingdom. It was none the less promulgated by the Emperor and his name is adorned with titles and epithets[36] which reveal that Frederick looked to Justinian for his model, imitating him too by prefacing the collection with a preamble on the origin and aims of the Emperor's authority. Here he expounded a broad analysis of the institution as the means by which Providence desired to save mankind from the original fall, a natural necessity and at the same time the instrument of God. As the argument develops it introduces the theme of the Emperor who derives his power from God alone, who is the intermediary by which the transcendent law can shed its light on the earth, and who is also the creator of earthly law, and is himself the law made live on earth. If ever the expressions *Sacrum Imperium, divus imperator, sacra maiestas imperialis* had a full meaning in the West during the Middle Ages, it was surely in a setting such as this. The state was completely penetrated by the concept of empire, which transformed it into what was virtually a lay Church, the *imperialis Ecclesia*, ruled over by an emperor who was the high priest of Justice and whose assistants, the justiciary, were as much priests as officials – they inevitably recall the *ulemas*, functionaries with whose duties Frederick had become familiar in the East.

(*b*) These visions can, however, be disregarded here for, though they remained a part of the background to the concept of empire, they could never be realised except in Sicily. Frederick was not merely Justinian –

---

[36] *Imperator Fridericus secundus Romanorum Caesar semper Augustus, Italicus, Siculus, Hierosolymitanus, Arelatensis, Pius, Victor ac Triumphator* (*Constitutiones regni Siciliae, proæmium,* Huillard–Breholles, *Historia Diplomatica Friderici secondi,* IV, I, p. 3).

he was Augustus. As such, for tactical and political reasons and with more enthusiasm and conviction than his predecessors, he adopted as his own the programme of the *Renovatio Imperii Romanorum*, and gave it a real meaning. In fact, he regarded Rome and Italy as the centre of his Empire. In his eyes the rôle of Germany, whose feudal disintegration he hastened by his own actions, was simply to be a reservoir of forces, a place where the Emperor could draw on the means to carry out his policies. On the other hand, Frederick turned his whole attention to the Romans, whose *amour-propre* he flattered. He declared Rome the capital of the monarchy. It was the Quirites who, by virtue of the *Lex Regia*, had spontaneously handed over the Empire to Frederick. For four generations the Hohenstaufen family had been linked with the institution. It was the *stirps caesarea* in which the line of the *divi imperatores*, founded by Aeneas,[37] lived again. Let *felix Roma* then play a part in carrying out the tasks which the Emperor must perform – in return she will be associated in his triumphs. Victorious over the towns of Lombardy at Cortenuova, Frederick dispatched the most illustrious trophy of the battle to the Romans, the *carroccio* of Milan.[38] When his struggle against Gregory IX was at its height he multiplied his appeals – 'Do not sleep, wake up, O citizens of Rome!' – as though he were anxious to revive the ancient *virtus* to the profit of his Empire. It was, in fact, from within the Roman aristocracy that he intended to recruit his 'proconsuls' who were to administer Italy in his name. However, these inflammatory proposals and promises did not cancel out the basic facts – even while he was repeating that Rome was *caput et auctrix Imperii nostri*, Frederick regarded the Romans as his subjects, of whom he could dispose at will.[39] The concept of the empire as a Roman institution was the foundation of his absolute power, just as Roman Law served him in his struggle against the claims of the papacy.[40]

(c) As Roman Emperor, Frederick demanded universality. His vision extended far beyond the dualism which was evolving in Germany between the dream of a universal empire and the reality of a territorial empire. The domination of the world which was his aim had a good

---

[37] On the *Lex Regia*, *Constit. regni*, I, 31, loc. cit., p. 33; on the imperial race, cf. the letter from Frederick II to Conrad IV – *O caesarei sanguinis divina proles* – Huillard–Breholles, V, 761 and the manifesto to the Romans, *Mon. Germ. Const.*, II, No. 424, pp. 559 *et seq.*

[38] See Documents, XX, p. 203.

[39] This he demonstrated in 1234, for example, by allowing Gregory IX to regain, in Rome, the authority which Luca Savelli had, for a brief spell, snatched from him.

[40] Evidence of this absolutism: Huillard–Breholles, V, 161 and 307; it should also be noted that at certain contested episcopal elections Frederick invoked the *Lex Regia*; see, for example, *ibid*, IV, 912.

deal in common with that which the papacy was striving to achieve: he was obviously following the example of Innocent III, of Gregory IX and their predecessors in the twelfth century, when he sought to gather various countries around him and to convert their alliances with him into support for an entirely spiritual empire, the *respublica universae christianitatis*. Some aspects of this project are particularly instructive.

It is significant that with the exception of the attempt he made towards 1236 to draw closer to Henry III of England, he never at any time followed any external policy or sought any alliance which could possibly risk shaking Christian unity.

But the concept of empire had also to take account of national aspirations in the various countries concerned. There was no longer any question of exercising an *auctoritas* of an arbitrary nature over them – this would inevitably have provoked them into re-grouping around the Church. On the contrary, it was important to associate them with the Empire in the struggle it was carrying on to defend its own existence against the aims of the papacy. This explains the very special tone perceptible in the manifestoes of the imperial chancellery after 1236, during the years when the struggle between the Empire and the papacy reached its maximum intensity. The Emperor appealed to the rulers for solidarity. He acknowledged that they, like him, proceeded directly from God and he invited them to defend their independence against the encroachments of the Church, as he himself was doing.[41] In order to battle together against the rebels within (among whom were the heretics) and the Church with its ambition to dominate, he suggested the establishment of a *corpus saecularium principum*. The idea was original and bold – had it been realised it might perhaps have been the means of saving the principle of universal monarchy.

III. VISIONS OF THE END OF TIME

No description of the concept of empire under the Hohenstaufens would be complete without some mention of the prophetic and messianic background of which we can obtain some impression, if rather inadequate, from the evidence of writers in the twelfth and thirteenth centuries: it consisted of a number of ideas which at first developed simultaneously on parallel lines and ultimately were intermingled and fused.

---

[41] See, for example, the encyclical letter of the 20th April, 1239, *Mon. Germ. Const.*, II, No. 215, p. 291; cf. No. 233, p. 318 and 263, p. 365.

A. *Eschatological speculation*

The importance of this in the years which preceded the restoration of the Empire by Otto I has already been made clear above. After that time the prophecies multiplied. They contributed to the development of a 'crusade-mentality' although at the same time they were strongly influenced in turn by the repercussions of the Holy War. At the end of the eleventh century, Benzo of Alba had tried to make Henry IV let himself be cast in the rôle of the last emperor,[42] but it was a vain effort since the Emperor, already overburdened by his dispute with the papacy, was determined not to become involved in the movement for the liberation of the Holy Land.

This helps to explain why the Germanic rulers took so long to incorporate the idea of a crusade into the vision of the Empire, and also why the various prophecies about the end of time took so long to turn in the direction of those rulers. Thus Italian speculation remained until the end of the twelfth century faithful to the image of an emperor of Greek origin, Constans, who was to unite the two separated halves of the Empire. A short time before the first crusade the interpolator of Adso announced that this function would fall to a king of the Romans who would first capture the Holy Sepulchre. The prince was designated by the single letter C – was he to be Constans or a new Charlemagne? For his part Otto of Freising was aware that some people were announcing that Louis VII, King of France, would be the universal monarch at the end of time.[43]

In this field too, as in so many others, the restoration of the prestige and glory of the Empire by Frederick had important consequences. On the one hand it induced the Germans to imagine that the person who was to be emperor at the end of time would be one of their rulers, another Frederick. This theme was elaborated on the stage in the *Ludus de Antichristo*, composed in the Bavarian abbey of Tegernsee about 1160–1162 – certainly one of the most striking pieces of evidence concerning the imperial ideology of the time.[44] In addition, it is probable that the distant perspectives unfolded by the mystical memory of Charlemagne, first and legendary crusader, together with the Emperor's duty in his rôle of advocate of the Church and protector of Christendom, supported by the ideals of chivalry, a soldier in the service of Christ, all combined to cause Frederick I to take up the Cross – it was

---

[42] See Documents, XII, p. 191 (e).
[43] Text of the interpolator of Adso in Erdmann, *Endkaiserglaube*, p. 411; evidence of Otto of Freising in *Gesta Friderici*, preamble, *op. cit.*, p. 10.
[44] See Documents, XVII, p. 197.

on the road to Jerusalem that the Emperor died in 1190 at the end of a glorious reign.

After the death of Frederick I great hopes were pinned on his successors. Henry VI was announced as the ruler who would unite the Greeks and Romans under his rule; his reign would see the baptism of the infidels carried out, the conversion of the Jews, the destruction of the infidel peoples of Gog and Magog; after 122 years the Emperor would go to Jerusalem to place the Empire in the hands of God.[45] The prophecy also referred to Otto of Brunswick himself, doubtless on account of his homonymy with Otto II, whose battles against the Saracens were remembered. But it was above all Frederick II who became the hero of numerous predictions, all tangled and confused. As early as the time of the third crusade it was announced that despite the death of the two Fredericks (Barbarossa and his son, the Duke of Swabia) a third would arise who would save Jerusalem from the infidels. After the fall of Damietta in 1217, there was a story of a king of Calabria and a mysterious Christian prince – David or Prester John – supposed to be reigning over some distant countries in the South or the East, who would enter the Holy City together. In the course of the years which preceded the frequently postponed departure of the Emperor for the East, a text from the eighth century, the Apocalypse of Peter, reappeared. It was full of allusions to battles which would be waged in Syria by a king of the South and a king of the East and it announced also that the Christians would be avenged by the victorious son of the Lion – in the literature of prophecy the Lion symbolised the Emperor – who would establish the universal monarchy.[46]

Thus when Frederick II embarked for Palestine in 1228 he was the object of joyous and confident expectation. When he returned he was adorned by the prestige acquired from the crown he put on in the Church of the Holy Sepulchre and he had been deeply influenced by the absolutism and messianism in which the East was bathed.

B. *Messianic hopes*
Hopes of a Messiah were built on disparate elements in which were mingled memories attached to the great oriental monarchies, mythical and mythological stories and prophecies of the Byzantine Empire.

---

[45] *Interpretatio sibyllinorum librorum,* in P.L., 110, 1181–6.
[46] Principal texts in Kampers, *Die deutsche Kaiseridee in Prophetie und Sage*; see also the references to the sources given by Kantorowitz, Vol. II.

During the reign of Frederick II, in an atmosphere peculiarly inclined towards the Beyond and hungry for signs which would herald the end of time, this hope of a Messiah burst forth. The opponents of the Emperor did indeed denounce him as the *infelix praenuntius Antichristi*, if not indeed the Antichrist himself,[47] but his partisans saw him equally certainly in quite another light – for them he was the *immutator mirabilis*,[48] the Emperor who would inaugurate the Golden Age, the saviour of the world.

Two figures, each in turn celebrated in the records of the Emperor's reign, were connected with this myth of the salvation of mankind. One of these was Adam, created in the image of God, who, before his sin, wore a diadem of glory and was the lord and master of nature, literally *Kosmokrator*. The other was Augustus in whom men recognised the *Soter par excellence*, founder of the Golden Age, the Emperor whose reign had witnessed the Redemption. To evoke Adam was to suggest the possibility of rediscovering in this world the harmony of paradise lost; to be inspired by Augustus was to restore the order of the universe in justice and peace. These speculations were not, however, directed only towards the past – they looked also to the present and the future. In Frederick's eyes, the universal Roman Empire, his Empire, was the Empire of the Fulfilment of Time, which must be restored once again to its state at the time when Christ passed through it – Christ who had recognised its authority when he directed people to render unto Caesar that which was Caesar's.[49]

But the Emperor's mission extended just as much to the Church, which, since the end of the twelfth century, had been undergoing an intense religious fermentation. The Cistercian Abbot, Joachim of Floris (who died in 1202), had announced the coming of the Third Kingdom, that of the Spirit. Another group, of which leading figures were Arnold of Brescia, the Waldensians and Francis of Assisi, strove to lead the Church back to evangelical poverty. Coming for the most part from Franciscan monasteries the Joachites looked to the Third Age to destroy the Church as a property-owner. Taking advantage of all these forces, Frederick II became the spokesman of the reformers, denounced the cupidity and secular interests of the papacy and the clerics and preached a return to apostolic times. Was he not henceforth the

[47] See, for example, Gregory IX's indictment, *Ascendit de mari* (*Mon. Germ. Epistolae pont. rom.*, I, p. 646).
[48] The expression is found among others in the Chronicle of Matthew Paris, *Mon. Germ. Script.*, XXVIII, p. 319.
[49] Cf. for example, the preamble to the *Constit. regni Siciliae* and a letter of Peter of the Vine (Iselius [Basle, 1740], II, p. 39).

Messianic King announced by the Sibyls, and the instrument whereby the *Renovatio* of the world would be carried out? What is more, Frederick seemed to be drawing nearer to Christ himself, at least in the eyes of his faithful followers who hailed in him the Co-adjutor,[50] who had received word of God's plans. And the Emperor, playing on the symbolic conception of the universe, gave credence to the idea that he was a representation of the Saviour, celebrating his birthplace Jesi as his own Bethlehem.[51]

The great reign of Frederick II ended in disaster. The catastrophe put an end to the Empire as an institution, but it could not eradicate from men's minds the hope which continued to inspire them, crystallised in the name of the last Hohenstaufen.

[50] *Cooperator Dei*; see, for example, the complaint of Master Salvus in Huillard-Breholles, *Vie et correspondance de Pierre de la Vigne*, Paris, 1865, p. 428.

[51] Decree dated August, 1239, in the *Histoire diplomatique* of Huillard–Breholles, V, I, p. 378.

BOOK IV
The Concept of Empire
Beyond the Realm of Reality

10

The Concept of the Empire as a Roman Institution: at the Time of the Great Interregnum (1250–1268)

In order to find out what was to be the fate of the concept of empire after the fall of Frederick II, we must remain in Italy and ask whether the moment had come for its representation as a Roman institution to take on a new lease of life. In Italy, in the Emperor's lifetime, the concept of empire had gradually become detached from its Germanic sub-stratum and had taken on a Roman colouring, the brilliance of which had reduced Germany to a secondary rôle. Indeed, since the Council of Lyons, Germany had been in a state of complete anarchy and her kings, urged on by the Church or at the mercy of the papacy, were no longer capable by themselves of maintaining the old imperialism. Italy had become a battlefield where the Ghibellines and the Guelfs, partisans and adversaries respectively of the Empire, confronted each other in a fierce struggle. Meanwhile, a new political structure was emerging, particularly in the North and centre of the country, where a purely nominal link with the Empire was maintained. The papacy, having won a victory over the Hohenstaufen Emperor, was at first quite incapable of exploiting the advantage so gained. Neither Innocent IV nor Alexander IV succeeded in settling the problem of Sicily or in preventing Frederick II's illegitimate son, Manfred, from becoming ruler of that kingdom. Furthermore, their authority was disputed even in Rome itself. Since the end of the twelfth century the administration of the town had depended on co-operation between the papacy and the Roman aristocracy and now, in 1252, when a democratic revolution brought Brancaleone of Andolo (a Bolognese) to power and aimed at restoring the town's sovereignty, it collapsed. In 1259 the Guelf nobles once more seized power, but the Roman *popolo* proved to be, temporarily at least, sufficiently influential to prevent the immediate reinstatement of the former régime; in 1260 Alexander IV left Rome and it was not until 1272 that a pope (Gregory X) returned to the city.

Thus the situation now was that the Germano-Roman doctrine concerning the Empire was dead; Italy was in ferment; there was a popular revolution in Rome. This picture inevitably recalls the situation in the middle of the twelfth century, when the idea that the Empire was a Roman institution first emerged.

In fact, we can observe that idea coming to life again during the Great Interregnum, despite the numerous difficulties which threaten to hinder its development. In itself, the idea of a Roman empire remained an archaic notion which was difficult to reconcile with the actual facts existing in the Middle Ages. Germanic competition may indeed have been swept away, but the imperial doctrine of the papacy was being disseminated over the ruins of the former Empire, and this, incidentally, with all the more energy because the successors of Innocent IV claimed that, in the absence of an emperor,[1] they had the right, in Italy at least, to administer the Empire themselves. Two questions must now be asked: was it possible for the idea of a Roman Empire to establish itself in the face of such an adversary? And, the political situation being as it was, what changes would it be forced to undergo?

. THE AWAKENING

The democratic revolution of 1252 was at the outset contained within the same restricted frontiers as all Roman movements of this type, which did not normally go beyond the immediate surroundings of the town. The Roman Empire was for some time a mere notion, expressed

---

[1] See the instructive texts in Böhmer (2) *Regesta Imperii*, V, 3–4, Nos. 9054, 9770, 9759, 9785, the last three relating to the administration of Tuscany which Clement IV took into his own hands 'in these times when the Roman Empire is wavering in uncertainty'; or Martène-Durand, *Thesaurus anecdotorum novus*, Paris, 1717, II, p. 587, the nomination, by the same Pope, of Charles of Anjou as vicar of the Empire in Tuscany (*Nos qui fluctuantis imperii curam gerimus*).

in certain classical phrases, such as the motto *Roma caput mundi* which appears alongside the sign SPQR on the coins of the time, while the seals depict a female figure with a lion beside her, symbolising the Roman people. Brancaleone at first sought to suggest that the notion of universality had a moral import, and tried to play the rôle of mediator, in the name of Rome, between the two supreme powers of Christendom, Pope Innocent IV and Conrad IV, who, on the death of his father, had come to Italy in order to defend his rights to the Empire.[2]

Very soon, however, it appeared that the notion of a Roman Empire was to be extended over the whole political scene, not as a result of any initiative or stimulus from Rome itself, where the public mind was slow to grasp the perspectives open to the city, but from outside. In 1254, on the grounds that when there was no emperor sovereignty reverted to the Roman people, the Pisans brought before Brancaleone a dispute which they had with the Florentines.[3] Two years later, at Soria in Castile, Bandino di Lancia – a Pisan again – chose King Alfonso X, to be King of the Romans and Emperor. This was a very bold innovation: Bandino acted in the capacity of *negotiorum gestor*, that is to say, 'representative of the interests and managing the affairs' of the whole of Christendom and the Roman Empire.[4] It must be noted that Alfonso abandoned this revolutionary project almost immediately and had himself elected King of the Romans by a group of German princes; he became, first, the mouthpiece of the Hohenstaufen policy and then, after Manfred's death, of the Italian Ghibellines, but he was never really closely involved with the idea of a Roman Empire.

By the end of the decade the idea had been revived and become sufficiently strong in Rome itself to survive, as did the party which supported it, the ultimate suppression[5] of the régime of Brancaleone in 1258. In the years which followed, it occupied the foreground of political interest. It naturally became a weapon in the hands of the Ghibellines of the town, but the Guelf aristocracy, who had now returned to take control of the affairs of the community, were for their part also obliged to come to terms with it. What is remarkable, however, is that the idea did not ever impose itself – it had to seek

---

[2] This point is brought out by Schmitthenner, *Ansprüche*, pp. 7 *et seq.*
[3] *Annales Januenses* in *Mon. Germ. Script.*, XVIII, p. 233.
[4] Text of the proclamation, in *Mon. Germ. Const.*, II, No. 392, p. 490; see the commentary in Jordan, *Dante et l'idée romaine de l'Empire*, third article, pp. 351–3.
[5] Brancaleone had been overthrown for the first time in 1255, but had returned to power three years later; thenceforth he waged a more aggressive policy in relation to the papacy and allied himself with Manfred.

supporting bases and thus to take on varying aspects, depending on the political temperament of its champions.

II. EXPLOITATION BY THE GUELFS AND THE GHIBELLINES OF THE CONCEPT OF THE EMPIRE AS A ROMAN INSTITUTION

It was now 1261. In that year the Romans established a custom which was contrary to former usage but which was to persist, notwithstanding some interruptions, for nearly two decades – they decided to confer the status of senator on foreign princes. What actually happened was that Richard of Cornwall, rival of Alfonso of Castile, and Manfred were simultaneously elected life senators.

This event was a reflection of the conflict between the Guelfs and the Ghibellines of Rome, which had been particularly acute since Manfred's coronation as King of Sicily in August, 1258, and which was pursued even within the sacred college itself, the members of which were divided over the major problem of the day, the Sicilian question: should the kingdom be allocated to Edmund, son of Henry III of England, whose candidature had been under discussion for some time, or ought they to come to terms with Manfred? Another thing had to be taken into account also; the spiritual atmosphere, evidently extremely tense in 1260-1, demanded that two should be elected. According to the Joachite prophecies, these were the years during which the persecution of the Church by a Germano-Roman emperor would attain its culminating point. Throughout the country, processions of flagellants were organised, who prayed for peace and general reconciliation. These prayers seem to have been associated with the hopes or fears which the Empire aroused, and the result was that the double Roman election was held.

Nevertheless the election of Richard of Cornwall was most unusual and had the greatest consequences for the future. He was elected because he was already King of the Romans and the Guelf electors were thus integrating the status of lord over the municipal area with that of emperor: by the election of their senator the Romans intended indirectly to determine who was to rule over the Empire. Their action must certainly be seen as a public affirmation of the concept that the Empire was a Roman institution, an attempt to make it clear that the Emperor's authority had its legal foundation in its genuine ties with Rome. But the effect of this was simultaneously to give an unmistakable Guelf colouring to the Roman representation. The letter to Richard, informing him of his election,[6] described Rome as both *creatrix Imperii, incitamentum vestrae promotionis* and *tronus apostolicae dignitatis*: the status of the new senator had its origin in the dual function of the town, birthplace of the Empire and seat of the papacy. Moreover, the active right of the Romans to decide who was to rule over the Empire, provided for by the true doctrine, had been transmuted into the right of their lord to claim it; neither of the two competing powers had been eliminated from the scene: kingship over the Germans still constituted the first stage towards elevation to the imperial throne, while the papacy alone possessed the right to crown the king after the Romans had first raised him to the rank of senator. In the event, this attempt by the Romans to intervene in the imperial succession proved unavailing, for Urban IV warned Richard that he could not accept the idea of a senator being elected for life and he thereupon made over the administration of Rome to a provisional committee of *boni homines* who remained in office until 1263.[7]

This forceful reaction by the Pope harmed Manfred, however, much more seriously than his rivals. By getting himself elected senator of Rome, Frederick II's son had reached the apogee of his power. He was King of Sicily and since his victory at Montaperti on 2nd September, 1260, he had functioned as the leader of the Italian Ghibellines; in 1257 he had allied himself with Brancaleone and he had control of a group in Rome. He too regarded the possession of a seat in the senate as being a necessary preliminary step towards the Empire at which he aimed; an empire free from any ties with Germany, based on possession of the town of Rome and receiving its principal support from a certain Italian nationalist sentiment which, since the end of the twelfth century, had been showing unmistakable though chaotic signs of germination.[8] Manfred's election, however, seemed to be inspired by quite different thinking from that of Richard: the Guelfs were fitting it into the traditional system of the Empire and thereby rendering homage to the

[6] *Mon. Germ. Const.*, III, No. 462, pp. 634–5.

[7] The epilogue to this story was the interdiction imposed in 1278 by Pope Nicholas III on the Romans to prevent them from putting into the senate any ruler or foreign prince whom they chose (cf. his bull *Fundamenta militantis Ecclesiae*; Liber Sextus I, 6, c. 17 [ed. Friedberg, II, 957–9]).

[8] This chaos was the concomitant of the struggle between the Empire and the papacy, both powers endeavouring to flatter the Italians' *amour-propre*. There are numerous pieces of evidence of this, cf., for example, the letter in which Innocent III informs the rectors of Tuscia that Italy has obtained the principate over all the provinces and the double universal dominion, because she is the seat of the papacy, sacerdotal and royal (P.L., 214, 377). Cf. also above, p. 87, the importance of the consent given by the Roman people referred to in Gregory IX's discussion of the subject of the *Donation*. Frederick II's advances to Rome will also be recalled.

concept of the Empire as a Roman institution; the Ghibellines, on the other hand, saw the same concept as providing them with the means to undertake radical changes in the actual structure of the institution.

But the election had no practical effect at all since it was annulled by Urban IV; moreover, Manfred did not dare attempt to enforce it, as he wished to avoid making the Pope ill-disposed towards him. It is also worth noting that from then on circumstances gradually turned against him. In fact, Urban finally solved the Sicilian problem by deciding that the kingdom was to go to Charles of Anjou. In 1263 the Guelfs of Rome elevated the Count of Provence to the senate even before the treaty of enfeoffment had been concluded. Confronted by this coalition, the opposition party broke up, and, as much from a desire for conciliation as to preserve Manfred's rights, they elected Peter of Aragon, his son-in-law, senator. The King of Sicily, for his part, adopted a policy of extreme procrastination. He subordinated everything to one major objective – the preservation of the kingdom – allowing all dreams of Rome and the Empire to sink into the background. Because of this Manfred went on trying to negotiate with Urban IV and then with Clement IV to the end, and failed to exploit to the full either his Italian alliances or the still vague position in Rome, where Charles of Anjou's representative was trying to administer the town, though he had insufficient means to take any real action and was all the time faced with an opposition which kept renewing its attacks. Too late, Manfred made up his mind to enter the lists once more and try to make the idea of a Roman Empire his own – on 25th May, 1265, the day after his adversary's arrival in Rome, he launched his famous manifesto announcing to the inhabitants his intention of coming into the town to receive the imperial diadem from them.[9]

This manifesto plainly constituted the most striking recognition ever given to the Roman theory of empire. Hitherto known only through some quotations in legal documents, it now took on the appearance of a well-arranged whole, with arguments taken from the Scriptures, from history and from Roman Law. The analysis starts off by contrasting the glory of the past and the poverty of the present, explaining that the latter was largely due to the way the Empire had been pillaged and that the Church had been guilty of this. It was the duty of Manfred and Rome to restore the splendour of former times by re-establishing the Empire and the authority of the town. The need for this restoration was to be deduced from 'the legal authority which requires that the fortunate – *felix* – people of the Roman republic be placed above all

[9] See Documents, XXI, p. 204.

the nations of the world'. The Romans were, in fact, still the reposi-
tories of full political sovereignty and the situation had not been altered
in any way by the Donation of Constantine. This must indeed be
considered as null and void, since an emperor could not impose the
mark of any servitude on his successors. The people of Rome should
exercise their own authority and put an end to this 'pestilential situation' by resuscitating the rights of the Empire and raising Manfred to
the pinnacle of power. It was indeed obvious that, while the *Lex Regia*
had transferred all the powers of the people to Caesar, these powers
were to be understood as being those of creating the Law and did not
include the power to elect the emperor or to change the external form
of the Empire, both of which remained under the control of the
people. The implicit conclusion was that headship of the Empire was
a transitory honour, elective, at the disposal of the Roman people.

Never before had such things been said so firmly. Manfred went
far beyond the terms of the letter written by his father to the Romans
in 1238. Nevertheless this text was not only an affirmation of the
concept of the Empire as Roman, it also contained many elements
which detract from its purity and authenticity. In fact, one thing
which emerges from this document is that Manfred's main interest
was not in the Empire but in the kingdom of Sicily. The two problems
were almost indissolubly linked, as the opening sentences show.
Manfred started by proclaiming that the objective of his policy was
the exaltation of the Empire; the Church had sought to block his
intentions by arousing enemies against him everywhere in Italy and
by trying to seize his hereditary kingdoms. He had defeated all his
adversaries: then the papacy had had the idea of calling Richard and
Alfonso to the Empire; because of this he himself had occupied Tuscany
and the March of Ancona. And now along came Charles of Provence,
a new tool being used by the Church 'against his honour and also
against the honour of the Republic, the Senate and the Commune of
Rome'. There can be little doubt that Manfred saw in the seizure of
the Empire the best method to defend the kingdom of Sicily; in
consequence he treated the concept of empire as in every way subordinate to his plans for furthering his own private interests.

What was still more serious was that the concept of empire had lost
its original Roman character; it had not been born in Rome – where
the majority of the inhabitants were at the least indifferent if not
positively hostile to Manfred; and it was not the result of a democratic
movement, as it had been after the events of 1143, or even as it might
have been between 1252 and 1258. It made its appearance outside

Rome, in the service of Manfred and his Ghibelline allies, and was on that account subtly changing its character, by acquiring two new elements: first it was appealing to Italian national sentiment, seen as an extension of Roman patriotism and aimed at flattering the *amour-propre* of the allies – 'What German, what Spaniard, what Englishman, what Frenchman, what Provençal would dare, O Rome, assume the service of thy government against our wish?'[10] – and, secondly Manfred was affirming that he had a double personal right to the Empire, both on grounds of heredity and also because he could, if need be, become Emperor of the Romans by force.

III. FINAL DEFEAT

Manfred was killed at the Battle of Benevento on 26th February, 1266, and his death laid the kingdom of Sicily open to Charles of Anjou. His triumph, which was simultaneously a victory for the papacy, was, however, compromised briefly by the last convulsions of the idea of a Roman Empire, from which Henry of Castile, the new senator of Rome, and Conradin, the last of the Hohenstaufens, both profited: in 1267 these two personages concluded an alliance. Henceforth the spirit of Manfred lived again, and this time it was more dangerous for the papacy, because it appeared not only outside, but also within Rome itself.

From his base in Rome Henry of Castile joined up with the Ghibelline league of Tuscany. They made him captain-general and gave him the right to acquire for himself and his descendants such properties of the Empire as lay in that province. This action was directed both against the papacy[11] and against any pretensions which Conradin might make and it is possible that it should be regarded as a new version of the theory which had inspired the Pisans in 1254: i.e. the principle that in the event of there being no emperor, the administration of the imperial territories reverted to the representative of the Roman people. This theory is all the more acceptable since, according to a communication sent by Clement IV to Charles of Anjou, Henry of Castile was said to have called the Pisans and the Sienese allies of the Romans *et alteram partem urbis*:[12] if this expression is to be understood

---

[10] Cf. the appeal by Manfred in the same spirit to the Ghibellines of Tuscany, in Winkelmann, *Acta Imperii inedita*, I, 420.

[11] Clement IV reacted by appointing Charles of Anjou, first, *paciarius generalis* in 1267 and then, on 2nd May, 1268, vicar of the Empire in these areas; see the references given in Note 1 of this chapter.

[12] Text in Martène-Durand, *Thesaurus*, II, 548.

as anything more than a mere rhetorical formula it would offer extremely clear evidence of a wider conception of what the Roman people represented – doubtless the same as that which inspired Bandino di Lancia in 1256 to proclaim Alfonso of Castile emperor. But it is Henry's behaviour in Rome which is particularly important, as it reveals certain incidental features of the concept of the Empire as a Roman institution, in particular its anti-clerical character. For example, the installation of the envoys in the Lateran Palace must be noted as a truly revolutionary act which struck at the papacy through what was the most significant symbol of its imperial authority; also the confiscation of some property belonging to Guelf cardinals; the arrest of some clerics; and the plundering of churches.[13] It seemed as though these measures might herald some imminent and even more radical action.

Conradin had come down into Italy primarily in order to recapture the kingdom of Sicily, but almost imperceptibly he began to cherish hopes of gaining the Empire also.[14] He sent representatives to Rome who were welcomed in the Capitol and who made proposals to the inhabitants, the exact terms of which are not known but which may be guessed from the indignant message addressed by Clement IV to the Romans on 5th April, 1268:[15] let not the City, daughter of the papacy, cover itself with the infamy of matricide by docilely lending its ear to the 'doctrine' of Frederick II reflected in the words of Conradin's envoys! From such allusions it can be assumed that the proposals concerned the re-establishment of the Empire in favour of Frederick's grandson, who would receive the diadem of Rome, *caput et creatrix Imperii*. On 24th July, Conradin entered Rome in triumph and was received with imperial acclamation by the people *qui naturaliter imperialis existit*.[16] But the actual proclamation of the Empire did not take place: no doubt chiefly because of the opportunism of Henry of Castile, who considered that the rebirth of the Empire was less important than the reconquest of Sicily, but also because of Conradin's hesitations, for his legalistic sentiments made him uneasy at the idea of such revolutionary action.

His defeat a few weeks later at Tagliacozzo, on 23rd August, 1268,

[13] Cf. Clement IV's encyclical to the Romans dated 5th April, 1268, and Henry of Castile's writ of accusation dated 17th May, in *Mon. Germ. Epistolae saec. XIII*, III, No. 675, pp. 699–702 and No. 684, pp. 715–16.

[14] Cf., for example, the document which he issued on 7th June to Siena where we can read *i.a.*: 'We who ascend with God's help towards the summit of the imperial dignity at which we aim, not without right, while following in the steps of our ancestors,' *Regesta Imperii*, V, 2, No. 4857.

[15] *Mon. Germ. Epistolae saec. XIII*, III, No. 675, pp. 699–700.

[16] So said the chronicler Saba Malaspina, in Muratori, *Rerum italicarum Scriptores*, vol. VIII, p. 842.

was at the same time a defeat for the representation of the Empire as Roman.

In brief, in the course of an era which apparently offered it unlimited possibilities, the concept of the Empire as a Roman institution met with total defeat; it gave birth to aspirations which were frequently enthusiastic but which never succeeded in altering the facts – which were hostile or indifferent. This fundamental impotence arose from a number of understandable reasons.

The representation of the Empire as Roman was a heritage of antiquity and it conflicted with the mediaeval tradition of the Empire. The proclamation of the Empire by the Roman people ran counter to two other doctrines of superior weight – the doctrine that the Germanic rulers, successors to the Franks, had a right to the Empire based on both heredity and conquest, and the doctrine that the Pope, because he crowned the prince, played a prominent part in the accession to the monarchy and had the right to dispose of the Empire (however one interpreted this term). Because of this, the third doctrine concerning the Empire seemed anachronistic and in practice unrealisable. It could not acquire any influence except by becoming an instrument of combat in the hands of the forces which faced each other during the period when the imperial throne was unoccupied, which was, in fact, its fate. This was responsible, moreover for the variety of aspects which it presents to us – from Brancaleone to Conradin, via the Roman Guelfs, Manfred and Henry of Castile, down the scale from universality to a Romano-Italian view of the Empire. So the map of the Empire seemed to shrink until ultimately it comprised no more than the town of Rome and Italy, and, at that, a very ill-defined Italy, but in any case one annexed by the *Urbs*. It seemed natural that the whole concept would thus inevitably tend towards an Italian empire; but national sentiment in the middle of the thirteenth century was far from being sufficiently mature to afford it a solid foundation.

In addition to this first stumbling block there was the resistance put up by the papacy to the idea of a Roman Empire. Victorious over the Hohenstaufens' concept of empire, the papacy used its last ounce of energy to combat every attempt to create an empire from which it would be excluded. The view held by the papacy of the supreme office was absolutely monolithic and because of this Clement IV was able, in a message to the Romans, to deny that there was any link, even of ideas, with the former empire, and to represent the Empire of the Middle Ages as a completely new entity.[17] The Rome of the Apostles

[17] See Documents, XXI, p. 204.

was the opposite of the Rome of the Caesars – it was not its continuation: an abyss separated Clement IV from Leo the Great.

Lastly, the indifference of the Roman people in this story must not be forgotten. From 1259 at least, they showed a passivity which deprived the concept of empire of its natural setting. Doubtless the underlying cause of this ineffectualness can be traced to the fact that the Roman Commune was an unsatisfactory and incomplete organisation, which never succeeded in achieving ultimate control of the nobility. In the last analysis too, the failure of the idea of the empire as Roman was a consequence of the failure of the Roman Commune. The utter passivity of the city was striking. After Tagliacozzo Rome was administered by Charles of Anjou, whom the Pope had appointed a senator for ten years from 3rd April, 1268,[18] and at that date the town entered into the orbit of the Angevin monarchy, where it was to remain for a long period.

The concept of the Empire as a Roman institution was henceforth incorporeal and became an object of speculation: as such it was to undergo a great resurgence.

[18] *Regesta Imperii*, V, 3–4, No. 9889.

11

The Controversy over the Concept of Empire

After the fall of the Hohenstaufens, after the demonstration of political importance given by the Roman doctrine, when theocracy was progressing towards victory on all levels, the concept of empire became an object of discussion – intense discussion, which presented a sharp contrast with the disintegration of the Empire as an institution, and which increased steadily from 1270, attaining its maximum in the first quarter of the fourteenth century, when it flourished alongside the last attempts to restore the Empire. Speculation was of two kinds – political and philosophical – on the one hand an effort to justify the institution while taking account of the crisis through which it was actually passing, and on the other an attempt, regardless of the factual situation, to adapt the concept of empire to the intellectual movement of the time.

I. THE POLITICAL LEVEL

A. *The Empire as an institution reaches a crisis*
The weakness of the ties which held the Empire together was revealed by the period of the Interregnum. It had comprised three territories. In one of these, Burgundy, developments varied from region to region: in the North, and especially east of the Jura, the feeling of belonging to the Empire proved to be fairly strong, but in the South (the Kingdom of Arles) the rivalries of the territorial powers served the interests of the French monarchy. In Italy, the Empire was first and foremost

a name and a party label. As for Germany, the tendency to break up into separate lands continued and the country was unable by its own strength to put an end to the crisis which had been devastating it since 1245.

So the Empire seemed to be no more than a huge disjointed body. Moreover, the picture it presented of a monarchy divided into two groups, differing greatly from one another, began to grow more and more vivid from the middle of the century and contributed to its ruin. The two sections were the *regnum* (*Alamaniae* or *Theotoniae*) and the rest (i.e. Burgundy and Italy, often called *imperium* in the restricted meaning of the expression). A corollary to this distinction was the principle that Italy was reserved, or rather that the rights of the Empire in Italy, were reserved, to the Holy See – a principle which stood out clearly enough in the time of the Interregnum. This tendency to differentiation had only to be reaffirmed for the idea to emerge that national monarchies might take the place of the Empire and, although in fact such a project was not explicitly set out in any document until the eve of the Council of Vienne in 1311, we can be fairly certain that it was discussed on several occasions in the *Curia* in the last quarter of the thirteenth century.[1]

Side by side with this tendency to disintegrate, the old notion of the institution nevertheless continued to exist – what is more, a Pope arose who was to resuscitate it. But Gregory X himself, who put an end to the Interregnum, did not envisage the Emperor as anything more than a dependant of his supreme authority. In the name of the doctrine of Innocent III, he insisted on himself approving the king elected in Germany and, in 1273,[2] he conferred the title of King of the Romans on Rudolf of Hapsburg. While awaiting his imperial coronation, which was frequently discussed but which never took place, Rudolf was merely the acting administrator of the whole of the Empire, by the grace of the Holy See. Abandoning the Romagna to Nicholas III in 1279, he proclaimed the superiority of the papal authority over that of kings, while on the same occasion the prince-electors publicly recognised that their prerogative had been granted to them by the vicar of Christ, 'the major luminary of Christendom'.[3] So it seemed that the papacy might be able to co-exist with the Empire on condition that the former dominated the latter, the essential point being to make people recognise that the exercise of an emperor's rights was derived

---

[1] For the history of this plan, cf. Folz, *Souvenir et légende*, pp. 382–3.
[2] *Mon. Germ. Const.*, III, No. 66, p. 56.
[3] *Ibid*, No. 222, p. 207, and No. 225, p. 213.

exclusively from the coronation which was conferred on the King of the Romans in Rome. But implicit in this principle was the possibility that the Holy See could make the emperor and need not be bound by the tradition according to which the King of Germany was the emperor to be. This was also the view of those who thought that the moment had come for a *Translatio* of the Empire to the French.

At this point the concept of the empire as a French institution began to emerge and it grew steadily stronger during the second half of the thirteenth century. It had its roots in the great memories of the past, especially the legend of Charlemagne, enshrined in the *Chansons de Geste – Charles li reis, nostre emperere magne* – which had gradually become associated with the royal house of Capet. For the Capetians the legend was, along with the prestige of the anointing at Rheims, an incomparable moral force by contrast with the actual potentialities of the monarchy in the eleventh and twelfth centuries. Its most noticeable effect was to preserve, in the collective memory, the existence of the notions of empire and of France combined, and at the same time to act as guarantor of the independence of the kingdom vis-à-vis the Empire in power, which similarly drew life and strength from the memory of Charlemagne. This twofold influence was well recognised in Germany in the time of Frederick I, as is shown by efforts made at that time to revive the Frankish tradition.[4] But whereas Germany abandoned the political theme of Charlemagne from the beginning of the thirteenth century, the Carolingian tradition continued to make irresistible progress in France. It cast its shadow over Philip Augustus, renowned among his contemporaries as the *alter Karolus*. His second name, or rather his nickname, signified that the King had a share in the imperial title, and the accession of his son Louis VIII, whose mother was Isabella of Hainault, a lady well known to be descended from Carolingian ancestors, was hailed as the return of the Kingdom of the Franks to the race of Charlemagne.[5] Henceforth, the King of France was a candidate for the Empire.

After 1250, all such hopes on the part of the French seemed admissible. There was the precedent of the Interregnum during which foreign (i.e. non-German) princes had been elected Kings of the Romans; the internal weakness of Germany and the possibility of exploiting the rivalry and cupidity of the electors; steady territorial progress achieved by the kings in the Western part of the Empire, its

---

[4] See above, p. 101.

[5] Principal evidence: Giles of Paris, *Carolinus*, Book V, in *Recueil des historiens des Gaules*, XVII, p. 289; *Gesta Ludowici, ibid*, p. 302.

area of least resistance; finally, in the background, the persistence since the middle of the thirteenth century of a prophecy foretelling the accession of a king of France to the Empire.[6] This explains why Charles of Anjou put forward his nephew, Philip III, as a candidate for kingship over the Romans in 1273. Charles was in control of Sicily and of part of Italy, and perhaps had a vision of the universal monarchy for the Capetian dynasty, but the attempt failed because of Gregory X's reservations; anxious to maintain a safe balance of power in the West, he refused to have a French emperor. But the idea was not lost sight of and it re-emerged in 1281–5, during the pontificate of the very French Martin IV, and persistently reappeared in years to come, e.g. in 1308, 1324, 1519 and even later.

To sum up: what with plans for dismemberment, vassalisation by the papacy, eventual transfer of the institution to the French – the Empire in the last quarter of the thirteenth century faced a very serious crisis which threatened simultaneously its unity, its authority and its nationality. Such was the background which inspired Alexander of Roes,[7] a canon of the church of St Mary of Cologne and a member of the household of Cardinal James Colonna, to advance his plea for the Empire in two treatises composed in 1281 and 1288.

B. *Justification of the Empire as a positive fact*

Alexander of Roes's apologia on behalf of the Empire was directed essentially towards the preservation of the old order. Although it showed a certain degree of adaptation to the realities of the age it was impregnated with archaism, as is plain from the main features of his arguments.

Faithful to the old tradition, Alexander attributed the foundations of the Empire firmly to the design of Providence. Given legal recognition by Christ who was one of its subjects, the Empire was the instrument of mankind's salvation; were it to disappear the field would be left clear for the Antichrist: the Empire was therefore necessary. It was, moreover, sanctified by its mission, a mission which extended far beyond its territorial framework and attained universal scope – not indeed Roman universality, the *dominium mundi*, as Frederick II had put it, but the service of the Universal Church, in the

---

[6] See below, p. 162.
[7] *Memoriale de praerogativa Imperii Romani* (1281) incorporating in its text the *Tractatus super Romano Imperio*, drawn up, during the Interregnum, by Canon Jordan of Osnabrück; *Noticia saeculi* (1288): can be consulted in the edition of Grundmann-Heimpel, *Die Schriften des Al. von Roes*, Weimar, 1949.

manner envisaged by the Carolingians, the Ottonians, Henry III and doubtless Frederick I (at least on occasion). In fact, Alexander did not recognise any one sphere as proper to the Empire, since for him the Empire was a service or a function i.e. the defence of the Church, with which it was so intimately linked that Alexander, when referring to the Empire, used terms which are, to say the least, ambiguous, such as 'Kingdom of the Roman Church, republic of the Christian faith', *sanctuarium Dei.*

This important function – and here we have his second thesis – had fallen to the *regnum* of Germany since the date of the *Translatio* of the Empire, through which it, in the person of Charlemagne, had profited. The *Translatio* was a definitive one and entailed as a corollary both the maintenance of the principle of election of the king (the future emperor) and at the same time the indissolubility of the Germany–Italy–Burgundy group as a whole. This explains why Alexander spoke out against the establishment of a hereditary monarchy in Germany;[8] hereditary kingship would break the link between the *regnum* and its universal mission, and might place the Pope in a position to crown as emperor any ruler whatsoever of his own choice. By insisting with such force on the imperial mission of the *regnum*, Alexander of Roes gave the empire-function a national tinge.

This acknowledgment of Germanism rested on an interpretation of history which fitted in with the ideas of Frederick I's contemporaries. The Empire belonged to the Germans because it was won by the Franks, but like Charlemagne's Empire, it was simultaneously the Roman Empire, which continued without change: the Germans, descendants of the Franks, were also, by virtue of the Trojan legend, the brother nation of the Romans. This reference back to Frankish tradition is undoubtedly the most instructive feature of Alexander of Roes's line of thought[9] and one cannot avoid assuming that he envisaged it as a possible way to resist French expansion, which he could observe taking place, and to demonstrate that the Germanic kingdom was the direct heir of the Frankish monarchy, so that its rulers were the true and only authentic successors of Charlemagne.

But beyond the frontiers of Frankish Germany there was the supreme order of the world and from this our cleric never allowed his attention to be deflected. This order was the Christian order which could be made to endure permanently if each nation retained the function which Charlemagne had attributed to it and which corresponded to its own

---

[8] A project which was attributed, apparently not without reason, to Rudolf of Hapsburg.
[9] For more detail on this subject, cf. Folz, *op. cit.*, pp. 386 *et seq.*

ethnic character and temperament. So the Germans, political heirs of the Franks, ought to retain the imperial mission irrevocably, whereas the Romans (or the Italo-Romans) had a right to the papacy, that is to say the spiritual government of the Church, which was protected by the Emperor's sword. However, times had changed and no longer did all Christendom gravitate around the Emperor and the Pope; national states had been born. These Alexander of Roes omitted from his scheme of things, with the exception of one, the Kingdom of France, which he considered to be also an heir, although to a lesser degree than Germany, since the French were not true Franks, not being of Carolingian descent. According to Alexander, Charlemagne granted the French state a hereditary monarchy together with full independence in relation to the Empire; and to the French people he gave the third function of universality, namely *studium*, that is to say, study and higher education. Germany, Italy, France; Empire, priesthood, education – the heritage of ancient Rome,[10] which had passed into the hands of the Franks and their successors; three pillars on which the order of the world, identified with the order of the Christian faith, was based; the Pope was the guarantor of the faith, the Emperor defended it by the material sword and France defended it by the weapons of dialectic forged at the University of Paris.

Admittedly a grandiose vision; an intelligent concession made to the changes which had taken place, in the course of which the Empire had evolved and become a factor in the order of the world, whereas it had formerly been identified with it; a subtle and skilful plea which gave rise to only one serious objection: it was the work of one who based his line of thought stubbornly on the past. How could it be otherwise? In his treatises Alexander of Roes assessed simultaneously the greatness and the weakness displayed by the concept of empire at a time when it was being shaped in such a way as to form a defence of the Empire in the political and institutional sense of the expression.

II. THE INTELLECTUAL LEVEL

A. *Forces opposed to imperial ideology*

Alexander of Roes's efforts seem all the more compromised when regarded in the light of the trends of contemporary thought, for a new conception of the state was arising, which based it on new

---

[10] Cf. *Memoriale*, chapters xiv and xv: Charlemagne transferred *studium* from Rome to Paris.

foundations and which had the effect of enabling the theocratic views of the papacy to reach their apogee.

Perhaps the most important contribution to this process was the victory gained by the schools of philosophy, which started by rediscovering Aristotle, then evolved a conception of the state which was a negation of the traditional theory of the Empire. First, its origin – the Empire had its foundation in God: the state by contrast had arisen out of the nature of man as a political animal. Then its aims and objects – the Empire aimed at being, as it were, the vestibule of the City of God; the state sought to realise on earth the general will of the people as interpreted by the rulers. Lastly, in the scheme of the world, the Empire, a reflection of the heavenly *ordo*, strove to achieve unified control of mankind, in theory at least – an aim which was incompatible with the diversity and multiplicity of rulers and, if pressed to its extreme, likely to lead to the suppression of the Empire as an institution: speculation thus arrived at the same conclusion as political evolution.

Taken together all such ideas greatly benefited the Western monarchies, at that time moving towards unification under the leadership of their kings. In France particularly, they were the chief weapon of the kings in establishing centralisation.

But they were just as helpful to the papacy. Supporting the Canon Law they provided remarkable reinforcement for earlier conceptions which had hitherto been conveyed by symbols. For the canonists, the primacy of spiritual authority was an indisputable fact. All they needed to know was just how far this principle could be applied. Henry of Susa, cardinal bishop of Ostia (*Hostiensis*), the most illustrious of them all, argued in his commentary on the Decretals of Gregory IX[11] that the Pope was the true source of secular authority, making use of the civil authorities for those tasks which he could not accomplish himself; the Emperor held his authority from the Church and could therefore be called the Pope's agent or vicar. And now the schools of philosophy began – at first with caution – to provide rational foundations for these theses. Following up the *De regimine principum* of St Thomas Aquinas, Ptolemy of Lucca used the idea of Being and the principles of Causality and Finality to demonstrate in what way papal authority was preeminent – being simultaneously sacerdotal and regal, essentially spiritual but also touching on temporal matters of order, as, for example, when Innocent IV deposed Frederick II. But by the end of the century

---

[11] *Lectura sive apparatus super V libris Decretalium*, pub. Strasbourg, 1512; cf. also the *Summa aurea super titulis Decretalium*, pub. Lyons, 1568.

much more radical ideas were being advanced in the great syntheses of Giles of Rome and James of Viterbo:[12] in these the penetration of temporal authority by spiritual authority was strengthened to such a degree that it is extremely difficult, if not impossible, to isolate them from one another and that the Pope figures in every respect as a universal ruler.

It was ultimately Boniface VIII who expounded these doctrines most strikingly, on the strength of the authority which he claimed *super reges et regna*. Unlike Innocent III who, when pursuing a moral aim, was capable of imposing limits on his will, Boniface pursued to their rational end with the umost rigour and relentlessness all the principles which had been formulated over a century of controversy. He seized on all the old arguments, secularised them and applied them to the political field. His thinking achieved a rare power in the Bull *Unam Sanctam*;[13] it was supported by a philosophy which was half-rationalist, half-mystic, inspired simultaneously by Aristotle and Pseudo-Dionysius, who together provided Boniface with the means of producing a synthesis of the pontifical *auctoritas* which, because it was the most spare and the most concise, was also the most striking ever made.

This *auctoritas* in turn was based on the purest universalism, the idea of the community of men, fused in the one Church – *una columba, una perfecta, unum corpus mysticum*. Inevitably this doctrine resulted in the postulate of control over mankind by one authority, which must be the exclusive right of the Roman pontiff, priest and king. Although Boniface was thinking of the figure of Melchizedek, he did not actually mention him, as he was anxious to delve deeper into an even more distant past. It was Noah to whom he looked, single head of the Church, symbolised by the Ark, haven of mankind. The Roman pontiff, sole head of the mystical Body, being the vicar of Christ and the successor of Peter, and also keeper of the Two Swords, exercised full jurisdiction in both the spiritual and the temporal field: 'judge of all, he cannot be judged by any person';[14] he was pre-eminently the *homo spiritualis* as defined by St Paul.[15] Thus Boniface used for the benefit of the papacy the great spiritual current flowing at the time of his

[12] *De regimine principum, De ecclesiastica potestate*, both by Giles of Rome; *De regimine Christiano*, by James of Viterbo. Cf. also, the same sort of thinking in the *Determinatio compendiosa de jurisdictione Imperii*, by Ptolemy of Lucca. There is an analytical study of these treatises in Rivière, *Le problème de l'Église et de l'État*.

[13] On the 18th November, 1302, feast of the Dedication of the basilicas of St Peter and St Paul; C.I., *Extrav. comm.*, I, 8 (Friedberg, *Corpus Juris Canonici*, II, 1245).

[14] In his second sermon *in consecratione pontificis* (P.L., 214, 657–8), Innocent III had similarly pronounced this formula but without drawing from it the conclusion reached by Boniface VIII.

[15] I *Cor.*, ii, 15.

pontificate, a current which was slowly moving towards the idea of the freedom of the believer, filled by the Spirit, in the eyes of God. Boniface appropriated this freedom for the Pope alone, as the bearer of the unity of the Christian community and he transformed it into *potestas spiritualis* – an intensification of the idea of *auctoritas* – superior to any earthly power; those who held the latter must, like all human beings, be subject to the Roman pontiff – it was a condition of their salvation.

And so the old Gelasian idea of the pontifical *auctoritas* had now reached its culminating point. Although it was soon to be brilliantly denounced by Philip the Fair, there was a short period – at the time of the elevation of Albert of Hapsburg to the Empire – when facts enabled it to prevail. On that occasion, in the consistory[16] on 30th April, 1303, the Pope pronounced a discourse which was a long dissertation on the *Translatio* of the Empire, which he saw as a tangible sign of the imperial authority of St Peter's successor, formally approved by the envoys of the King of the Romans in the name of their master. They affirmed in addition the unlimited authority of the Pope, from whom all power was derived, simultaneously recognising also that the Roman Empire, because it was universal, was integrated with the domain of the Church. Albert went still further, declaring himself to be the liege-man of Boniface, *homo papae*.

An emperor who was a vassal of the Holy See and thereby and therefore universal – this was the picture which Boniface, the Pope-Emperor,[17] bequeathed to his successors.

B. *The philosophical foundations of the Empire*

It was in the first third of the fourteenth century that the Empire, having passed through the era of kings, and the era of pontifical theocracy, received its philosophical justification. This first appeared about 1308, under the pen of Engelbert,[18] the Cistercian Abbot of Admont in Styria. Then, at a date which cannot be fixed precisely but which was apparently sometime between 1312 and 1313, it appeared in Dante's *Monarchia*:[19] thus this great work was contemporaneous with the setback to Henry VII's efforts to achieve universality and can be regarded as pleading for an institution which was condemned by the political situation.

---

[16] *Mon. Germ. Const.*, IV, I, No. 173, p. 138.   [17] See Documents, XXII, p. 207.
[18] *De ortu, progressu et fine Romani Imperii* (Goldast, *Politica imperiala*, Frankfurt, 1614, pp. 754–74).
[19] *Ed.* C. Witte, Vienna, 1874; text and French translation by B. Landry, Paris, 1933.

Reading those two treatises one is struck by the fact that in certain respects they resemble one another. First, both are inspired by purely speculative thinking: there is no allusion to the detailed factual situation of the time. They use one single historical point on which to base their theme of universal monarchy, i.e. that the Roman Empire had persisted without a break in its continuity since the reign of Augustus and would endure to the end of time. Similarly, there are points of correspondence between the main elements of the arguments in the treatises of both Engelbert and Dante, among which are the following:

1. *The need for one single authority.* Engelbert established this by reference to the principle of unity, which everywhere brings order to plurality, and of the order of the world, which demands an emperor, arbiter of kings, creator of harmony and of peace,[20] guarantor of general fidelity. These ideas reappear in Book I of the *Monarchia*, where they are expressed with greater philosophical vigour and with greater richness too. Thus the Emperor is represented as the prime cause of social order; he is everywhere; his authority gives princes and kings the capacity to rule and is therefore compatible with a plurality of governing bodies. Moreover, society is created by the Emperor and through him achieves its aims. In the third chapter of Book I the ultimate aim assigned to mankind is given as the full development of the intellect, *virtus aut potentia intellectiva*. But only in a hierarchal society, under the command of one single person, can human minds receive the divine intelligence to the full. It is bestowed on the Emperor and from him radiates over all men; he who holds the universal Empire incarnates, as it were, the universal intellect of mankind; he thus typifies a new conception of man, which is gradually elaborated – intellectual man or spiritual man.

2. *The legality of the Roman Empire.* This is demonstrated in the two treatises by means of more or less well-founded arguments: the Empire was created by men whose outstanding qualities predestined them to carry out this mission and whose success was equivalent to a Judgment of God; the Empire was founded in justice; the Empire was sanctified by the attitude of Christ towards it for he submitted to the census and when he appeared before Pilate, he recognised the universal jurisdiction of the Emperor.

[20] On the subject of universal peace, guaranteed by the Emperor, one can also very well turn to the writings of Pierre Dubois, where it is alleged that the King of France is able to make peace reign in the West; therefore he alone is competent to rule the Empire (cf. the brief analysis given by G. Zeller, *Les rois de France, candidats à l'Empire*).

Up to this point it might be said that the *Monarchia* was, so to speak, simply a more striking version of the theme elaborated in Engelbert's treatise, but when one examines the manner in which each envisages the relationship between the Empire and the Church one sees that this is not the case. Following the example of his compatriot, Alexander of Roes, Engelbert found it difficult to distinguish between the spheres proper to the two entities; for him, the basis of the universal Empire was the 'unity of the Body of Christ and of the entire Christian republic'. In other words, no universal Empire without universal Christianity. In that case who would be master? Would the Emperor rule over Christendom or would the Empire be controlled by the Pope?

Engelbert left this question open and it fell to Dante to reply in Book III of the *Monarchia*, the aim of which is to defend the complete independence of the Empire. All the arguments of the papal doctrine are demolished one after the other. Dante invokes the authority of St Augustine and in particular rebels against the abuses caused by the allegorical interpretations of Holy Writ: thus, according to him, the symbol of the Keys may not be interpreted in an absolute sense – no pontiff can unmake the laws of the Empire – but must be regarded merely as representing the relationships between man and Heaven. Incidentally, it is noteworthy that the poet himself did not escape committing the very fault of which he accused the Empire's adversaries. See, for example, his refutation of the Donation of Constantine: how, he says, could an emperor, whose mission was to impose one single will on the human race, destroy the unity of the Empire, this seamless robe of which the Gospel speaks? Thus Dante utilised one of the theses of the Bull *Unam Sanctam* to the advantage of the Empire.

All these arguments combined to emphasise the dual principle that the Church, which came after the Empire, was entrusted with the care of the purely spiritual order and that the Empire had its source in God alone. But man's nature has two sides: it has both a temporal and an eternal aim; its objective is happiness, simultaneously in this life (which it can obtain through reason) and in the future life (which it can obtain by observing the teachings of Christ). This dualism requires that humanity be governed by two separate masters, the Emperor and the Pope, ordained by God, 'from Whom, as from one point, there is a bifurcation of the power of Peter and the power of Caesar'.[21] Two equal powers, two suns, as Canto XVI of *Il Purgatorio*[22] says so marvellously – contrary to the classic theme that there is a

---

[21] *Letters*, VIII, 5.   [22] See Documents, XXIV, p. 209.

major and a minor luminary – it requires two authorities, which are equal because they are both alike instituted by God and are both responsible for guiding mankind, the Pope in respect of the life beyond and the Emperor in this present life, a guide to man, a restraining rein for his soul in its uncertain steps, *cavalcatore della umana volunta*.[23]

None the less this perfect equality does not exclude a certain degree of submission by the temporal supreme authority to the spiritual authority from which grace radiates, that is to say, the moral influence which permits the monarch to fulfil his mission more effectively: the Two Luminaries are indeed equal, but there must also be co-ordination and harmony between them. These then seem to be the major principles set out by the *Monarchia*.

Thus the concept of empire moved on a stage from Engelbert of Admont to Dante, reflecting the general trend of thought of the time. From the principle of absolute unity – exploited by the papal theocracy and simply adapted in favour of the Empire by Engelbert – there evolved imperceptibly a degree of distinction between philosophy and theology, the Church and the State: it was as though Dante had just been using, for his own arguments, certain theses of Averrhoism.[24]

By contrast, the Averrhoist attitude of mind took over completely in the *Defensor pacis*, written towards 1324 by Marsilius of Padua in collaboration with John of Jandun.[25] This treatise is first and foremost a general doctrine of the state, a social philosophy, constructed on foundations laid by Aristotle and strongly marked by the example of the Italian *constitutiones* and the writings of Philip the Fair's legal advisers. Though it goes beyond the scope of the Empire proper, it must be mentioned here because of the influence which it had on Louis of Bavaria: it was perhaps even written for him.

Marsilius's starting point was the dualism of man's aims, which relate to two different kinds of life – life in one's own time and eternal life. The priests, with the aid of Revelation, led one to the latter while the former, on the other hand, was controlled exclusively by the state, in accordance with the teaching of philosophy.

The main theme of the *Defensor* was meanwhile that all authority – including the authority of the priests – was of human origin and that divine intervention was necessary only to ensure its operation. From this Marsilius deduced that all priests were equal and delivered himself of a violent criticism of the hierarchy and the papacy, for being guilty

[23] *Convivio*, IV, 9.　　　[24] E. Gilson, *La philosophie au Moyen-Age*, p. 578.
[25] Ed. R. Scholz, in *Fontes iuris germanici antiqui*, 1932.

of a long series of usurpations at the expense of the people and the state. Moreover, he said that the Church existed only in and through the state; it was but the community of the faithful, priests and laymen, completely subject to the prince, who was the interpreter of the general will and was charged with the supervision of spiritual life. Supreme control within the Church was the prerogative of the Œcumenical Council, convoked by the Emperor 'who has no person above him.' Acting in the name of the Council and under the order of Caesar, the Pope was no more than a kind of chairman, presiding over Christendom, a Christendom fragmented and divided into separate states. His weakness was in striking contrast to the prestige of the Emperor's authority, based on the handing over to the Emperor of all the authority exercised by the 'supreme human legislator of the Empire', i.e. the Roman people. Marsilius rejected the papal theory of the *Translatio* of the Empire and showed it to be an act which the Romans ordered Leo III to perform for the benefit of Charlemagne.[26]

Though the inspiration of the three treatises which we have just reviewed may differ greatly, they nevertheless present one common feature – they were all trying to free the Empire from the pontifical grasp which bid fair to stifle it and were all striving to hold fast to the ancient Roman doctrine. From the ruins of the imperial institution there had just emerged an ideology which seemed to have a solid foundation, with sufficient flexibility to permit of a variety of nuances, enabling us to distinguish a moderate tendency in Engelbert of Admont and Dante and a radical tendency represented by Marsilius of Padua. The most serious drawback of these three apologias was that they took no account of political developments which were moving in the opposite direction from their thoughts. In consequence, their influence could be no more than indirect, affecting simultaneously those who were dreaming of a restoration of the past and those others whom circumstances were to lead towards an attempt to adapt the Empire to the needs of the time.

[26] This question is studied in the *Defensor*, Book II, chapter xxx, and he devoted a special treatise to it (Goldast, *Monarchia*, Frankfurt, 1611–13, II, pp. 147–53).

12

The Concept of Empire on the Threshold of Modern Times: Realities and Aspirations

In assessing the position of the concept of empire towards the middle of the fourteenth century, it seems to be necessary to concentrate on three essential facts. First, the last attempts to revive the universal Roman Empire had failed. Secondly, the concept of empire had become restricted in scope and had been deprived of part of its most profound substance, in order that it might be in a position to guarantee the independence of the state which bore the title. Lastly, the concept survived in the minds of men, as an aspiration, which was to persist long beyond the Middle Ages, so great was the influence that the very word 'empire' was able to exercise on people's imaginations.

I. THE FAILURE OF ROMAN UNIVERSALISM

In the first half of the fourteenth century several attempts were made to resuscitate the concept of a universal and Roman empire before it was finally crushed by the sheer weight of facts. Though they differed from one another, the experiments with which the names of Henry VII, Louis of Bavaria and Cola di Rienzo are connected nevertheless had one feature in common: they were all more or less marked by the atmosphere of the period.

A. *Some features of the intellectual background which existed in Italy during the fourteenth century*

In a general way this background is that of the first Renaissance, in which there was an inextricable mixture of features typical of mediaeval mentality and a renewed interest in classical antiquity. First there was the great movement inspired by the Spirituals, urging men to be born again in the life of the spirit. The concrete expression of this current was the famous Jubilee of 1300. Originating in a deep collective feeling of need among Christians and organised by Boniface VIII, the great Roman pardon took place before a symbolic figure, that of the Emperor Constantine: his bath was no longer regarded as merely the means of providing for his physical healing but was seen to be the instrument of his conversion and, even more, the emblem of his spiritual regeneration. This is the explanation given for the bath of penitence, to which the Pope invited all Christians and which appeared to be a replica, on a collective basis, of the baptism of the legendary Emperor.[1] Thus the Emperor became, as it were, a symbol of the rebirth of the life of the spirit; it is easy to see how this movement 'dematerialised' the Empire and started its gradual evolution towards the concept of an empire of the spirit.

Another element which assisted this evolution in much the same way was the rediscovery of the past: for the purposes of this study, that meant in particular the re-awakening of Rome's consciousness of her civilising mission, a mission made possible by her outstanding status, her *virtus* and her cultural and moral superiority over all nations. Such ideas greatly influenced Jacques de Voragine, who presented the last version of the Constantine tale in his *Golden Legend*, putting the accent much less on the Donation itself than on the quality of Roman men and women and their superiority over the barbarians.[2] Thus, under the influence of humanism – and in this connexion Petrarch's is the name which must be mentioned before all others – thoughts were moving towards a spiritualisation of the idea of Rome: the Eternal City became the symbol of a glorious ancient time when she was free and thus able to enlighten and educate the whole of human society.

Such visions were at the root of what might be called Roman patriotism in the fourteenth century. But it was a patriotism not

[1] Strikingly brought out by C. Burdach (*Rienzo*), the relationship between the two rebirths is illustrated by the fresco with the baptism of Constantine which was painted, shortly before 1300, by Giotto in the loggia of the benedictions of the Lateran; cf. also the treatise written for the Jubilee by Cardinal James Stefaneschi, *De centesimo seu iubilaeo anno, Bibliotheca Patrum*, Lyons, 1677, vol. XXV, pp. 936 *et seq.* (see in particular chapter ix).

[2] See Documents, XXIII, p. 208.

restricted by the boundaries of the town: it was moving towards an
Italian national sentiment which was gradually taking shape regardless
of the territorial and political fragmentation of the peninsula. Events
suggest that national forces, isolated from one another within the
framework of each city and each seigneurie, were none the less tending
to be regrouped in a synthesis, as yet purely ideal: the notion of an
Italian empire. On the same grounds as the Romans, the Italians considered they were the heirs of ancient Rome, united among themselves
by the tie of Latinity and alone in a position to restore the Empire of
that universal Latin culture which the Germans had allowed to perish.[3]

The abyss which lay between these aspirations and the facts was,
however, such that they were impossible to realise and were ultimately
transformed into purely intellectual ideas. But the interesting thing
about the first half of the fourteenth century is the fact that the political
sap of the Empire was apparently not yet exhausted; in consequence
when two ultramontane rulers advanced a fresh policy of empire,
these ideas blended easily with it and later directly inspired Cola di
Rienzo when he started to pave the way for a Romano-Italian empire.

B. *Henry VII's great plan*

Inspired by the loftiest imperial ideology, Henry VII, who succeeded
Albert of Hapsburg, had decided to recreate the universal Roman
Empire as a living reality, notwithstanding the numerous obstacles
which such an undertaking was likely to encounter. Universality of the
Empire did in fact run the risk of being held in check by the papacy,
for the popes did not admit its existence, except when they wished to
favour a 'good' emperor (which meant a prince approved and confirmed by them and one who would agree to be their defender). Even
if no objections were raised against the Emperor on the part of the
Pope, the attitude of the various national states still had to be considered. France was a typical example: there the long-affirmed principle
that the king was completely independent in relation to the Empire
had just been triumphantly established by Philip the Fair.[4] On the
southern boundaries of the imperial territories the Kingdom of Naples
was resolutely and openly hostile towards any attempt to restore the
Empire, since this might compromise the influence which Naples
exercised in Italy beyond her own frontiers: in a way, Naples

---

[3] See very significant passages in M. Villani, *Histoire de Florence*, Muratori, *Rer. ital.
Scriptores*, vol. XIV, Book III, chapter i; IV, lxxvii; V, 1.
[4] See below, p. 156.

incarnated the negation of the concept of empire.[5] To revive the Roman-ness of the Empire seemed to be equally difficult. As for the actual facts of the situation, the most important was that the Emperor was created in Germany. Dante tried indeed to weaken this argument by showing that a Caesar did not effectively begin to reign until he entered Italy – *il giardin dell' Imperio*[6] – when on his way to Rome, Rome the spouse who would make him a gift of the Empire.[7] Then there was still the question as to how Italy would welcome this 'Roman' emperor: would he succeed in imposing his status as arbiter – and thus peace – on the Ghibellines and the Guelfs (the former being the allies of Frederick, King of Sicily, and the latter of Robert of Naples) or would he simply become the head of a party? Lastly, there was still Rome herself; without a pope since 1304, the town was oppressed by the nobles and divided into rival factions among which were the Ange-vins of Naples who disposed of a powerful party. However, the people, grouped in corporations which gave them once more an aware-ness of themselves, were finding this régime difficult to bear and had not lost hope of recovering their freedom; a democratic revolution could, as before, reopen the whole question of the Empire.

These various circumstances explain the diverse contradictory features of Henry VII's expedition into Italy. In order to obtain the promise of the imperial crown, he had submitted to all the tests and conditions laid down by Pope Clement V; he had forced himself to observe them as well as he could in the Italian maze, despite all the obstacles which his Guelf adversaries had piled up in his path. It was ultimately possible for his coronation to take place in the Lateran on 29th June, 1312, although at the time a battle was raging throughout the town between the imperialist party and the Neapolitans. Henry VII immediately left Rome, as he had promised the Pope he would do, but this did not prevent him from entering at once into a struggle against Robert, King of Naples, despite the truce which Clement V wished to make him accept, and on 26th April, 1313, the Pope declared the king deprived of his crown.

The stiffening of the king's attitude can be explained by the fact that he had now formed a higher opinion of his imperial title and of his own mission.[8] In the name of the spiritual and moral order of Christen-

---

[5] E. Jordan, *Dante et la théorie romaine*, third article, p. 369.   [6] *Purgatory*, VI, 105.
[7] The idea recurs frequently in the letters of the poet written at the time of Henry VII's expedition; cf. A. Werminghoff, in *Neue Jahrbücher für das Klass. Altertum*, 9, 1908, Leipzig, pp. 578–91. It will be noted also that this nuptial theme is the replica of that which Innocent III had used for similar ends – see above, p. 83.
[8] See, for example, *Mon. Germ. Const.*, IV, 2, No. 801 (manifesto announcing the imperial coronation), and No. 946 (sentence inflicted on Robert of Naples).

dom, of which he felt he was the guarantor – here we can recognise one of Engelbert of Admont's arguments – he went boldly forwards convinced of the justice of his cause. His action was defended fiercely by the Ghibelline jurists who laid the greatest emphasis on the theory that each of the two supreme authorities had complete independence – the necessity for co-ordination between the two, such as Dante was to note in the *Monarchia*, escaped them completely – and on the fact that all temporal questions (and thus the right of peace and war) were the business of the Emperor alone, in his capacity as holder of the sovereignty formerly wielded by the Roman people.[9]

In Rome itself the imperialist party was re-awakening. Rising against the domination of the Orsini and Colonna families, who had settled their differences, a mob had made Jacopo Arlotti Stefaneschi captain of the people, an appointment he held for several months; the chronicler who wrote about it added that the purpose of this revolution was to benefit the Caesars and that its instigators decided to invite the Emperor to re-enter Rome, so that they might carry him in triumph to the Capitol where he would publicly recognise that he held his authority from the Roman people alone.[10] It would admittedly be hazardous to guess what this movement might have led to if it had not been wiped out by the return to power of the Roman nobility, followed soon after by the death of Henry VII on 24th August, 1313; nevertheless, the idea that an Emperor ought to be proclaimed by the people of Rome had been raised afresh, a fact worth recording.

It is not the only item to be recorded in summing up the story of Henry VII. He failed to achieve universality for the Empire because the confusion of the notions of Empire, Church and Christendom, inherent in the concept of the Empire as a Germanic institution, had led him to exceed his powers by venturing into the field of Christian peace and by usurping prerogatives which were recognised to be the Pope's. But his supreme effort to compel people to restore something of its former strength to the concept of empire remained alive in men's minds and can be perceived in the background of Dante's *Monarchia* in the same way as the memory of the *Alto Arrigo* persisted undying in Ghibelline circles.

[9] Such were the Paduan Nicholas Branchazolus and the Sicilian John of Calvaruso; see their memoranda in *Nova Alamanniae*, I, No. 90, and *Const.*, IV, 2, No. 1248. Cf. also the very odd anonymous treatise written shortly after the death of the Emperor, in which the latter, *corpore absens, virtute autem Imperii praesens*, advances his own apologia (published by H. Heimpel, in *Nachrichten der Gesellschaft der Wissensch. zu Göttingen*, 1952).

[10] *Principatum ex sola plebe recogniturum*, Albertino Mussato, *Historia Augusta*, in Muratori, vol. X, p. 508.

C. *Louis of Bavaria's Roman and 'republican' Empire*

The proclamation of Louis of Bavaria's Empire on the Capitol was an event unique in the history of imperial accessions.

In the first place it illustrated the vigorous reaction of the King of the Romans against the papal doctrine of the Empire, which had been affirmed since the death of Henry VII and against which Louis had already protested in his Sachsenhausen appeal.[11] But the king had not kept within the limits of the traditional right which assured in theory the independent status of kingship – he had extended the debate by intervening in the quarrel which had brought John XXII into conflict with a break-away section of the Order of Franciscans: he accused the Pope of heresy and appealed to the general council. This attack bears the double stamp of the precedent set by Philip the Fair and the influence brought to bear on Louis by the Ghibellines of Italy and their advisers, Franciscans and jurists, authors of stern indictments against the papacy and of memoranda concerning the law of the Empire, inspired by the most absolute imperial ideology, obliterating all distinction between the king and the Emperor of the Romans, proclaiming the latter lord of the world, and supreme master over temporal affairs.[12]

In 1327 the Emperor went to Italy once more in response to an appeal by the Ghibellines. Excommunicated by John XXII, who was intriguing to raise up an adversary against him in Germany, he needed the Empire to save his kingdom – a situation reminiscent of Manfred's in 1265. This time, however, the candidate for the imperial crown had at his disposal a trump card which the son of Frederick II had lacked. In April, 1327, the officials of the King of Naples had been driven out of Rome by a democratic revolution, and the dictator Sciarra Colonna, the implacable enemy of Boniface VIII, had been installed in the Capitol. Although the leaders of this movement probably had not at the outset been inspired by the prospect of a realisation of the concept of the Empire as a Roman institution, there is no doubt that Louis's presence in Italy in such exceptional conditions gave fresh stimulus to the thought. So a Roman delegation visited Milan to invite

---

[11] On the subject of the simultaneous pontifical and Guelf attacks against the Empire, cf. the bulls *Romani principes* and *Pastoralis Cura* by Clement V (*Const.*, IV, 2, Nos. 1165 and 1166, pp. 1207 and 1211), the bull of John XXII confirming the King of Naples in his appointment as vicar in Italy (*Const.*, V, No. 401, p. 340) and a memorandum from Robert requesting that no further steps be taken to hold an imperial election, the Emperor being the hereditary enemy of the Church of Italy and of France (*Const.*, IV, 2, No. 1253, p. 1368). The Sachsenhausen Appeal (made on the 22nd May, 1324) is published in *Const.*, V, Nos. 909 and 910, pp. 720–54.

[12] Such as that of Ugolino da Celle, written in 1313 (*Nova Alamanniae*, I, No. 123).

the king to come to Rome and have the imperial crown placed on his head. Louis, being then much influenced by the thesis propounded in the *Defensor pacis*, was not at all disinclined to listen to these advances.

Thereupon events succeeded one another rapidly. On 11th January, 1328, a few days after his entry into Rome, Louis of Bavaria promised to a parliament, which he had himself been careful to summon to the Capitol, that he would defend and promote the honour of the people of Rome; in accordance with the precedent of 1261 he then received from them the titles of senator and captain of the people. The imperial coronation took place on 17th January: two bishops anointed Louis in accordance with the traditional rites, after which Sciarra Colonna set the diadem on his head in the name of the Roman people. In the course of the following weeks the Emperor intensified his homage to the idea of Roman sovereignty by holding a series of assemblies in March, at which he promulgated edicts against John XXII and all heretics and traitors to the Empire; finally, it was with the aid of a council composed of both clerics and laymen that the Pope was deposed. A member of the Spiritual party, Peter of Corbara, was then elected to replace him and compelled to reside in Rome. Thus in April–May the town seemed to have become once more the seat of the two highest authorities of Christendom.

And so this coalition of Italian Ghibellines, Roman imperialists, revolutionary Franciscans and Marsilius of Padua (appointed at Rome to be vicar of the Emperor in the spiritual field) succeeded in carrying off a brilliant victory. The Empire seemed to be reborn, a Roman and a people's Empire. 'In this town', proclaimed Louis of Bavaria, 'by the grace of Providence, we have lawfully received the imperial diadem and the sceptre, from our Roman people, who are particularly dear to us,[13] and, thanks to the invincible power of God and to our own power, we rule over this town and the world.' But the picture soon became blurred; Louis left Rome in August, 1328, never to return, and the remainder of his reign evolved along different lines. Nevertheless, the great days which the Capitol had seen persisted in the memory of the inhabitants of Rome, as evidence to remind them that their city might, in favourable circumstances, have the power to create the Emperor.

---

[13] *Peculiaris populus,* an expression used ordinarily by the popes to indicate the people of Rome. The quotation is an extract from the constitution *Gloriosus Deus,* which proclaims the downfall of John XXII; *Const.,* VI, I, No. 436 of 18th April, 1328, p. 345.

D *Cola di Rienzo, or the dream of the Empire*

Less than twenty years later, in 1347, the dream of a Roman empire began to grow more definite. Cola di Rienzo's tribunate appears to have been the first stage towards its realisation. From 20th May to 15th December, Rome lived through days of waiting, full of glittering ceremonial designed to prepare men's minds for the restoration of the Empire. Yet the year had scarcely closed when everything vanished, except perhaps the faith of the tribune in his mission to be henceforth the guide of the Emperor who would restore the Empire to its former glory: and this second plan was to fail like the first. Here we need only note a few of the aspects of the tribunate of 1347 which throw light on the multiplicity of notions which people in Rome attached to the concept of empire.

1 *The timing* of Rienzo's appearance is in itself instructive. In 1346 Louis of Bavaria had been stripped of his imperial title by Clement VI. Charles of Moravia, the future Charles IV, elected by five electors to replace Louis, was not yet uncontested master: by comparison with the Bavarian, who still had control of a fairly strong party in Germany, he appeared more like an anti-king – the imperial throne appeared then to be vacant. It seemed as though the time had come for Rome to act independently of foreigners and herself to proclaim the Empire. Yet it must not be forgotten that Rienzo's tribunate occurred at a date only a little earlier than the second Jubilee, that of 1350:[14] and his actions were therefore also regulated by the necessity to wait for the spiritual renewal which was estimated to be due in the middle of the century. Preparation for the Empire, preparation for a new life – such themes had a profound influence on the tribune's actions.

2 *Titles, symbols and deeds.* Rienzo came on the scene on Whit Sunday, the 20th May, 1347. In the Capitol he declared the abolition of rule by the nobility and had himself invested with truly dictatorial powers to enable him to govern and reform Rome. The title he took was that of 'tribune of freedom, peace and justice, and liberator of the Holy Roman Republic'.[15] Rienzo's rule was then, in its first form, strictly limited to the town; it looked back to the pre-imperial era; it was based on delegation by the people of the authority with which he was

---

[14] Incidentally, Rienzo had been a member of the Roman embassy which begged Clement VI to advance the date of the second holy year from 1400 to 1350.

[15] First piece of evidence: a letter from Rienzo, informing the city of Viterbo of his elevation to the tribunate; cf. the letters of the tribune, published by Burdach and Piur, No. 7, p. 17.

invested to struggle against the tyranny of the nobility and resuscitate freedom, justice and peace, to which Rome was entitled by right. But he soon went beyond this. It appears that even before he took power, Rienzo had discovered an epigraphic fragment of the *Lex Regia*,[16] brought to light under Boniface VIII and concealed by him behind the high altar of the Lateran. From the clause which gave the Emperor the right, *inter alia*, to alter the boundaries of the original plan of the town, he boldly deduced the principle that the authority of the Romans could go beyond the *pomerium*[17] and be extended to the whole of Italy. As early as 20th May, therefore, he announced that the liberation of Rome was to be the prelude to the freeing of Italy. The idea that the good old days were to be restored then ceased to have a purely Roman setting and the extension of its scope resulted in the superimposition on it of the concept of a Romano-Italian Empire, deeply marked by the spiritual and religious atmosphere of the time, as is shown by the rites performed by the tribune during the month of August.

On 1st August, which was in Rome the most celebrated day of the year – it was, according to the *Mirabilia Urbis*,[18] the anniversary of the day Octavius took the title of Augustus, and, five centuries later, of the arrival in the town of the chains of St Peter – Rienzo took the Constantinian bath of individual renewal in the Lateran baptistry, at the same time as the ablution which was the essential preliminary to being received as a knight. After spending the night in the baptistry on a soldier's bed – as a sign of his soul's spiritual marriage to the spirit of God – he put on a crimson mantle, duplicate of the *chlamys* of the Donation, took the insignia of chivalry, and henceforth called himself *Candidatus Spiritus sancti miles*, adding 'Augustus' to his title of tribune, as well as the epithets *zelator Italiae* and *amator urbis*. The concrete expression of this 'Augustate' was the coronation of the tribune at the Capitol on 15th August, after an evening during which the procession wound its way through the town, bearing the then venerated archetypal image of the Saviour, which had, since the eighth century, symbolised the freedom of the town.[19] This coronation ceremony recalls that accorded to Petrarch in 1341. One after another

---

[16] *Foedusve cum quibus*, C.I.L., VI, 1, No. 930, p. 167.

[17] Rienzo, as it happens, read this as *pomarium*, a word which became *pomario* in Italian, was assimilated to *giardin dell' Imperio* and described the district in which the Empire had its origin.

[18] See above, p. 94.

[19] In the past this procession had often given rise to political manifestations; according to the life of Pope Gregory IX, Frederick II's supporters were said to have hailed the image on 14th August, 1239, with cries of *Ecce Salvator veniat Imperator* (Muratori, III, p. 586).

the six crowns were set on Rienzo's head, crowns of which the prototype figures in the *Libellus de caerimoniis*,[20] and which represented the number of preliminary steps leading to the status of emperor.

3 *Prospects*. These diverse manifestations obviously presaged the imminent proclamation of the Emperor. Several of Rienzo's decrees throw light on his conception of the process. On 1st August, after proclaiming the Holy City of Rome capital of the world and seat of the Christian faith, he declared that all the cities of Italy were free and their inhabitants Roman citizens. Since the government of the Holy Empire belonged of right to the City and to Italy, the tribune called before him the two persons who had been elected, Louis of Bavaria and Charles of Moravia, also their electors and all authorities who claimed to have any right in the election of an emperor.[21] The motives behind this programme became clear some weeks later. On 19th September,[22] having first held a conference with Roman and Italian experts, Rienzo declared that the senate and the people of Rome now re-assumed all the authority and all the jurisdiction over the world which they had possessed in olden times, that is to say, before the *Translatio* of the Empire to the Germans, revoked everything done to their prejudice and declared null and void all transfers of powers and of appointments carried out before this date. Moreover, the two elected rulers would have to appear before a parliament which would examine their titles; lastly, all the towns in the peninsula were called upon to nominate electors who would select, on 24th June, 1348, an Italian patriot to be elevated to the imperial throne, where his task would be to give peace to the country and protect it against all intrusion from outside.[23]

This new *Translatio* of the Empire never took place. The death of Louis of Bavaria on 11th October, 1347, shortly after all these preliminaries, completely revolutionised the situation. In Rome, Rienzo was opposed by both the papal legate and the aristocracy. Though he won a victory over the latter in the battle at the Porta San Lorenzo, he preferred to surrender his insignia and leave the town.

The plan to establish a Romano-Italian empire marks the last attempt to transmute the concept of the Empire as a Roman institution into a

---

[20] See above, p. 67.   [21] Burdach-Piur, *op. cit.*, No. 27, pp. 102–4.
[22] *Ibid* – No. 41, pp. 152–7.
[23] This plan, which was intended to rally the Guelf towns like Florence, aroused varying reactions: applause from Petrarch, opposition from Queen Joanna of Naples, who was directly threatened by Rienzo's intrigues, as they aimed at causing the surrender of the kingdom to the Roman people.

reality. Its failure was due to several causes, some of which arose from the fact that Rienzo never succeeded in freeing himself completely from the past. Moreover, because he also could not bring himself to break away from the theme of Roman sovereignty over the Empire (indeed, it was his dream, as his prior transformation of the Italians into Roman citizens proved) he planted the seed of a misunderstanding which could have caused a fatal conflict between the pretensions of Rome and the *amour-propre* of the Italian cities. He was also unable to cut himself off from the papacy: Rienzo was very different from Arnold of Brescia and the Romans of 1143; he took care to keep up his links with the Court of Avignon and he kept silent about the events of 1328, always hoping he would succeed in reconciling the two elements – the revolution, which he had carried out, and the rights of the papacy – which, incidentally, he never defined, but which he always seemed to acknowledge. Those were the prime reasons for his failure, but it must be added that there were others: for one thing, not only were his aims imprecise and frequently obscure, but also – most important of all – he sought to achieve the impossible by combining the notion of an empire which had a political content with the idea of a community of culture. In the last analysis, the tribunate of Rienzo was a form of transition between the Middle Ages and the Renaissance; the concept of empire was doomed on the political level, and was destined henceforth to live, in Italy at least, a completely spiritual life.

II. FROM UNIVERSAL EMPIRE TO NATIONAL EMPIRE

It was in the thirteenth century particularly that the idea of an empire embracing a group of territories began to make its appearance. And as it became more and more obvious that the conception of a universal empire was unrealisable, this new notion gradually grew in strength and gained acceptance in men's minds. It first came to maturity at the end of the thirteenth century in France and there is no doubt that the image of a *rex-imperator* which existed there affected the image of imperial authority which ultimately became reality in Germany in the middle of the following century.

A. *France's contribution*
Apart from the fact that her kings had an interest in the Empire by virtue of its being the heritage of Charlemagne, France made a

contribution to the concept of empire which included a principle of considerable importance: the establishment of equivalence between the King of France in his kingdom and the Emperor.

We are here faced with one consequence of the theme of absolute independence of the monarchy, guaranteed by Carolingian tradition. This idea was so strongly established that at the beginning of the thirteenth century Innocent III, breaking away from the theory of the Emperor's general supremacy, could actually say that the King of France did not recognise any authority as superior to his own in temporal matters.[24] This was a statement of fact and not as yet a declaration of right, and it was so understood by several canonists in the thirteenth century. On the other hand, Alan of Bologna, glossator of the first collection of Innocent III's Decretals, interpreted it quite differently: when he came to comment on the famous Gelasian canon, dealing with the distinction between the two authorities, he took account of the *divisio regnorum*, which had taken place since the canon was issued, using it to support his declaration that every king or independent prince possessed as much authority in his own territory as the Emperor in the Empire.[25] The original feature of this thesis was that the author combined in it the aspiration to full sovereignty and a recognition of the universal scope of the Empire, without mentioning how those two notions were to be reconciled with one another.

In the last third of the thirteenth century, however, the disintegration of the Empire, and simultaneously the increasing study of Roman Law in France, made it possible for the jurists to take a fresh step forward. Bishop William Durand of Mende, contemporary of King Philip the Bold, recognised in his *Speculum* that the Emperor held sway over the whole world and that all the 'provinces' were under his authority, yet he made an exception in respect of the King of France, who, he admitted, was *princeps in regno suo*.[26] The expression *princeps* is close to, though not entirely identical with, that of *imperator*, in that a certain number of rights were recognised as reserved to the exclusive possession of the *imperator*.[27] It was during the dispute between Boniface VIII and Philip the Fair that the assimilation became complete – we find it formulated almost simultaneously in the memorandum by William

[24] Decretal *Per Venerabilem* in the collection of Gregory IX, Book IV, tit. XVII, chapter xiii (Friedberg, *Corpus Juris canonici*, vol. II, 714).

[25] Texts in Rivière, *Le problème de l'Église et de l'État*, p. 428.

[26] *Speculum Judiciale*, Frankfurt, 1592, Book IV, Part III, paragraph 2.

[27] Thus a certain number of practical rights were reserved to the Emperor, such as the creation of notaries and the legitimisation of bastards; in addition, reserved prerogatives included the Emperor's right to declare a *bellum iustum*, to issue edicts about taxes and to change the currency, also the possibility, in certain cases, of going back on ecclesiastical immunities.

Durand the Younger and in the *Quaestio in utramque partem* (1302): the King of France is emperor in his own kingdom.[28] Emperor or an emperor? In view of the former conception of the one and only Empire, one must ask this question and enquire whether there were several empires. But, fundamentally, the shade of difference matters little, since without any doubt the interpretation given to the statement by the contemporaries quoted was that the King of France was completely emancipated from the imperial jurisdiction and at the same time possessed of full sovereignty. It must be stressed that the latter naturally included the reserved rights[29] and that the pronouncement was aimed at least as much against the Pope as against the Emperor – a premonition of the situation which reigned for a brief period in 1303 – the conjunction between a pope who claimed universal authority and an emperor, with the title of 'universal', who was the vassal of the sovereign pontiff.

This equivalence between the king who was an emperor at home and the titular emperor, continued to be accepted from the fourteenth century onwards, and provided one of the main arguments for monarchical authority in France. Political theoreticians in the reign of Charles V and, in particular, the author of the *Somnium Viridarii*, reaffirmed it when they glossed over the absence of the official imperial title in France by emphasising the importance of the title of king. So far as the Empire was concerned, the final consequence of this theory was to destroy the former doctrine of imperial œcumenism and to contribute towards the influences which resulted in a general acceptance of the notion that there could be at one and the same time a multiplicity of sovereign countries[30] and a territorial empire.

B. *The German doctrine of the Empire*

The question now was whether the Empire could be completely 'territorialised' and whether the Emperor could enjoy in his Empire an authority as complete as that of a national king in his kingdom. Although the problem was infinitely complex, it was clear that great efforts were continuously being made to resolve it, particularly during the last phase of the dispute between Louis of Bavaria and the papacy,

[28] *Quaestio* (ed. Goldast, *Monarchia*, vol. II, p. 98). Durand the Younger's memorandum is quoted in Rivière, *op. cit.*, p. 426.
[29] Possession of which – particularly those concerning financial prerogatives – seemed particularly necessary to Philip the Fair during the battle he was waging against the papacy.
[30] On this point see John of Paris, *De potestate regia et papali* (J. Leclercq, *Jean de Paris et l'ecclesiologie du XIIIᵉ siècle*, Paris, 1942) chapter xviii.

which largely revolved around a definition of the scope of the two notions of *regnum* and of *imperium*, and an effort to achieve a harmonious regulation of their relations with each other. Attacks were at first directed against the pretensions of John XXII and Clement VI, but as a corollary they were also aimed at certain aspects of the Roman doctrine of empire. For greater convenience the questions being debated can be grouped under three main headings: the source of the Emperor's authority; its independence; the framework within which it was exercised.

I *Source of the Emperor's authority*. With the exception of certain publicists who remained faithful to the doctrine according to which an emperor was created by his coronation, which the Pope, by virtue of his superior authority, accorded to the King of the Romans,[31] Louis of Bavaria's supporters were agreed in recognising that the authority of the Empire was founded on the election of the King of the Romans by the seven electors whose rights had been progressively established in the course of the thirteenth century. They were also agreed that in theory the status of those electors was derived from a delegation of power to them by a sovereign authority which had in the past possessed the right to elect the emperor. In the eyes of Marsilius of Padua, this sovereign authority was the 'supreme legislator', that is to say, the whole (*universitas*) or the effective part (*valentior pars*) of the citizens of the Roman Empire,[32] whereas William of Occam explicitly named the inhabitants of the town of Rome as being representatives of all the people who were within the jurisdiction of the Empire.[33] Between these two points of view about the meaning of *populus romanus*, there is a fine shade of difference in interpretation, the point of which was, in the writings of Marsilius, opposition to the exclusive right claimed by the townspeople, and an attempt to base the Emperor's authority on a wider supporting foundation than the vote of a single town.[34] The same concern led the more subtle commentator of the 'Law of the Kingdom and the Empire of the Romans' (the title of a treatise by Lupold of Bebenburg)[35] to interpret in a very personal manner the

[31] Such as Konrad von Megenberg, *De Translatione Imperii* (1354) (R. Scholz, *Unbekannte Kirchenpolitische Streitschriften*, vol. II, pp. 249–346).
[32] *Defensor*, II, 30, *op. cit.*, p. 604.
[33] *Dialogus*, Book IV, *tract.* II, part III, chapter xxix (Goldast, *Monarchia*, vol. II [Amsterdam, 1631], pp. 901–2).
[34] At this point it is worth recalling that Charlemagne had, from the year 800, instinctively wished to be, not Emperor of Rome, but Emperor ruling over the Roman Empire; see above, p. 23.
[35] *De Iure regni et Imperii Romani* (Schard, *De iurisdictione imperiali et potestate ecclesiastica*, Basle, 1566, pp. 323–429; see especially chapter xii, pp. 384–6).

problem of the *Translatio* of the Empire – which was the very heart of the matter at issue. While recognising that in former times the authority of the Emperor was based on the *Lex Regia*, voted by the inhabitants of Rome in the name of all the people within the jurisdiction of the Empire, Lupold showed that in the year 800 the Romans were in a position where it was absolutely impossible for them to exercise their rights, Rome being then no more than a town subject to Byzantium, which was the seat of the Empire. In view of this impossibility, the *Translatio* was carried out by the Pope, not by virtue of his political prerogatives, but as a matter of expediency, because the Roman people of the Empire could find no one to act in their name. Admittedly this is an artificial interpretation, but it is a clever one, not its least merit being that by this twist it maintained the original link between the Empire and the papacy.

2 *Independence of the Emperor's authority*. In the last dispute between the priesthood and the Empire this was in fact what was at stake. The principle of independence could be imposed because it was founded on the election of the Emperor by the electors, who, in the historical and juridical thinking of the time, had, generally speaking, taken the place either of the senate or of the Roman army,[36] as the case might be, and whose vote was deemed to represent God's choice. Notwithstanding the fact that from the time of Innocent III the papal doctrine had had a considerable degree of success, the principle (so dear to Frederick I) that the Empire was held *a Deo solo per electionem principum* gained a victory about the middle of the fourteenth century. Two declarations by Louis of Bavaria and a decree made by the electors meeting at Rhens in 1338,[37] proclaimed that the King of the Romans, elected unanimously or by a majority of votes, had no need at all to have recourse to the confirmation or the approbation of the Holy See; in 1356 this principle became part of the fundamental law of the Empire, the Golden Bull.

3 *Framework of the Emperor's authority*. Once the independence of the electoral body and of the King of the Romans in relation to the papacy was thus proclaimed, the logical corollary was a definitive conception

---

[36] For the succession of the senate – see above, p. 107. For the succession of the army, see, for example, the commentary on the *Sachsenspiegel*, by Jean de Buch, cf. Folz, *Souvenir et légende*, p. 405.

[37] *Fidem Catholicam* and *Licet iuris* by Louis of Bavaria, in *Nova Alamanniae*, I, No. 522, p. 343, and in Zeumer, *Quellensammlung zur Geschichte der deutschen Reichsverfassung* (1913), No. 142, p. 184. Decree of Rhens, in *Nova Al.*, I, No. 583, p. 390.

of the Empire as divided into two entities. On the one hand, was the Empire in the restricted sense of the expression: all the territories which had formed part of the Carolingian Empire, with the exception of France, i.e. the three kingdoms. But henceforth Italy and Burgundy are scarcely mentioned except as surviving titles and when cited in support of arguments. This was one obvious consequence of contemporary political thought, out of which the idea had evolved that the two kingdoms were almost completely detached from the *regnum Teutonicorum*: the political conception of the Empire thus coincided practically entirely with this last entity,[38] and in this respect the expression 'Holy Roman Empire of Germanic nationality', which was current from the fifteenth century onwards, is very significant. The Germanic Empire then appeared as a *regnum* in which the Emperor recognised no authority superior to himself and where he was king by the same right as, for example, the King of France.

Outside of this restricted empire there remained the universal Roman Empire, to the throne of which the King of the Romans acceded by the coronation which the Pope accorded to him. But in the middle of the fourteenth century people knew very well that this universality was no more than a memory and was not conceivable except in close liaison with papal universality.[39] In practice, what people chiefly wanted to know was, whether the Roman rites conferred a real increase of authority on the ruler of the restricted Empire. No, thought the imperialists, and in Louis of Bavaria's proclamation, *Licet iuris*, it was affirmed that election by the princes created the *verus rex et imperator Romanorum*. The full import of the expression *verus* was doubtless the sum total of the rights reserved to the Emperor, which he was entitled, even before his coronation, to exercise within the Empire in the restricted sense of the term, since the same text laid down that the *verus imperator* was to be obeyed by all subjects of the Empire. For Louis of Bavaria and the radical polemists, the Roman coronation was thus no more than a simple ceremony without political significance. Lupold of Bebenburg drew finer distinctions: first, he

[38] It is nevertheless important to draw attention to some survivals, such as the fact that Charles IV in 1361 detached the county of Savoy from the former Kingdom of Arles (which was abandoned to France in 1378) and incorporated it into the 'Roman Empire'; the efforts made by the rulers in the fifteenth century to preserve the northern part of the former Kingdom of Burgundy under their authority; Maximilian's establishment in 1512 of a Burgundy circle, comprising the Low Countries and the Franche-Comté. Similarly, until the Revolution, south of the Alps, Milan, Mantua and other fiefs of northern and central Italy were regarded as forming part of the Empire.
[39] This emerges in particular from the treatise by Konrad von Megenberg already cited (note 31), and, in the fifteenth century, from that of Peter of Andlau, *Libellus de caesarea monarchia*, in *Zeitschr. für Rechtsgesch. Kan. Abt.*, 1892–3.

recognised the Emperor's entitlement to exercise the reserved rights in his realm from the time of his accession; secondly, he emphasised that Charlemagne was emperor in his empire long before 800[40] – Lupold was thus in reality taking a further step towards the assimilation of the Empire to national *regna* whose rulers were, according to him, invested with this prerogative. The imperial coronation did, however, give each emperor who acceded to the universal monarchy the right to exercise the reserved rights within the nation-states and did make him the advocate and pre-eminent protector of the Church. If the first of these consequences remained a simple expression of principle which he was excluded from putting into practice, the second still remained a reality, capable of suggesting grandiose images up to the end of the Middle Ages – for example, when the Emperor Charles IV and Pope Urban V gave a display of harmony by deliberating in common at Rome in 1367 on the affairs of Christendom, and when, in 1414, Sigismund presided over the inaugural session of the Council of Constance convoked by him to put an end to the great schism.

Nevertheless, even when faced by political realities, the traditionalist clerics still maintained their view that the Roman coronation constituted the real starting point of an imperial reign, because it transformed the King of the Romans from an acting administrator of the Empire into a true emperor, the holder from that moment only of all the reserved rights, both in his own states and on a universal scale; for those who held to this line of thought the Pope therefore remained in the last resort the controller of accession to the imperial throne.[41]

Thus, up to the end of the Middle Ages, no unified view of the Empire had yet come into being. The future belonged, however, to the ideas which were being expressed in circles around Louis of Bavaria. The visible sign of this was that on 19th March, 1452, when Frederick III had himself crowned emperor at Rome, he was the last King of the Romans to do so. Maximilian was to take the title of emperor elected by the Romans and, with the exception of Charles V, none of his successors was in future to ask the Pope for the imperial diadem.

From the middle of the fourteenth century it can be said that, without achieving complete success on the plane of ideas or any success at all on the plane of reality, the Holy Empire was tending to become more and more like the nation-states.

---

[40] *De Jure*, chapter xii, *loc. cit.*, p. 384, and chapter v, p. 351.
[41] See, for example, in the *De Translatione* of Konrad von Megenberg, chapters xiv–xviii, *loc. cit.*, pp. 297–310.

III. HOPES FOR THE FUTURE EMPIRE

A political conception of the Empire had now been established, but hopes for its future development continued to be extremely fluid and to be centred on the idea of universality. Those who speculated about the future started out from the expectation that an emperor would arise who was destined to be the last one and this ruler was represented alternately as a persecutor and as one who would restore Christendom. The vision of this last emperor spread from Italy into France and Germany and in each country took on the complexion of the special aspirations cherished by each according to its temperament and tradition. This long process would merit a study in itself: here only the essential features can be distinguished.

A. *The two prophecies about the Empire*
The first feature of importance was the appearance in Italy of a local legend, immediately after the death of Frederick II, in the tense atmosphere which surrounded the struggle between the party of the Empire and the party of the Church. According to this legend, which took hold of men's imaginations, Frederick survived in Etna – an echo of the legend of King Arthur. At the same time the Ghibellines of the peninsula announced that he himself or one of his descendants would revive the Empire in all its glory.[42] The Joachites for their part predicted that the world would end in 1260–1, after an emperor of the House of Hohenstaufen[43] had waged a general persecution against the Church. This vision was soon embroidered by an additional element: the same circles (the Joachites and the Guelfs) foretold that an emperor descended from Charlemagne would liberate the Church from all its opponents and would introduce a long period of peace. This prophecy became connected with Charles of Anjou and persisted henceforth in the background of every French candidature for the Empire; until the end of the Middle Ages it retained its anti-Germanic aspect and had the effect of keeping in view the prospect that a French emperor would arise, one of Carolingian descent, a faithful servant of the Church, who would prepare the second coming of Christ.

The Ghibelline prophecy was destined to evolve quite differently. Immediately after the death of Conradin in 1268 it took a hold in

[42] See, for example, the text concerning Conrad IV, published by K. Hampe in the records of meetings (*Sitzungsberichte*) of Heidelberg Academy, Philosophy and History Section, 1917, No. 6.
[43] Cf. above, p. 124, the influence of this version on events in Rome.

Germany where it offered the popular imagination a persistent vision of a Hohenstaufen emperor who would give new life to an empire which was in process of succumbing to its enemies: the character appropriate to such an emperor was that he should be hostile towards the papacy and to the land-owning Church in general. Even before 1268 confused hopes were seeing the light of day in Germany; in particular there was a current of thought, related to the doctrine of Arnold of Brescia, which recognised the Antichrist in Innocent IV and assigned to the Roman Emperor a great purifying mission in the Church, sometimes with the assistance of the mendicant orders. The Germanic countries were thus predisposed to welcome the predictions which had issued from Italy, according to which the eagle would conquer the lion (Charles of Anjou) and a descendant of Frederick II (given the name of *Fredericus Orientalis*) would extend his power to the ends of the earth after first humbling the papacy and the simoniacal clerics.

The prophecy in this form became associated temporarily with the young Landgrave of Thuringia, Frederick the Valorous, grandson of the Emperor through his mother. But its main feature was belief in the survival of Frederick II himself, who was pictured as wandering through the world, like the old god Woden, until (apparently about the middle of the fourteenth century) a fixed residence was assigned to him in the mountain of Kyffhäuser, the Thuringian equivalent of Etna, out of which he would one day re-emerge.[44]

From then on the two prophecies persisted along parallel lines, both – the French and the German alike – incorporating the theme of the Emperor's final victory over the nations of the East and his voyage to Jerusalem where he was to surrender his insignia to God. Apart from their different religious orientation they had, however, one other noteworthy divergent feature, which was to become more accentuated as time went on: the French prophecy, dominated by the memory of Charlemagne, was noticeably the more universalist, whereas the German one had a more pronounced national, even social character. Thus these two predictions can be seen to be a most striking sign of the competition for the Empire in the fullest sense of the word, which was to break out between France and Germany.

B. *Rivalry between the two prophecies in the middle of the fourteenth century*
In this movement, however, one occasion must be noted when a

[44] This is the explanation for successive appearances of false Fredericks. The most celebrated, if not the first, was the famous impostor, Tiele Kolup, who was installed at Neuss and for some time held Rudolf of Hapsburg in check (1285).

Carolingian prophecy became associated with a ruler of the Empire. The name of Louis of Bavaria's successor, Charles IV, his forebears, his initial status as King of the Romans elevated by the Church against a heretical and insubordinate emperor, the very name of Charlemagne conjured up by Pope Clement VI in favour of his protégé – all these circumstances favoured the projection of the myth of the universal Emperor, descended from Charlemagne,[45] on the new reign.

An attempt was indeed made to effect this connexion. Not, incidentally, in Germany: there, for a variety of reasons, the theme of Charlemagne as a political figure had been abandoned since the beginning of the thirteenth century and between 1346 and 1348 the prophecies about the Empire's future, stimulated perhaps by the fact that the Wittelsbach party at one time envisaged supporting the candidature of Frederick the Serious (son of the Valorous), Landgrave of Thuringia, persistently foretold that a new Frederick would appear and be crowned emperor. But once this hope had faded away the prophets had to take account of Charles IV and they reacted by demonstrating deliberate hostility towards him, pointing out the contrast between the present poverty of the Empire and its future glory when a new Frederick would have assembled around him the people of God in order to reconquer the Holy Sepulchre.[46]

Other circles, however, thought differently. The Spiritual party and the Italian Fraticelli gave great credence to an oracle which was probably composed at the very end of the thirteenth century in the group around Peter-John Olivi, General of the Franciscans (who died in 1298), an ardent opponent of Boniface VIII. The text announced the coming of an angelic pope – a new Celestine V[47] – who would inaugurate the age of the Holy Spirit and, in co-operation with the Emperor of the Romans, would reform the world. The name of this emperor was not uttered, but everything led people to understand that the expected messianic prince would be a Germanic ruler. This oracle, called the oracle of Cyril, was known in several versions: for the purpose of this study the most important is the one, of which Brother Jean de la Roquetaillade was the author, shortly before 1350. Nurtured

---

[45] For more about this occasion, cf. Folz, *Souvenir et légende*, pp. 422–30, with reference to the texts.

[46] Signs of the persistence of this way of thinking were that in 1369 the people called the leader of a sect of Thuringian flagellants 'Emperor Frederick and King of Thuringia', and in 1376, just when Charles IV was negotiating the election of his son Wenceslas to the royal throne, an oracle pointed to Frederick, Duke of Bavaria, descended on his mother's side from Manfred, as candidate for the universal monarchy.

[47] A spiritual hermit, elected to the papacy in 1294, he abdicated after a few months and was replaced by Boniface VIII. The latter's enemies accused him of having forced Celestine V to abdicate by extortion.

in the French Carolingian tradition, influenced moreover by all that the name of Charles evoked, Roquetaillade steered the prophecy to point to Charles IV, bringing out his kinship with the Valois dynasty (and with another Charles IV) and arguing that his election under the auspices of the Church would seem to have reserved for him the rôle of emperor of the future.

In 1350 Cola di Rienzo conveyed this great hope of the Spiritual party to Charles IV in Prague. Immediately after his defeat in Rome Rienzo had stayed for two years among the hermits of Mount Majello in the Abruzzi and this turned his dreams of the Empire in another direction: to win the future Emperor to the programme of *Renovatio* of the Roman Empire, universal and messianic, and to cut a path for him through Italy. He was unfortunate; the man he addressed was a man of prudent and realistic mind, deaf to prophecies, not at all eager to be flung into an adventure of this sort. Charles did, it is true, go to Rome, to have the diadem placed on his head in 1355, but he had no intention of undertaking any reforms. To be brief, he escaped from the Carolingian prophecy: in consequence the later writings of Jean de la Roquetaillade – in particular his *Vademecum in tribulatione* – concentrated anew on the King of France.

C. *The dream of a Messiah*

At the end of the fourteenth century and during the whole of the fifteenth, the duel between the two prophecies became more and more acute, on account of the very serious crises through which the West was then passing; the great schism, the Turkish peril, the French intervention in Italy, the disintegration of the Empire, considerable social ferment in Germany: all circumstances of the type to favour oracles expressing popular hopes or the ambitions of ruling powers.

Shortly after Jean de la Roquetaillade's time, the Italian hermit Telesphorus of Cosenza prophesied that a Holy Pope would be persecuted by a Germanic emperor; he would be recognised by a King Charles of France, whom he would crown emperor; both would then work together for the reform of the Church. Between 1378 and 1380 another prophecy foretold the great deeds of a King Charles, son of Charles (Charles VI) born of the nation of the Lilies: after getting rid of all the tyrants infesting his kingdom he would set forth to conquer all enemy nations – the English, the Spanish and the Lombards. Rome would be captured by him and liberated from the clerics who had usurped the papacy. After this, Charles would receive the imperial crown. He would cross the sea, would be hailed as king by the Greeks and would subject all the nations of the Orient to the authority of Christ. Because of these victories people would call him the Saint of Saints: finally he would go to Jerusalem, to the Mount of Olives, and would there lay down his crown and die in the midst of great events.[48] This text was not forgotten: a century later, in 1494, it was to reappear in relation to Charles VIII, whose entry into Naples was considered as a prelude to the great imperial undertaking: on his entry into the town he was acclaimed as King of France, Emperor of Constantinople and King of Jerusalem. He was a new Charlemagne, the last of the Emperors, uniting East and West – this was the picture of the King of France which formed a background to popular belief up to the end of the Middle Ages.

A different shadow hovered over his Eastern neighbour. The prophecy of Telesphorus provoked a vigorous national reaction in Germany, of which, in the years following the Council of Constance, 'Gamalion's prophecy' gave an indication. The latter prophecy received its name from the 'Holy Pope', to whom a strange vision had been vouchsafed: that the Germans would elect an emperor of *Almania alta*, that is to say, one coming from the upper valley of the Rhine. He would assemble a council of laymen about him at Aix, then he would establish a patriarch at Mainz, who would be crowned pope. The Emperor would fight and put to death the Roman pontiff and Rome would lose its position as capital of Christendom, which would be taken over by Mainz. This gives a valuable indication of growing nationalism and at the same time a glimpse of the transformation of the Roman Empire into the Germanic Empire and the end of Rome's spiritual primacy: testimony in such precise form was, however, exceptional. The main element of the dream of empire continued to be above all the need to wait for the messianic Emperor, reformer of ecclesiastical and civil society, who would utterly overcome all forces opposing the establishment of the Kingdom of God on earth. These hopes were centred successively on Sigismund, under whose name a whole programme of radical reforms was listed in the *Reformatio Sigismundi*, and on Frederick III, whom a popular song at least hailed as the Hohenstaufen who was reborn. The last-named, however, showed such inertia that he soon lost all hold on the imagination of the people, who turned from him and appealed in all their prayers to the Emperor, universal and German at the same time, who would endow

---

[48] This prophecy was found in the archives of the Côte d'Or, by M. Chaume, and published in the *Revue du Moyen-Age latin*, 3, 1947, pp. 27–42.

his country with the benefits of the Golden Age. He would be called Frederick and would emerge out of the mountains. But this Frederick was no longer the Sicilian and Roman prince, who was indeed scarcely German: he was, as the poet has said in a famous ballad, *Der alte Barbarossa*, the truly Germanic Emperor, the conqueror of Rome, covered with glory, the Emperor marching towards the Holy Land, Frederick I, whom the men of the fifteenth century confused with his grandson. It was he whom the innovators awaited: as late as 1519 the myth of Frederick I still formed the background to the German revolution which broke out in that year.

But it was in that year also that an *alter Karolus*, Charles V, acceded to the Empire, his election being largely ordained by national Germanic sentiment. Under the influence of humanism, the Germans had rediscovered Charlemagne as a political theme. It had gradually emerged from the multiple aspects of the long and brilliant survival of the memory of that emperor throughout the Germanic countries and had also shared in the general evolution of the Empire, of which this Charles had, now, particularly since the reigns of Frederick I and Charles IV, become the guardian saint.

Thus, on the threshold of modern times, the concept of empire was incarnated in two heroes, Charlemagne and Frederick I, who represented its two main aspects: universality and the national aspirations with which it had steadily become charged.

Conclusion

Conclusion

This study began with men's belief in the survival of the Roman Empire and it comes to an end with their evocation of the dream of a Universal Empire. For ten centuries the concept of empire was always present in men's minds, with a bias towards universality derived from its dual origin, Roman and Christian: this was its purest aspect.

However, the achievements to which it contributed far surpassed this ideal. In the West the Roman Empire, as an institution, was dead. When restored in the year 800, it had to establish itself in the face of the Empire still in existence at Byzantium, where the Roman Empire was always regarded as a manifest usurpation. The reaction of the West was to deny that the 'Empire of the Greeks' had any Roman character and thereafter to formulate the theory of the *Translatio*, without at the same time quite giving up all hope of a conquest of the East, which would restore the Roman Empire to its former unity. None the less, the existence of two empires side by side was the very negation of Roman universality. Christian universality could perhaps have been developed as its successor in the West, but Charlemagne's Empire, which came closest to achieving this, did not comprise all the Christian lands of the region. His Empire was first broken up, then regrouped and finally disappeared. In its turn the concept of empire deteriorated to such an extent that in the tenth century, and even up to the twelfth century, it came to be attached to territorial empires which had no connexion at all with the former Roman dominion. After the latter was re-established in 962 by what was then the most powerful European nation-state, the concept of empire was progressively elevated towards the notion of universality. Because vast areas of the West and North-West lay outside its boundaries it did appear at one time as though the Empire of Otto III was to be greatly expanded towards the East, but the grandiose vision of Otto I's grandson vanished with him.

From that moment the possibility that the Empire could achieve universality was no more than an idea largely based on the need for it to put up a defence against the spirit of independence which was now growing strongly in the various national states. Indeed, the impression one gains from about the middle of the eleventh century is that the notion of a Christian Empire had been superseded by a Christendom in which the independent states were grouped under the spiritual control of the papacy. This conception of universality gradually became compatible with the actual situation and it advanced steadily at the expense of older ideas, compelling those who still clung to the latter to fuse the notions of empire and of Christendom right up to the threshold of the fourteenth century, in order to maintain a programme at all: this fusion was the main cause of its political failure.

In the West the concept of empire encountered other difficulties, as a by-product of its inability to come to terms with the changing times, which hindered its advance and which can be seen to be part of its opposition to Byzantium. It was no longer attached to a permanent centre – mediaeval Rome was neither ancient Rome nor the new Rome on the shores of the Bosphorus, but the city of the apostles, whose prestige was exploited by papal imperialism. Yet the city's political prestige was so great that when the rebirth of the Empire took place, it was at Rome that it was proclaimed and, after a short period of hesitation, Rome became the place where emperors came for their inauguration. But the city's function was more or less limited to giving a legal blessing to the accession of various emperors. The inhabitants ceased to play any active part, even later, when the revival of juridical studies facilitated access to texts which demonstrated that the Empire was the result of a delegation of the powers of the Roman people who gave them into the hands of a supreme overlord. The few attempts which were made to put this theory into effect were either frustrated by failures (1143-54) or were not followed up (1328); the juridical weapons were manipulated outside of Rome. In such conditions the city itself played a very limited part in developing the concept of empire. Rome was able to create the image of an emperor but never the concrete representation of an empire; on several occasions Rome tried to free herself from papal domination, but those revolts affected only the area confined within the city boundaries, a field whose narrowness contrasted strangely with the inapposite dream of empire superimposed on it; it was not until the fourteenth century that a Roman raised his eyes to the Italian level. In consequence, the concept of empire was never able to become deeply rooted in the city where the

Empire was traditionally born; when it is spoken of as the Roman Empire this name never signifies a special link with the town of Rome but always (from 800 onwards) the fact that in a given field it was the heir to the former Empire.

The moral force of the concept of empire resided in the sacred character which it conferred on the institution, reputedly derived directly from God. From ancient times this inheritance remained inviolate in the East and no ecclesiastical authority emerged there to seek a position superior to the Empire and its representative. In the West, on the other hand, Caesaropapism, in the precise meaning of the expression, did not ever succeed in taking root. The Empire had had to be restored; the Pope had resuscitated it; it was the Church which endowed the new authority with its sacred character, by virtue of the coronation and, from the year 816, the anointing of the Emperor by the Pope. Thus, although barely a century had elapsed since Charlemagne had become emperor, John VIII was already attributing a creative value to the inaugural act and this interpretation was never allowed to die out: it persisted and finally triumphed in the doctrine of Innocent III and his successors. Furthermore, from the end of the eleventh century, the Church made a point of detracting from the value of the Emperor's anointing and depriving the rite of its sacramental character: nothing could be more effective in diminishing the status of the Emperor's person and preventing him from ever participating actively in ecclesiastical affairs.

The concept of empire in the West was universal in theory only, Roman in name alone, holy only at the will of the Church, and in the end no one could set out a doctrine of empire which was anything other than very incomplete and, at that, applicable only to the last centuries of the Middle Ages. What is the Empire? How and by what means does one become Emperor? Is the Church in the Empire or is the Empire a branch of the Church? How far do the respective powers of the Pope and the Emperor extend? To what extent can the imperial title exist without its Roman associations? So many are the questions, so bitterly debated and about which agreement has never been reached! As one studies them, one realises that the history of the concept of empire is not only that of the divorce between myth and reality, but also that of a very great divergence of views on the institution itself.

As a result of these uncertainties the mediaeval concept of empire in the West draws its most original and vital characteristics from the contingencies which shaped it and the individuals who stamped their personality on it.

The strongest influence was undoubtedly that of Charlemagne. His empire was a 'renewal' of the Roman Empire, but its most profound element was the Christian religion, Christendom under the sway of the Empire. Afterwards, people never forgot his unique epoch and, by thinking of the *pacificus* and of the *orthodoxus imperator*, of St Charlemagne, they interpreted his high status as a gift made by God to the elect and saw in the Empire a preview of the celestial city. After Charlemagne, the concept of empire was extended to include the Frankish monarchy and presided over its various regroupings. Yet at the same time it began to take on a stronger imprint from the papacy. Under the Ottonians and the Salians it struggled, with incomplete success, to resuscitate the Carolingian standards once more: it then became concentrated on the most important territorial group in Europe and, although it was not able to embrace the whole of Christendom, it did at least succeed in turning the Pope into a subordinate of the Emperor. It was already taking on a Roman complexion. In order to combat the imperial pretensions of the papacy, emancipated since the Investiture Contest, it adopted every possible means to put up a defence under the Hohenstaufens, who for their part, by restoring the honour of the Empire, conferred considerable glory on it. Under Frederick I the concept of empire took on simultaneously the complexion of Frank and Roman; under Frederick II, who claimed that he was the reincarnation of Caesar, Augustus and Justinian, it took on a more pronounced secular look, which was due as much to the stronger influence of Roman law as to the fact that Innocent III occupied the throne of St Peter for a period between the two Fredericks: according to this Pope the empire belonged to the papacy *principaliter et finaliter* and he strove to diminish the sacred character of the institution. Henceforth, though the concept of empire still retained its traditional character and was based on the rôle of the Emperor in the Church, it clearly displayed certain features imprinted on it by Frederick II, which it had begun to acquire in the time of his grandfather: the Empire was an end in itself; its origin was independent of the papacy; it was, in its own right, and not as a result of a blessing by the Church, the *sacrum imperium*; the Emperor's function went beyond the classic 'defence' of the Church (in the course of his dispute with Gregory IX and Innocent IV, the Emperor no longer had recourse to the former procedure of setting up a pope created by himself in opposition to the lawful pontiff – he simply drew the attention of Christendom to the vices of the hierarchy and himself assumed coercive and punitive powers over the clerics). Such ideas made a deep mark on the image of the empire, and the political successes of Frederick I, the aims of Henry VI, the plans of Frederick II for a federation of princes, all helped to restore something of its former universality to this picture.

From the great duel between the imperialism of the Hohenstaufens and the imperialism of the papacy, the latter emerged victorious and was able, until the fourteenth century, to put its ideas into practice. The concept of empire, no longer tied to the institution with which it had been associated, once more took on the appearance of an intellectual theory and became a distant hope in the background of men's minds. The last occasions on which it caused any activity in the political field were no more than the result of momentary recollections of its two fundamental characteristics – its theoretical universality (Henry VII) and its Romanism (Louis of Bavaria, in 1328, and after him, Cola di Rienzo).

Present or latent, the concept of empire played a part, which should not be underestimated, in the life of those countries in which it took root. In England, as in Spain, it acted as a call to unity. In France, it became a factor in the consolidation of the monarchy. In Italy, regardless of territorial fragmentation, it aroused a feeling of community of culture which can be regarded as a first manifestation of patriotism. In Germany its rôle was more complex: there is no doubt that the immensity of the tasks laid on the Empire diverted its rulers from the construction of a monarchic state, but if this seems a somewhat negative balance, the consolidation of the bases of the German state can positively be ascribed to the concept of empire, by means of which it was possible to establish the principle of election of the *verus imperator* and of his full sovereignty within the Empire. Outside the separate states the concept stimulated the universality of the Church and enabled its head to become the pope-emperor.

Such in brief was the history of the mediaeval concept of the Empire in the West. It penetrated the religious body of society and established itself, temporarily or permanently, in different countries, attracting personalities to itself, inspiring attempts at achievements which could never be fulfilled, or intellectual doctrines which were indeed seductive but incapable of realisation. Its attraction to the human mind cannot be explained merely by the sentimental link which it permitted men to maintain with an idealised past or by the hope it aroused of a better future: it also responds to one of the most profound features of the intellectual mentality of the Middle Ages, the aspiration towards unity, the need for the *ordinatio ad unum*.

Documents

I   THE UNIVERSALITY OF CHRISTIANITY AND OF ROME

1 *Prayer for the Church*, dating apparently from the time of the persecutions [from the Roman Missal – Good Friday]: 'Almighty and everlasting God, Who in Christ hast revealed Thy glory to all nations; preserve the works of Thy mercy; that Thy Church, spread abroad over the whole world, may with a steadfast faith persevere in the confession of Thy name.'

2 *Examples of prayers for the Empire and the Emperor* [selected from the old sacramentaries and edited by G. TELLENBACH, *Römischer und christlicher Reichsgedanke*, Heidelberg, 1934, pp. 45 *et seq.*].

(a) 'Let us pray also for our very Christian Emperor, that our Lord and God may, for our perpetual peace, make all the barbarian peoples subject to him.'

(b) 'Almighty and everlasting God, in Thy hands are the powers and rights of all kingdoms; look down graciously on the Roman Empire, in order that those who put their trust in their own brute force may be conquered by the power of Thy right hand.'

[The Roman Missal, for Good Friday, still contains paragraphs based on these last two texts, in the part following the prayers for the ecclesiastical hierarchy.]

(c) 'O God, Thou hast created the Roman Empire in order that the preaching of the Evangel of Thy everlasting rule might be carried on; grant now to Thy servants who are our Emperors such heavenly weapons that the peace of Thy Churches may not be troubled by the storms of wars.'

II   CONTINUITY OF ROME'S UNIVERSAL MISSION

Leo the Great, Sermon 'in Natali Apostolorum'. [P.L. 54—this sermon is still read at the second Nocturn of the feasts of 29th June and 18th January.]

(From: *A select library of Nicene and post-Nicene Fathers of the Christian Church*, 2nd series. Translated into English with prolegomena and explanatory notes (Oxford, 1895, James Parker and Co.). Vol. XII: 'The letters and sermons of

Leo the Great, Bishop of Rome', translated with introduction, notes and indices by the Rev. Charles Lett Feltoe, M.A.).

'Sermon LXXXII: On the Feast of the Apostles Peter and Paul (29th June). [The Pope first invites his audience to celebrate the feast of the apostles Peter and Paul with particular fervour. He continues in the following terms:]

'For these are the men, through whom the light of Christ's gospel shone on thee, O Rome, and through whom thou, who wast the teacher of error, wast made the disciple of Truth. These are thy holy Fathers and true shepherds, who gave thee claims to be numbered among the heavenly kingdoms, and built thee under much better and happier auspices than they, by whose zeal the first found-ations of thy walls were laid: and of whom the one that gave thee thy name defiled thee with his brother's blood. These are they who promoted thee to such glory, that being made a holy nation, a chosen people, a priestly and royal state,[1] and the head of the world through the blessèd Peter's holy See thou didst attain a wider sway by the worship of God than by earthly Government. For although thou wert increased by many victories, and didst extend thy rule on land and sea, yet what thy toils in war subdued is less than what the peace of Christ has conquered. . . . For the Divinely-planned work particularly required that many kingdoms should be leagued together under one empire, so that the preaching of the world might quickly reach to all people, when they were held beneath the rule of one state, that the light of Truth which was being displayed for the salvation of all nations, might spread itself more effectively throughout the body of the world from the head itself. What nation had not representatives then living in this city; or what peoples did not know what Rome had learnt?'

III   THE DONATION OF CONSTANTINE

[Ed. K. ZEUMER, *Der älteste Text des Constitutum Constantini, Festgabe für R. von Gneist*, 1888, pp. 47 et seq.]

[English version – see E. F. HENDERSON, *Select Historical Documents of the Middle Ages*, 1892, pp. 319–29.]

ANALYSIS

The text is drawn up in the personal form: Constantine speaks in the first person. The main points in his proclamation are as follows:

1 Profession of faith.

2 A long recital in which the Emperor relates how he was led to become a Christian. He was ill with leprosy; the pagan priests recommended that in order to get rid of the disease he should bathe in the blood of young children.

---

[1] *I Peter*, ii, 9.

During the night preceding the projected slaughter of the children, Constantine was visited in a dream by two mysterious persons, whom he recognised the next day as the apostles Peter and Paul, who advised him that, in order to be healed, he should turn to Sylvester, Bishop of Rome, who was at that time in concealment on account of the persecutions. The Emperor went to see the Pope, who baptized him; when Constantine emerged from the water he was free not only of the leprosy, but also of paganism, which he abjured in solemn terms.[2]

3 Subsequent arrangements.

(a) Desirous of showing his gratitude to the apostles and Sylvester, both in his own name and in that of the senate, of his 'satraps', of the nobles and of the people of Rome, Constantine proclaims the Pope and his successors vicars of Christ and representatives of the chief of the apostles, who have received their supremacy from Heaven; he declares himself ready to accord to these pontiffs a power wider than that which he himself possesses in his capacity as Emperor.

(b) Accordingly, he makes a gift to the Roman Church of supremacy (*principatus*) over the four patriarchal sees of the East and over all the churches in the world; the Pope is proclaimed *princeps* (emperor) over all the priests in the universe.

(c) After reminding his hearers of the fact that he has built the churches of St Peter and St Paul, and drawing attention to their sumptuous decoration and their endowments, Constantine, anxious to assure to Sylvester, supreme and universal pontiff of the city of Rome, a residence worthy of him, announces that he is relinquishing to him the imperial palace of the Lateran, and authorises him, as also his successors, to wear the diadem and all the insignia of the Empire.

(d) Similarly he allocates senatorial decorations and privileges to the Roman clergy.

(e) 'We did also decree that our venerable Father Sylvester, supreme pontiff, and likewise all his successors, should wear the diadem, that is to say the crown of purest gold and precious stones, which we took from our own head and handed over to him. But the most Holy Pope refused to place a crown of gold over the clerical crown (the tonsure) which he wears to the glory of the blessèd Peter. Therefore, we placed on his most holy brow, with our own hands, the *phrygium*, whose white colour proclaims the glorious Resurrection of our Lord. Then holding the bridle of his horse, we rendered to him, by way of homage to the blessèd Peter, the duty of groom (*stratoris officium*), while at the same time we ordained that all his successors should make use of this same *phrygium*, following the example of our Empire.'

(f) 'And, in order that the prestige of the papacy should not deteriorate in

[2] The whole of this account is drawn from old documents which appeared in Rome at the end of the fifth century, when Symmachus was pope: apocryphal instruments of Pope Sylvester; records of a Roman Council which was supposed to have been held before the Nicene Council and which included, *inter alia*, an account of the healing of Constantine, and an enactment made by Sylvester and countersigned by the Emperor and the Empress, according to which the Holy See could not be judged by anyone.

any way, but on the contrary should shine even more brightly than the honour of the Empire and its power and glory, we hereby concede and confer to the blessèd Sylvester, our father, the universal Pope, not only our palace of the Lateran, already mentioned, but also the city of Rome, and likewise all the provinces, districts and cities of Italy and the Western regions, so that they may be held by him and his successors in their power and under their guardianship. ... By this charter and constitution [enactment of an emperor] they are handed over to and shall lawfully remain with the Roman Church for ever.

(g) 'Accordingly we consider it opportune to transfer our Empire and our sovereign power into the Eastern regions and to construct in the province of Byzantium, on a most fitting site, a city which shall bear our name and which shall be the capital of the Empire. For it would indeed not be right that an earthly emperor should exercise his power in the place where the supremacy of priests (*principatus sacerdotum*) and the capital of the Christian religion has been established by a heavenly ruler.'

IV   GALLO-FRANKISH LAUDES

Formula used in the years 796–800 [ed. E. H. KANTOROWICZ, *Laudes regiae*, Berkeley, 1946, pp. 15-16.]

1 Christ is conqueror, Christ is king, Christ is emperor (*three times*).

2 Hear us, O Christ![3]

3 (a) To Leo, supreme pontiff and universal pope: life! Saviour of the world, aid him.[4] St Peter, St Paul, St Andrew, St Clement, St Sixtus.

(b) To the most excellent Charles, crowned by God, great and pacific King of the Franks and the Lombards, patrician of the Romans: life and victory! Redeemer of the world, aid him. St Mary, St Michael, St Gabriel, St Raphael, St John, St Stephen.

(c) To the most noble royal family: life! Holy Virgin of the Virgins, aid them. St Sylvester, St Lawrence, St Pancras, St Nazarius, St Anastasia, St Genevieve, St Columba.

(d) To all those in authority and to the entire army of the Franks: life and victory! St Hilary, aid them. St Martin, St Maurice, St Dennis, St Crispin, St Crispinian, St Gereon.

4 Christ is conqueror, Christ is king, Christ is emperor.

5 Our liberation and redemption: Christ is conqueror.[5] King of kings, our king, our hope, our glory, our mercy, our succour, our valiance, our liberation

---

[3] Invocation repeated before b, c and d.
[4] In these four paragraphs, the invocation follows the name of each saint.
[5] This phrase is repeated after all the invocations.

and redemption, our victory, our most invincible armour, our unassailable wall, our defence and our exaltation, our light, our way and our life.

6 To him alone be empire, glory and power through the undying ages. To him alone be virtue, strength and victory in all the ages of the ages. To him alone be praise and jubilation through the ages without end.

7 Hear us, O Christ (*three times*)! Lord have pity (*three times*).

8 [Addressed to the king] Mayest thou be fortunate (*three times*)! Mayest thou know prosperity (*three times*)! Mayest thou reign many years! Amen!

The reader should refer to the scholarly analysis of this masterpiece of Frankish liturgy given by E. H. KANTOROWICZ. Only one comment need be made here. Although the Pope is placed first in the list of acclamations, he is supported by saints of a lower rank than those who are called to the aid of the Kings of the Franks. On Byzantine ivories the Virgin, the three archangels and the Precursor are gathered around Christ enthroned in majesty (the theme of the *Deisis*). It is as though the King (and not the Pope) were elevated to the same level as the Saviour; he is in every respect the image of the latter.

It appears that this arrangement was slightly altered in Rome during the first quarter of the ninth century. The *Laudes* which resulted from the changes survived until the end of the twelfth century. In them the Pope's position is on the same level as, and side by side with, that of the Emperor, under the direct protection of Christ; the Emperor is under that of the Virgin; the two other categories – the last now reduced to the army of the Romans and the Franks (and later the Teutonici) – are each under the protection of one saint only. The wonderful final invocations, in particular No. 5, remain. The order of the world, of which, exceptionally, Charlemagne had been the sole guarantor, was henceforth the responsibility of the Pope and the Emperor, placed on an equal footing: the formula *a Deo coronato* referring to the Emperor corresponds to *a Deo decreto* relating to the Pope.

V   THE THREE SUPREME AUTHORITIES ON THE EVE OF THE YEAR 800

Letter written in June 799 by Alcuin to Charlemagne, *Domino pacifico David regi* (published in *Monumenta Germaniae, Epistolae*, Vol. IV, No. 174, p. 288).

'Until now, three persons have been at the summit of the hierarchy of the world.

'1 The representative of apostolic sublimity, vicar of the blessèd Peter, prince of the apostles, whose throne he occupies. As for what has happened to the person at present occupying this throne, you have been kind enough to let me know.

'2 Next comes the holder of the status of emperor, who exercises secular power in the second Rome. The news has spread everywhere of the impious manner in which the head of this Empire has been deposed, not by foreigners, but by his own people and fellow citizens.

'3 Thirdly, there is the sovereign status which Our Lord Jesus Christ has reserved to you in order that you may govern all Christian peoples. This status is higher than the two others, eclipses them in wisdom and surpasses them in power. It is now on thee alone that the Churches of Christ depend, from thee alone they await their salvation, from thee, avenger of crimes, guide of those who stray, comforter of the afflicted, support of good men. . . .'

VI   THE ACCESSION OF CHARLEMAGNE TO THE EMPIRE AS DESCRIBED IN THE *ANNALES LAURESHAMENSES*

(Published in *Monumenta Germaniae, Scriptores*, Vol. I, p. 37)

'Since there was no longer an emperor in the country of the Greeks, and the imperial power was in the hands of a woman, it seemed to Pope Leo himself and to all the holy fathers who were at that time assembled in council, and also to all other Christian people, that it would be fitting to give the title of emperor to King Charles, who held in his power the town of Rome, where the Caesars were always accustomed to reside, and the other towns of Italy, of Gaul and not just those of Germany. Since God Almighty had thus permitted all these places to be placed under his authority, it seemed right to them that, in accordance with the will of God and the request of all Christian people, he should in addition bear the title of emperor. Charlemagne did not wish to oppose this request and, submitting humbly to God, as well as to the wish expressed by the priests and all Christian people, he received his consecration from Pope Leo and along with it the title of emperor.'

VII   A LETTER FROM THE EMPEROR LOUIS II TO BASIL I, EMPEROR OF BYZANTIUM

Writing immediately after the capture of Bari in 871, Louis II was asking that a Byzantine fleet should be sent into Italian waters. In the letter, Louis justifies his imperial title to Basil I. The author of the letter was almost certainly Anastasius, the librarian of the Holy See, who was a protégé of Louis II (published in *Monumenta Germaniae, Epistolae*, Vol. VII, p. 385.)

EXTRACTS

'What thou hast said about the title of emperor – that it was not inherited from father to son and was not suitable to our people – makes me smile. Why should it not be inherited by a son from his father – this title which our grandfather already inherited from his father? Why should it not be suitable for our people, since we know that the Spaniards, the Isaurians, the Khazars[6] – and we omit the others in order to keep this letter brief – became Roman emperors? Thou canst not in truth affirm that those people are, by their religion or their qualities, more illustrious than the Frankish people and yet thou dost not refuse to admit them (to the honours of the Empire) and thou dost not disdain to praise highly the emperors who have come from those nations.

'As for thy objection that we do not hold sway over all Francia, I shall reply briefly as follows. Our empire does indeed extend over all Francia for there is no doubt that we hold what was held by those with whom we are but one flesh and one blood and one spirit in the Lord.

'Moreover, thou, our belovèd brother, declarest that thou art astonished that we do not call ourselves emperors of the Franks, but of the Romans;[7] it is fitting that thou shouldst know that if we were not emperors of the Romans we should not be emperors of the Franks either. We have received this name and this title from the Romans, among whom the pinnacle of such great sublimity and such a distinguished appellation first shone with a brilliant light; it was the decision of God which caused us to assume the government of the people and of the city, as well as the defence and exaltation of the mother of all the Churches, who conferred authority, first as kings and then as emperors, on the first princes of our dynasty. Indeed, it was only those of the Frankish princes whom the Roman pontiff consecrated for the purpose by means of the holy oil who bore the royal and then the imperial title. It was through this anointing also, dispensed to him by the sovereign pontiff, that our great-great-grandfather, Charles the Great, first of our nation and of our family, came to be called emperor and became the Christ of the Lord, by reason of his great piety. In your country on the contrary there have been individuals who seized the status of emperor quite without any divine action being taken by the bishops, and solely by being designated by the senate and the people, who did not pay any attention to the pontiffs; some did not even become emperors by this means, but simply through acclamation by soldiers; others were brought to the government of the Roman Empire by women or in many other ways. . . .

'The people of the Franks finally offered numerous and rich fruits to God, not only by coming swiftly to believe in him themselves but also by converting many other peoples to salvation. And the Lord had good reason to announce to you that "the kingdom of God would be taken from you and given to a nation bringing forth the fruits of it".[8] For just as God was able "of the stones to raise up children unto Abraham"[9] so he was able to raise up successors to the Roman empire from this rock-like people the Franks; just as, if we are "Christ's,

---

[6] Here Louis II was referring in turn to Theodosius and his sons; to Leo III and the three immediately preceding emperors; and to the mother of Leo IV, who was a member of the Khazar dynasty.

[7] A letter addressed by the Emperors Michael and Theophilus to Louis the Pious bore the superscription: 'To their brother Louis, glorious King of the Franks and of the Lombards, and called emperor of those nations.' (*Mon. Germ. Concilia*, II, p. 475).

[8] *Matthew*, xxi, 43.

[9] *Matthew*, iii, 9, and *Galatians*, iii, 29.

then we are also" – in the words of the Apostle – "the seed of Abraham", so, if we are Christ's, we can, through his grace, do all things which can be done by those who seem to proceed from Christ. Just as, by virtue of our faith in Christ, we belong to the race of Abraham (which the Jews have ceased to do because of their perfidy), so we have received the government of the Roman empire, by virtue of our right thinking and our orthodoxy. The Greeks, on the other hand, because of their "cacodoxy", that is to say their heretical opinions or wrong thinking, have ceased to be emperors of the Romans; indeed, not only did they abandon the town and the seat of the empire, but, losing Roman nationality and even the Latin language, they established their capital in another city and transformed entirely the nationality and the language of the empire.'

To these extracts let us add now the heading to the letter – 'Louis, by order of Divine Providence, Emperor Augustus of the Romans, to our well-beloved spiritual brother Basil, very glorious and very pious Emperor of the new Rome' – and thus all the essential elements of Louis II's concept of empire are gathered together.

1 Absolute parity of the two Empires; no tendency towards universality.

2 Denial to the Byzantine Emperor of the title of Roman Emperor, because it did not correspond to the facts.

3 Sublimity of the Empire: the allusion by Louis to the 'pinnacle of great sublimity. . . .' which takes up the point he made a little earlier: 'the status of emperor is not just a word; it resides gloriously side by side with God at the pinnacle of piety.'

4 The source of the Empire is in Rome. Not with the Romans, in relation to whom the Emperor recognises that he has certain duties, but in the mother Church, whence the Frankish sovereigns received, through their anointing, the status of king and of emperor. This is an extremely serious statement, recognising that the anointing has a constituent value and going so far as to present Charlemagne himself as an emperor consecrated by the Pope. This view, absolutely contrary to the facts, is indeed significant and demonstrates the evolution of the concept of empire in the ninth century; it is, moreover, an argument in favour of denying the rank of emperor to the Byzantine sovereigns who come to power 'without the participation of the pontiffs'. But in basing the authenticity of his authority on such principles, Louis II completely deprives his empire of independence in relation to the Church: the contrast between the two 'Roman' monarchies is thus clearly exposed.

5 Those entitled to the Empire (Roman) are the Franks, who have earned 'the pinnacle of monarchy' because of their scrupulous orthodoxy. This empire

of Frankish substance remains a whole, even though it consists of several separate countries.

To sum up, it seems indeed that in Louis II's view the real essence of the Western Empire's authority was 'the incorporation in one single substance of the Roman Empire and the Frankish Empire' which Pope Sergius had defined a third of a century before.[10]

VIII   DIATRIBES LAUNCHED AGAINST THE ROMANS BY LIUTPRAND OF CREMONA

[An account of Liutprand's mission to Constantinople, in June 968, from the *Works of Liutprand of Cremona* translated for the first time into English with an introduction by F. A. Wright (George Routledge & Sons, London 1930), pp. 242–3, 'The Embassy to Constantinople'.]

The Emperor Nicephorus Phocas has just said to Otto I's envoy: 'You are not Romans, but Lombards.' Liutprand replies:

'History teaches us that Romulus, from whom the Romans get their name, was a fratricide, born in adultery. He made a place of refuge for himself and received into it insolvent debtors, runaway slaves, murderers and men who deserved death for their crimes. This was the sort of crowd whom he enrolled as citizens and he gave them the name of Romans. From this nobility are descended those men whom you style "rulers of the world" ["cosmocratores"]. But we Lombards, Saxons, Franks, Lotharingians, Bavarians, Swabians and Burgundians so despise these fellows that when we are angry with an enemy we can find nothing more insulting to say than – "You Roman". For us in the word Roman is comprehended every form of lowness, timidity, avarice, luxury, falsehood, and vice. You say that we are unwarlike and know nothing of horsemanship. Well, if the sins of the Christians merit that you keep this stiff neck, the next war will prove what manner of men you are, and how warlike we.'

There is no need to stress the violence and irony of these diatribes. Nevertheless it is worth noting that criticism of the Romans was a common political and literary theme throughout the Middle Ages, side by side with a whole-hearted admiration for Rome.

IX   POPE AND EMPEROR TOWARDS THE YEAR 1000

A poem by Bishop Otto of Vercelli addressed, in 998, to Pope Gregory V and the Emperor Otto III (ed. P. E. SCHRAMM, *Kaiser, Rom und Renovatio*, Vol. II, pp. 62–4).

[10] *Mon. Germ. Epistolae*, V, p. 583.

Christ, hear our prayers, look down on thy city of Rome; in thy goodness, revive the Romans, reawaken the strength of Rome; let Rome arise again under the rule of the Emperor Otto III.

1

We greet thee, our Pope, hail, very worthy Gregory; with Otto Augustus, thy apostle Peter has welcomed thee; thou ascendest towards sublimity, humble thyself.

2

Thou hast gone out from the house of the bride, thou returnest to it as the bridegroom and thou recoverest the gifts of thy venerable father.[11]

3

Thou art Peter, thou ordainest the praises of Peter, thou revivest the rights of Rome, thou restorest Rome to Rome in order that Otto may become the glory of the Empire.

4

May Otto succeed in all things, may he prosper always, he who has carried thee away from Gaul and has led thee to Rome; God has made thee very great and has raised up thy arm.

5

Thou art the mouth in the Churches, in the holy mysteries, thou art the master of all, thou art the link of the people, thou judgest many cases, thou freest captive souls.

6

Otto takes care of thee, attentive and vigilant, he who, according to the apostle, is responsible for the body; for the punishment of sinners, he carries an invincible sword.

7

Ancient Antioch reveres thee in everything, antique Alexandria runs anxiously towards thee, all the Churches in the world follow in thy wake.[12]

[11] Advanced to the papacy by Otto II who had brought him out of 'Gaul' with him in 996 (verse 4) – that is to say, out of Western Germany into Italy – Gregory V was driven out of the city the following year by a revolt of the Romans. He returned in 998, in the Emperor's retinue. The 'venerable father' is the apostle Peter; the Pope is the spiritual spouse of the Church of Rome.

[12] Perhaps SCHRAMM is right in guessing that we have here a reply to the discourse pronounced at the Council of Rheims, in 991, by Arnulf, Bishop of Orleans, in which he stressed that the Church of Rome had lost all superior authority over the patriarchates of the East; see the text in *Mon. Germ. Scriptores*, III, p. 676.

8

Babylon of iron and gilded Greece fear great Otto and serve him with bowed head; he rules throughout the whole world as emperor, he who sets free the king of kings.

9

Rejoice, noble Pope, thou doest honour to the first throne by the majesty of thy name, thou raisest up the second; thy wisdom is resplendent in the right hand of Gerbert.[13]

10

Rejoice, O Pope; rejoice, O Caesar; let the Church exult most fervently, let joy be great in Rome, let the imperial palace rejoice. Under the power of Caesar the Pope reforms this age.

11

O you, two Luminaries, send your light across the space covered by many different lands; lighten the churches, put the darkness to flight. May one of you prosper by the sword and the other make his words sound round the world.

12

O lord Pope, raise up what is lying on the earth, consider the gift of God; God has made thee very great and the aid given by Peter is thy support; keep the memory of what is thine and of thy glory.

All this is significant evidence of the hope of a *Renovatio* both of the Church and of the Empire, by a return to the past of the apostles and of the former emperors. This *Renovatio* will be accomplished by the two supreme powers in the world, the two Luminaries working in close co-operation. Nevertheless, the more considerable of the two is the emperor, source and support of the papacy, bearer of the temporal sword which permits him to carry out his mission. Verse 8 gives an idea of the nature of the imperial authority of Otto III: he exercises supremacy in the world. (See also pp. 7, 63, 67.)

X   THE REJECTION BY OTTO III OF THE DONATION OF CONSTANTINE

[Document No. 389 published in *Monumenta Germaniae, Diplomata regum et imperatorum Germaniae*, Vol. II, p. 819; dating from the first days of the year 1001, drafted apparently by Otto of Vercelli.]

Otto, slave of the apostles and, in accordance with the will of God the Saviour, Emperor Augustus of the Romans.

---

[13] The first throne is the pulpit of Peter at Rome; the second is that of the archbishopric of Ravenna, to which Otto III had nominated his teacher Gerbert.

We proclaim Rome capital of the world, we recognise that the Roman Church is the mother of all churches, but also that the negligence and incompetence of its pontiffs have for a long time tarnished the brightness of its titles. In fact, they have not only, by certain dishonest practices, sold and alienated some of the property of St Peter outside the city, but – and we do not make this statement without sorrow – they have behaved with even greater licence and have caused some property, which they held in our own imperial city, to pass into common usage, in return for money; they plundered St Peter, St Paul and even their altars and, instead of making reparation, they have done nothing but sow confusion. Scorning pontifical precepts and disdaining the Roman Church, certain popes pushed their arrogance to such a point as to confuse the greater part of our Empire with their apostolic powers; without caring about what was lost through their fault, without showing any concern for what their personal vanity caused them to waste, they replaced their own property, which they had dilapidated, by turning to the property of others, namely, in particular, our property and that of our Empire, as though they wished to cast their own faults on our Empire.

Such indeed are the lies invented by them, by means of which the cardinal-deacon John (nicknamed 'the one with the mutilated fingers') drew up in letters of gold the 'privilege' which he mendaciously caused to be back-dated very far in time and placed under the name of the great Constantine.[14] Similarly, such are the texts by means of which they would like to prove that a certain Charles gave to St Peter all the property of our public domains.[15] To which we reply that that Charles could not lawfully give anything away, since, put to flight by a better Charles,[16] he had already been deprived and dispossessed of the Empire and his authority was therefore annulled; he therefore disposed of something which did not belong to him at all, or, again, which he could not give away except as someone does who has acquired a thing wrongfully and therefore cannot hope to keep for a long time what he has appropriated.

In consequence, we reject these mendacious 'privileges' and these fictitious writings and, through our generosity, we confer on St Peter those properties which are ours, not the properties which belong to him as though they were ours. Just as we have, for the love of St Peter, chosen as pope the Lord Bishop Sylvester, our teacher, and as God willed, have ordained him and brought him to the supreme pontificate; in the same way, for the love of the Pope Sylvester, we offer to St Peter some properties which are part of our public domain, in order that the master may possess what he offers to our Emperor Peter on the

[14] This is an allusion to the copy of the Donation of Constantine, in letters of gold on a crimson background, which was presented to Otto III and doubtless before that to Otto I.
[15] This is no doubt a reference to the pact concluded between Charles the Bald and Pope John VIII after the Assembly of Ponthion, which, towards the middle of the tenth century, roused the indignation of the anonymous author of the *Libellus de imperatoria potestate in urbe Roma* (*Mon. Germ. Scriptores*, III, 719), one of the sources of the official document issued by Otto III.
[16] Carloman, son of Louis the German, whose intervention in Italy compelled Charles the Bald to leave the peninsula in 877.

part of his disciple. We therefore offer and make a gift to St Peter of [eight] counties, for the love of our master, Pope Sylvester, in order that he may hold them for the honour of God and of St Peter, his own salvation and ours, and that he may administer them for the prosperity of his pontificate and that of our empire. . . .

XI   THE NATURE OF THE EMPEROR'S AUTHORITY IN THE OTTONIAN PERIOD

Acclamations to the Emperor [ed. P. E. SCHRAMM, *Kaiser, Rom und Renovatio*, Vol. II, p. 61].

'Let Slavs groan and Hungarians grind their teeth; let Greeks be stunned, let Saracens be troubled and take flight; let Africans pay tribute and Spaniards appeal for help. Let Burgundy venerate and cherish the Emperor and let Aquitaine run joyfully to meet him. Let all Gaul say: "Who has ever heard such things?" And the Italian people will raise their arms and cry aloud: "By God, this is the only son of the Caesar, Otto the Great." And let thousands of the poor say: "By our souls, this man is born of our mother and sovereign Adelaide."'

These verses are inserted in a letter written by Odilo, Abbot of Cluny, to the Emperor Henry II (about 1013–14). The three last lines seem to come from a poem, written in the reign of Otto II and dating from before his defeat at Cape Colonna in 982.[17] In general, though it is not of course free from hyperbole, this passage is evidence of the overwhelmingly superior status of the Emperor in the world.

XII   THE CONCEPT OF EMPIRE AT THE PERIOD OF THE INVESTITURE CONTEST

Benzo of Alba: *Ad Heinricum*. [*Monumenta Germaniae, Scriptores*, Vol. XI, pp. 590 *et seq.*]

Benzo, who was perhaps a native of southern Italy, was a cleric in the chapel of Henry III, who promoted him to be Bishop of Alba. He was a passionate supporter of Henry IV against Gregory VII and the most representative writer to offer evidence of the concept of empire at the height of the first conflict between the Empire and the papacy.

---

[17] This hypothesis has been contested by C. ERDMANN, *Studien zur Briefliteratur Deutschlands im 11. Jahrhundert*, 1938, where it is suggested that the son of Otto I and Adelaide might be, by poetic licence, Henry II himself.

1 *The Imperial 'scenopegia'*[18]. [Book I, chapters vii–xii, pp. 602–3].
Benzo first notes that the emperor of the world is crowned in very different
manner from the subordinate kings (*reguli*) of the provinces. He then describes
the ritual of the imperial inauguration, which according to him was spread
over four days.

(a) [Solemn procession] 'In front of the king is carried the Holy Cross, heavy
with the wood of the Cross of the Saviour, and the Lance of St Maurice. These
two emblems are followed by bishops, abbots and innumerable clerics. The
king is dressed in a tunic of *byssus*, embroidered with gold and precious stones,
and over this is thrown a *chlamys* in cloth of frieze, the imperial garment. His
shoes are gilded; he is girt with the sword; on his hands are gloves of linen; the
pontifical ring on his finger, the diadem on his head. In his left hand he carries
a golden orb, symbolising the universal monarchy; his right hand holds the
imperial sceptre, in the manner of Caesar, of Augustus and of Tiberius.
'On his right walks the Pope, on his left the Archbishop of Milan; dukes,
marquesses, counts and other great men bring the procession to a close. . . . A
tremendous shouting rises to the heavens. The clerics intone *"Jam bone Pastor"*.
The Germans cry out *"Kyrie eleison, helfo, St Petre heleyson."*[19] All the nations
present burst out into acclamations, each in their own language. . . . In the
course of Mass, the Emperor is crowned and blessed before the Evangel'. The
Mass is followed by a banquet after which 'the emperor puts on a *chlamys* of
brilliant green and covers his head with the white mitre, on top of which he
places the circlet of a patrician, thus adorned he goes to the vespers.'
(b) 'The following day, the Lord Pope takes the Roman crown from the
altar of the prince of the apostles and places it on the brow of Caesar. Caesar,
crowned by the will of God and at the request of St Peter, advances to the
great staircase where he is greeted by the Roman senate; mounted on a horse,
accompanied by the Roman, German and Lombard knights, he advances along
the triumphal way. On all sides he is hailed by the chants of the Romans. In
front of the doors of the Constantinian basilica (St John Lateran), chief of all
the churches in the world, he is received by the *scholes*;[20] . . . he goes to the
altar where Mass is celebrated amid general rejoicing. . . .'
(c) 'On the third day, the emperor, with his crown on his head and accompanied by a splendid train of nobles, visits St Paul's.'
(d) 'On the fourth day, as though he were returning from Bethlehem, he
enters Holy Jerusalem. . . . In the course of the last three days of the week he
holds a synod with the apostolic lord and together they remedy all that the holy
hierarchy has left undone. Lastly, helped by wise men, he deals with the affairs
of the Republic. . . .'

[18] This expression is borrowed from *John*, vii, 2, where it signifies the Jewish feast of
Tabernacles.
[19] Helfo: this is the German translation of *Tu illum adiuva* in the Laudes, an echo from
which can be recognised in the following invocation also.
[20] Benzo doubtless used this word to signify regional groups of clergy or notaries
coming from the various quarters of Rome.

P. E. Schramm believes that this passage can be accepted as an account of the *ordo* of the imperial coronation at the time of the Salian emperors,[21] but it appears more likely that it is Benzo's own free interpretation of the ritual. His description contains several recognisable factual features: the dress of the emperor, his insignia, the procession, the echo of the *Laudes*, the connexion, since the time of Henry III, between the status of emperor and that of patrician. The new features are, first, the dissociation between the anointing proper and the coronation and secondly, the visit to the Roman basilicas, which seems to have been suggested to Benzo by the papal liturgy. Bethlehem and Jerusalem stand for the churches of Santa Maria Maggiore and the Holy Cross, but at the same time they evoke the idea of the emperor as the figure of Christ.

2 *The Emperor of the Romans*

(a) The destiny of the empire: St Peter and St Paul acquired the empire and they may pass it, at their pleasure, to those who are to administer it in their name, to the Greeks, the Gauls, the Lombards and lastly the Germans, to be held forever by them. [Book III, chapter iii, p. 622.]

(b) The empire must be governed in such a way as to be favourable to the Romans. 'A good tree cannot bear bad fruit', said Henry IV, according to Benzo, 'the memory of their ancestors is a fire which burns brightly in the Romans ... they are the instruments of my battles and my counsellors; let them share my royal prerogatives among themselves for I shall make them leaders of all Italy. ....' [Book III, chapter xxiv, p. 631.]

(c) Not in any way disconcerted by the account he has already given of the imperial '*scenopegia*', Benzo relates one accession to the empire in different circumstances: he describes a scene taking place in 1081, when Henry IV is instituting a new curia under the walls of Rome, in which he is said to have recruited centurions, tribunes, senators, the urban prefect. After this he is said to have received the imperial diadem in the open air, surrounded by his troops, 'in accordance with a new ritual'.[22] [Book VI, Preface, p. 657.]

(d) Memories of the Romans of former days are revived and quoted in relation to the emperor; 'Caesar, thou art as great as is the world; both on this side and on the far side of the sea thou art a powerful lion; the dragon is crushed beneath thy heel; thou art victorious as was Scipio. He [Africanus] defeated the Carthaginians but thy right hand has put to flight the Romuleans [the Byzantines]. He destroyed the weak castles of Dido, thou, Caesar in person, thou hast captured the walls of Rome; thou transcendest the Fabians, the Ciceros, all the Fabricii, the Catos. Like Solomon, thou givest laws to the people: it is honey which flows from thy mouth and from his. The Christian and pagan kings, the Theodosiuses, the Justinians, the Charlemagnes and the Pepins, all of them are

---

[21] See his study in *Deutsches Archiv*, I, 1937.

[22] In this passage it is difficult to distinguish what is real and what is imaginary, but the most interesting point about it is that it is evidence of the notion that the Caesars came to the throne through the action of the Army and thus integrates it in the world of representations of the Roman Renewal (as SCHRAMM remarks in *Kaiser, Rom und Renovatio*, I).

surpassed by thy intelligence, strength and arms, for thou hast been sent from heaven, thou art not a man born of flesh'. [Book VI, chapter vii, p. 668.]

(e) Henry IV will be the emperor at the end of time: 'He will be seen by Byzas,[23] crowned in his own city. . . . He will then go to Jerusalem, where he will visit the Holy Sepulchre and the other sanctuaries, then he will receive the crown for the praise and glory of Him who lives in all the ages and whose tomb will shine in glory.' [Book I, chapters xiv–xv, p. 605].

3 The Anointed Emperor, Image of God

'God walks before His anointed and prepares for him an accumulation of victories. All the world awaits him as though he were the Redeemer; the crowd, going to meet him with palms and branches, opens the gates of the towns to him. . . .' [Book I, chapter xiv, p. 605.]

'Next after God, O Caesar, thou art king, thou art emperor: rule and command by means of thy redoubtable power; may fear of thy threats reduce to nothing those who rely on their own fierceness.' 'Thou, O Caesar, holdest the sword of vengeance from the hand of God.' [Book I, chapter xxiii, p. 608.]

'Before the face of Augustus, the pride of the rebels falls like a wisp of straw[24] . . . Let all Christendom therefore give praise to the Creator who renders the eagles of the very Christian Emperor terrible to the attacking enemies. . . .' [Book I, chapter iv, p. 601.]

'Vicar of the Creator, . . . he [the emperor] has been raised by God's favour to a position of great sublimity and exalted above all powers and laws of all kingdoms; my prayer is that he may project his thoughts upwards to God[25] and that he may exercise discretion, mother of all the virtues, in his actions, rendering honour and glory to Him Who has made from among human creatures, another creator in His own likeness.' [Book I, chapter xxvi, p. 609.]

XIII   THE IMPERIAL CORONATION OF ALFONSO VII (1135)

[*Cronica de Alfonso VII* (H. FLOREZ, *España Sagrada*, Vol. XXI, Madrid, 1766, pp. 345–7.)]

'After these events, in the course of the year 1173, the King summoned a meeting of a council to be held in the royal city of León, on the fourth day before the nones of June,[26] the feast of Pentecost. The first day of the council all the members, great and small, assembled in the Church of St Mary with the King and there took such steps as the clemency of our Lord Jesus Christ dictated to them, concerning the salvation of the souls of all the faithful. On the second day, when the descent of the Holy Spirit on the apostles is celebrated, the

---

[23] Legendary founder of Byzantium.
[24] An echo of *Psalms*, lxxxii, 14 (Psalm lxxxiii, v. 14, in A.V.).
[25] An echo of *Psalms*, liv, 23 (Psalm lv, v. 23, in A.V.).
[26] RASSOW (*Urkunden*, p. 356) considers that this date is incorrect and that it should in fact be 26th May.

archbishops, and the bishops, the abbots, all the nobles and those who were not noble and all the people met together once more in the Church of the Blessèd Mary, along with King Garcia,[27] and the King's sister. They all received from God the inspiration to bestow on King Alfonso the title of emperor, because King Garcia and Zafadola,[28] the King of the Saracens, and Count Raymond of Barcelona,[29] and Count Alfonso of Toulouse,[30] and numerous counts and dukes of Gascony and of France were in every respect his obedient vassals. After having clothed the King in a magnificent mantle, they placed on his brow a crown of very pure gold and precious stones and made him take a sceptre in his hand. Then, with King Garcia holding his right arm and Arrianus, Bishop of León, his left, the bishops and the abbots led him up to the altar of St Mary, all the while chanting the *Te Deum* to its end and then saying after that: 'Long live the Emperor Alfonso!' After the Benediction had been pronounced over him, they celebrated Mass according to the usage of the high festivals. . . .'

Statements made in the *primera cronica general* (which dates from the middle of the twelfth century) suggest that the new Emperor addressed Pope Innocent II, requesting that his new status be confirmed. The Pope is alleged to have agreed to his request, but this report is apocryphal.

In short, we have here a very sober account, which nevertheless gives a perfectly clear picture of the ceremony. It comprised a sort of imperial election, *divino consilio accepto*; the coronation was inspired by that of the Roman emperors but retained a certain originality (th re was no anointing: Alfonso VII had been anointed as king as long ago as 1111); there was a simple handing over of the insignia (as in Byzantium, in Rome on the 25th December, 800, and in Aix-la-Chapelle in September, 813) and an acclamation of the Emperor – *Vivat Adefonsus imperator* – which took the place of the Laudes and was an explicit recognition of the sovereign's imperial status. The juridical foundation of this Empire resided in Alfonso's plural authority, represented here by the many different lands over which he exercised suzerainty.

XIV   THE ROMANS AND THE EMPIRE IN THE MIDDLE OF THE TWELFTH CENTURY

I *Letter addressed by the Romans to Conrad III, in 1149.* [Preserved along with two identical missives in the collection of the correspondence of Wibald, Abbot of Stavelot: JAFFE, *Bibliotheca rerum germanicarum*, I, pp. 332–4.]

To the very excellent and illustrious ruler of Rome and of the whole world, Conrad, by the grace of God, King of the Romans, ever Augustus, the senate

[27] Garcia V Ramirez, King of Navarre (1134–50).
[28] King of Saragossa, an ally of Alfonso VII, who gave him the arms of a knight.
[29] Raymond-Berengar IV, Count of Barcelona, who became King of Aragon in 1137, as a result of marrying the daughter of King Ramirez.
[30] Alfonso-Jordan, Count of Toulouse, son of Raymond IV of Saint-Gilles (1105–48).

and the Roman people wish health and a prosperous and glorious government of the Roman Empire.

We have already set out most carefully in a number of writings, to your royal excellency, our deeds and actions, our perseverance in the sworn faith and our daily struggles to elevate and fortify in every way your imperial crown. Your royal majesty has not deigned to reply at all to our pressing letters and this is something which astonishes us, we being your sons and faithful subjects, you being our father and master. For we do nothing which is not evidence of our feeling of obedience and respect. Indeed, we desire to raise up and make great the Roman empire, the government of which God has entrusted to you, and to re-establish it in the condition in which it was at the time of Constantine and Justinian, who through the strength of the senate and the Roman people, held the entire universe within their power. With this object we re-established the senate, by the grace of God. The rebels who, always unamenable to your orders, had plundered the Roman Empire of its glory, were also crushed by us; in a word, we are making energetic and unanimous efforts to ensure that everything due to Caesar and to the Empire shall indeed be rendered unto you. . . .

But because they hate what we, on account of our attachment to you, are doing, the Pope, the Frangipani family, the sons of Pierleone (with the exception of Jordan our devoted standard-bearer),[31] the friends of the Sicilian[32] and many other people still attack us on all sides in order to prevent us from placing the imperial crown freely on your royal head. But, although we are afflicted by a crowd of ills . . . for love of you and your honour, we suffer them gladly. . . .

We pray that your imperial majesty will come to us, since you will be able to fulfil all our wishes in Rome. To put everything in one word, you will be able to reside in Rome, capital of the world, and because all objections on the part of the clergy will vanish, both for Italy as a whole and for the Teutonic kingdom, you will be able to found a much more settled dominion with less trouble than your predecessors. Come then without delay, I beg of you. . . .

> May the king be powerful, may he win over his enemies what he desires,
> May he have the empire, its seat in Rome, may he rule the universe,
> As a prince of the earth, as Justinian was.
> May Caesar receive what is due to Caesar and the Pope what is due to
> the Pope,
> Peter paying tribute, as Christ ordained it.

[31] The Frangipani and the Pierleoni were two of the most important families of the Roman aristocracy. Jordan Pierleone, brother of the former Pope Anacletus II, was the only one of his line to enter into a pact with the Commune, which, in 1144, made him a Patrician of the city. This title recalled memories of the tenth century and conferred on its holder a kind of imperial delegation in Rome. (Cf. Otto of Freising, *Chronicle*, VII, chapter xxxi: *omnes tamquam principi subiciuntur.*) At the request of Eugenius III, the patriciate was abrogated in 1145, but Jordan remained the standard-bearer of the Commune.

[32] *I.e.* Roger II, King of Sicily (1101–54) adversary of the two empires which, at that moment, had joined in a coalition against him.

II *Missive addressed by Wezel, very probably a German, a disciple of Arnold of Brescia, to Frederick I, in 1152.* [*Ibid*, pp. 539–43.]

As the text is very long, only a summary is given here, with a few quotations.

1 *Introduction*
I feel great joy because your nation has selected you as its king; but I am deeply grieved by the fact that, following the advice of the clerics and the monks, whose conduct has confused divine and human things, you did not consult the Holy City, mistress of the world, creator and mother of all the emperors, on this subject, as was your duty; that you did not ask this city, without which no emperor has yet reigned, to confirm your election; and lastly, that you did not write as a son to her, if indeed you propose to be her son and her minister.

2 *Argument*
Rome compared to Rebecca, making Jacob come forward to receive the benediction and sovereignty (*dominium*) from Isaac.

Violent attacks against the heretical and apostate clerics who overturn the Church of God and the secular world.

Denunciation of the Donation of Constantine; this is today so well recognised as a lie that 'the good women of Rome (*mulierculae*) are capable of arguing on this subject with the most wise men, and the Pope and his cardinals dare no longer, for shame, show themselves in Rome'.

What the Emperor ought to be: 'The imperial majesty ought not only to be well provided with arms, but ought also to be seen to be armed with laws, in order that people may be well governed in peace as in war.'[33] In addition, every decision of the Emperor ought to have the force of law, 'in view of the fact that the people hand over to his discretion all the power and all the authority which are in their charge.'

The right of the Romans to create the Emperor: 'As all the authority, all the dignity of the republic is in the hands of the Romans, as the Emperor depends on the Romans and not the Romans on the Emperor, what law, what grounds are there which could prevent the senate and the people from creating an emperor?'

3 *Conclusion*
'Send to Rome as soon as possible Count Rudolf of Ramesberg, Count Udalric of Lenzenburg and other enlightened men . . . who, accompanied by legal advisers, know and dare to negotiate for the rights of the Empire. Be careful to see that no new attack is made against you.'

---

[33] This quotation is taken from the preamble to the *Institutes*, but the author attributes the text to the Emperor Julian.

XV   THE TRADITION OF THE ANOINTED RULER
IN THE MID-TWELFTH CENTURY

1 The Anointing of Frederick I [from *The Deeds of Frederick Barbarossa*, by Otto of Freising and his continuator Rahewin, translated and annotated by Charles Ch. Mierow, Columbia University Press, 1953, Book II, chapter iii, pp. 116–17].

Frederick I has just been unanimously elected at Frankfurt, on 4th March (the Tuesday after the third Sunday in Lent), 1152, a fortnight after the death of Conrad III.

'When, therefore, all the princes who had thronged to that place had been bound by oath of fealty and homage, the king with a few men whom he considered suitable for the purpose, having dismissed the rest in peace, took ship, amid great rejoicing, on the fifth day of the week. He sailed by the Main and the Rhine, and disembarked at the royal seat at Sinzig. There taking horse, he came the next Saturday to Aix-la-Chapelle. On the following day, that is, on that Sunday [the fourth Sunday in Lent, i.e. the 9th March] on which *Laetare Jerusalem* is sung, he was escorted by the bishops from the palace to the church of the blessèd Mary ever virgin. With the greatest applause of all who were present, he was crowned by Arnold, archbishop of Cologne, the others assisting, and was seated on the throne of the realm of the Franks that was placed in that same church by Charles the Great. Not a few marvelled that in so short a space of time not only had so great a throng of princes and of nobles of the kingdom flocked together, but that some also had arrived from western Gaul, whither the report of this event was supposed not yet to have arrived.'

Here the author records an incident which happened 'after the completion of the sacramental anointing', then continues:

'But this too, should not be veiled in silence, that on the same day and in the same church the bishop-elect of Münster (also named Frederick) was consecrated by those same bishops who consecrated the king. So it was believed that the Highest King and Priest was actually participating in the present rejoicing; and this was the sign, that in one church one day beheld the anointing of the two persons who alone are sacramentally anointed according to the ordinance of the New and of the Old Testament, and are rightly called the anointed of Christ the Lord.'

2 The Honour of the Empire. An imperial manifesto pronounced immediately after the Diet of Besançon in October, 1157, during which a serious argument took place between the Chancellor, Rainald of Dassel, and Cardinal Roland, legate of Pope Hadrian IV, bearer of a message which described the Empire as being a *beneficium* [*Mon. Germ., Constitutiones*, I, p. 231 or Otto of Freising, *op. cit.*, Book III, chapter xi, pp. 184–6].

EXTRACTS

'. . . the Divine Sovereignty, from which is derived all power in heaven and on earth, has entrusted unto us, His anointed, the kingdom and the empire to rule over, and has ordained that the peace of the churches is to be maintained by imperial arms. . . .

'For when we were recently at the diet in Besançon and were dealing with the honor of the empire and the security of the Church with all due solicitude, apostolic legates arrived asserting that they bore to Our Majesty such tidings that the honor of the empire should receive no small increase.'

At this point there is a description of the astonishment and disturbance caused by the reading of this message. The Emperor then continues:

'And since, through election by the princes, the kingdom and the empire are ours from God alone, Who at the time of the passion of His Son Christ subjected the world to dominion by the two swords,[34] and since the apostle Peter taught the world his doctrine: 'Fear God, honor the king',[35] whosoever says that we received the imperial crown as a benefice (*pro beneficio*) from the lord pope contradicts the divine ordinance and the doctrine of Peter and is guilty of a lie. But because we have hitherto striven to snatch from the hand of the Egyptians[36] the honor and freedom of the churches, so long oppressed by the yoke of undeserved slavery, and are intent on preserving to them all their rights and dignities, we ask Your Universality[37] to grieve at so great an insult to us and to the empire, hoping that your unwavering loyalty will not permit the honor of the empire, which has stood, glorious and undiminished[38] from the founding of the City and the Establishment of the Christian religion even down to your days, to be disparaged by so unheard-of a novelty, such presumptuous arrogance. . . .'

XVI   SUPREMACY OF THE EMPIRE IN THE TIME OF FREDERICK I

Letter addressed in July, 1157, to the Emperor, by Henry II, King of England [quoted in *The Deeds of Frederick Barbarossa*, by Otto of Freising and his continuator, Rahewin, translated and annotated by Charles Ch. Mierow, Columbia University Press, 1953, Book III, chapter vii, pp. 178–9].

'To the friend dearest to his heart, Frederick, by the grace of God the most invincible emperor of the Romans, Henry, king of England, duke of Nor-

[34] This is an affirmation of the Gelasian doctrine of the co-existence and co-ordination of the two supreme authorities.

[35] I *Peter*, ii, 17.

[36] This was the usual metaphor, inspired by *Exodus*, xviii, 9, to describe the oppression which might be exercised against the new chosen people. Cf. in the liturgical office of St Charlemagne the prayer addressed to the Emperor *ut nos a palea et latere aegyptii torrentis eruamur*.

[37] The explanation for the use of this term is that the Emperor's manifesto was an encyclical.

[38] A striking affirmation of the principle of the continuity of the Empire.

mandy and Aquitaine and count of Anjou, greeting and the harmony of true peace and love.

'We express to Your Excellency the utmost thanks within our power, O best of rulers, because you have deigned to visit us through ambassadors, to greet us in letters, to anticipate us in bestowing gifts, and – a thing we cherish even more dearly than these – to enter into treaties of peace and love with us. We have exulted and have felt our spirit somehow grow within us and be carried to greater heights, since your promise, whereby you have given us hope in the matter of setting in order the affairs of our realm, has made us more alert and more ready. We have exulted, we say, and have with all our heart arisen before your Magnificence, making you this answer with sincere and heartfelt affection, that we are prepared to bring to pass according to our ability whatever we know tends towards your glorification. We lay before you our kingdom and whatever is anywhere subject to our sway, and entrust it to your power, that all things may be administered in accordance with your nod and that in all respects your imperial will be done.

'Let there be, therefore, between us and our peoples an undivided unity of affection and peace, safe commercial intercourse, yet so that to you, who excels us in worth, may fall the right to command (*imperandi auctoritas*), while we shall not lack the will to obey (*voluntas obsequendi*).'

XVII THE EMPIRE'S REPUTATION AND THE ESCHATOLOGICAL VISION OF FREDERICK I'S CONTEMPORARIES

Ludus de Antechristo. Stage play written about 1160–2, at the Bavarian Abbey of Tegernsee; it reflects the atmosphere in which the Emperor and his court lived [F. WILHELM, *Münchener Texte, Heft I*, s.d.].

A Summary. We are in Jerusalem, in front of the Temple of the Lord. The following come on to the stage (in order of appearance): the King of Babylon (representing the pagan world); the Synagogue; the Church, accompanied by Mercy and Justice, and followed by the Pope and his clergy; the Emperor of the Romans, accompanied by his troops; the King of France; the King of the Greeks (that is to say, the Byzantine Emperor); and the King of Jerusalem. The Emperor of the Romans requires all the kings to submit to him. The king of the Franks refuses haughtily but is defeated and made prisoner by the Emperor, whose vassal he becomes, whereupon he receives his kingdom from him. The Kings of the Greeks and of Jerusalem, on the other hand, give way without a struggle; as for the King of Babylon, who was preparing to attack Jerusalem, he is put to flight by the Emperor. Thereafter, the Emperor, followed by the Church, enters the Temple, where he pays homage to God for his crown and his sceptre. When he emerges, alone, he is no longer anything more than King of Germany, and he goes to occupy the seat reserved for the *rex Theotonicorum*.

Now the Antichrist arrives, with a retinue of hypocrites, charged with the task of seducing the laymen, and of heretics whose task it is to make the Church fall. Events succeed one another rapidly. The Antichrist, adorned with the royal insignia of Jerusalem, is enthroned by his supporters in the Temple from which the Church is driven out: the Church takes refuge with the Pope. One after another all the sovereigns are won over by the impostor, who uses the most diverse means to seduce them: menaces for the King of the Greeks, gifts for the King of the Franks, miracles for the King of Germany who had at first won a victory over the false prophet; even the King of Babylon abandons his idols in order to perform the act of submission. At last it is the turn of the Synagogue to be approached: it recognises the Messiah in the Antichrist and, as a reward, receives from him the Promised Land. But at this juncture, lo! the prophets Enoch and Elijah appear, to announce the return of the Lord; they succeed in snatching the Synagogue from the impostor. The latter martyrs them, but, though he has reached the pinnacle of power, he is nevertheless felled by the Word of the true God. As he collapses, the Church welcomes back into the faith all those present and invites them to praise God.

B The *Ludus* was inspired by two specific tendencies: a feeling of German patriotism which takes the form of a certain military pride, and a still deeper conviction of the supremacy of the Emperor, which emerges in the extremely characteristic scene of the King of France's submission.

(a) The general instruction which the Emperor disseminated among the Kings by means of his messengers, was on the following lines:

'As the history books have told us, the whole world was the property of the Romans. It was the zealous efforts of the first Romans which constructed the Empire; the weakness of their successors has led to its decadence. With the power of our majesty we undertake to restore it. Therefore let all Kings now pay to the Empire the tributes instituted for this purpose in ancient times. But, as the Frankish nation is valorous in battle, let their King render military service to the Empire. Command him therefore to offer us his homage and his vows of loyalty as soon as possible.'

(b) The Emperor's messengers appear before the King of the Franks and say to him:

'The Emperor of the Romans greets the illustrious King of the Franks, dear to his heart. For thy enlightenment, we would have thee know that thou art subject to Roman law: the redoubtable judgment of the powerful Empire reminds thee of this. Therefore, we invite thee to render service to it and we inform thee of the order to come and put thyself without delay at its disposal.'

The King of France replies to them:

'If the historians are to be trusted, it is not we who should be subordinate to the Empire, but the Empire which should submit to us. For the ancient Gauls possessed it and transmitted it to us, who are their heirs. As the Empire was taken from us by force there can be no question of our bowing down before our plunderers.'

(c) But after the battle between the two sovereigns, in which both sides conducted themselves well, and which ended as we have described above, the King of the Franks returns to his own kingdom and sings:

'We respect the honour of the name of Rome, we glory in serving Caesar Augustus. The strength of his Empire is redoubtable, may his honour and glory be ever an object of veneration. We proclaim thee, thee alone, rector of us all, and we shall ever obey thee with all our soul.'

XVIII   THE CONCEPT OF EMPIRE AT A CRITICAL STAGE UNDER INNOCENT III

I *The new form of the Laudes*, used for the first time on the occasion of the anointing of Otto IV as emperor in 1208 [E. H. KANTOROWICZ, *Laudes regiae*, p. 144].

'Hear us, O Christ! Health and victory to our Lord, the most invincible and ever august emperor of the Romans! (*three times*).
   'Saviour of the world, aid him.
   'St Mary, St Michael, St Gabriel, St Raphael, St John the Baptist, St Peter, St Paul, St Andrew, St Mark, St Stephen, St Vincent, St Laurence, St Alexander [aid him].
   'Have pity, O Lord! Have pity, O Christ! Have pity, O Lord!'

This excessively simplified version must be seen side by side with the form of the pontifical Laudes of which Innocent III was the author [the text is printed on p. 134 of the work quoted above]. The most striking feature is that in both cases each of the two authorities is mentioned separately and as though isolated from Christian society as a whole. But, whereas the Pope has himself acclaimed as *a Deo decretus*, the Emperor has lost his former designations – 'pacific' and 'crowned by God'.

II *The Emperor as the Pope's vassal*. Gervase of Tilbury, *Otia Imperialia*, Book II, chapters xviii–xix. [*Monumenta Germaniae, Scriptores*, Vol. XXVII, pp. 378 and 382.]

The author is explaining to Otto IV (shortly after his deposition in 1210 by Innocent III) what are the essential characteristics of the Roman Empire in the West.

'From that time [the time of Charlemagne], because the Empire of the Greeks had become weak, the title of Emperor returned to certain regions in the West. This fact led to some confusion since the dualism, created by the fact that two princes bore the title of emperor, diminished the power of each. While the Empire of the Greeks depends on God alone, the Pope asserts that the Empire in the West depends solely on the Roman see. This explains a new and unusual change – the Pope alone bears the imperial insignia, whereas the Emperor has at his disposal only the usual insignia borne by other kings, to demonstrate his status as emperor. The Pope appears as Lord of the City and of the seat of the Empire, and the Emperor, though he has the appearance of a sovereign, is called a minister of the Pope: in temporal matters he is the executor of the apostles while the Pope is the vicar of Christ and is called the successor of the apostles. . . . The princes of Germany have the right to elect the Emperor but it is the Pope who confirms the election and performs the consecration. Another innovation is that although he is called master, the Emperor is not consecrated as such. In fact, he does not receive the imperial insignia, which the Pope keeps for himself, as they were conferred on him alone. What is more, he is consecrated by the Pope alone, at a modest altar, on the right side of the basilica of St Peter, whereas on the other hand the Pope is given the imperial insignia and receives his anointing before the High Altar, reserved for this purpose alone. The Emperor at Constantinople, though he has changed his capital, has not altered his status and he bears the insignia as a right and not as a result of any kind of concession by the Pope. He does not call for the aid of the supreme pontiff in the capacity of one who grants the Empire, but enjoys his status fully in his own right.'

[Chapter xix] 'That is why the Empire is not thine – it is the Empire of Christ; it is not thy Empire but Peter's. Thou didst not acquire it thyself, thou dost but hold it from the vicar of Christ and the successor of Peter. It will not belong perpetually to thee, because thou art not perpetual, neither with nor in it. . . . The Pope . . . himself is thy judge, but he cannot be judged by any man. . . . Thou shalt lose nothing of what belongs to thee if thou abandon'st to Peter what is Peter's. To Peter Constantine surrendered the Empire of the West, which was served by the kingdom of the Franks, the kingdom of the Teutons, the kingdom of the Britons, and more than that, by the entire West and the parts of the world adjacent thereto. It was Constantine's wish that the entire West should serve Peter, under Christ. It was as a result of a concession by the Pope and not through her own efforts that Rome regained the imperial title in the time of Charlemagne; again, it was a papal concession which transmitted the Empire to the King of the Franks; and it is still as a result of a concession by the Pope that to-day the Empire is due to the King of the Teutons and not to the King of the Franks. The Empire does not go to him whom the Germans desire, but to him whom the Pope has chosen.'

This text reveals how much the author was under the influence of the doctrines of the Donation of Constantine and of the *Translatio* of the Empire, and also what conclusions he drew from Innocent III's policies. He describes most strikingly the contrast between the Empire of the West and the Byzantine Empire – and incidentally, like the Western historiographers as a whole, he denies the latter the right to the title 'Roman'. He makes some mistakes. For example, it was wrong to state that the Roman Emperor had not insignia of his own – perhaps this arose from his own trend of thought. On the other hand, what he says about the anointing of the prince before the altar of St Maurice is confirmed by the *ordo* of Innocent, which was used for the first time for Otto IV's anointing in October 1208: though it is not correct to say that the Pope alone performed the consecration – since the tenth century that had always in fact been the prerogative of the three cardinal-bishops of Albano, Ostia and Porto. The suggestion that Otto ought to render to St Peter what is his, is aimed at and condemns the policy adopted immediately after his coronation by Otto IV, when he sought to 'recuperate' the provinces of the Papal States and in particular to conquer the kingdom of Sicily (vassal of the Holy See). It was this policy which made the Pope depose his former protégé. Lastly, it should be noted how insistently the author uses the word *beneficium* in connexion with the Empire – a word which we have translated in as general a way as possible by 'concession'. There can scarcely be any doubt that in Gervase's mind this expression had a feudal significance and that the 'concession' implied that the beneficiary was bound by the obligations of a vassal.

XIX   THE ENTHRONEMENT OF GREGORY IX

[VITA GREGORII IX, P. FABRE, Le '*Liber censuum*' *de l'Église romaine*, II, Paris, 1905, p. 19, chapter iv.]

'On that day (19th March, 1227), to the great joy of the Romans, the people and the clergy rejoicing gaily, in the midst of a huge gathering of men and women, Gregory, wearing the pontifical mitre, was enthroned in the Lateran Palace. Then the Church took off her mourning-clothes and the walls of the city, which had been half-destroyed, were restored to their former splendour. The following Sunday, St Benedict's day (21st March), the blessèd Father, accompanied by the prelates doing homage to him, and in the presence of an innumerable audience of Romans, was greeted by tremendous demonstrations of joy in the basilica of the prince of the apostles, where he, who was also a venerable prince himself, received the *pallium*, symbol of his omnipotence. After Mass had been celebrated, the supreme pontiff, glittering with gold and precious stones, returned to the Lateran. On the Sunday of the Resurrection (28th March), after the liturgical mysteries had been celebrated in the basilica of the glorious Virgin, the Pope returned to his palace, wearing his crown and surrounded by rejoicing people. The following day, the Monday known as *in Albis*, in the basilica of the blessèd Peter, crowned with the double diadem, he appeared transfigured with radiance, as are the Cherubim; in the midst of a procession of cardinals clothed in crimson robes, surrounded by the clergy and countless prelates, preceded by the papal insignia, mounted on a horse which was adorned with a precious collar, he could be seen passing through the various quarters of the venerable city, exposed to the admiration of all. In one place people would burst out singing, in another they acclaimed him with jubilant cries, while the sound of people singing the *Kyrie eleison* with loud voice could be heard all over the town. The open places were decorated with gold and silver, and brilliant carpets from Egypt covered the ground . . . the air was fragrant with many soft perfumes. The crowd was excited by the noise of trumpets and enthusiasm overflowed – many people simply shouted in order to see who could make most noise. The judges and notaries were gleaming in silken garments; the legion of nobles wore tunics of cloth of gold and the colonies of Greeks and Jews paid ample tribute to the vicar of Christ by saying his praises each in their own language, while children improvised songs in his honour which they sang in their piping voices. And so, in the midst of an incredible multitude of people, carrying palms and flowers, preceded by the senator and the prefect of the great city, who walked on foot and held the bridle of the Pope's horse, the very holy man was led to the Lateran.'

The *Vita Gregorii* was written by a senior official of the Apostolic Chamber about 1239–40, at the request of the Pope who was at that moment engaged in a serious dispute with Frederick II. The translation above can give only an imperfect impression of the language in which it is written – rhythmic, flattering to excess, full of subtle metaphors, antitheses, associations of ideas, in which there are very many words which describe impressions on the senses – sight, hearing, smell and touch – the author has an astonishing gift for painting the scene.

Incidentally this account does recall the imperial '*scenopegia*' described by Benzo of Alba[39] who also showed the Emperor's accession as being spread over several days. Here the rites involved in the enthronement proper of Gregory IX are mingled with those of the stational liturgy of the festival of Easter, in such a way as to give an unequalled brilliance to the pontiff's inauguration. Thus we have:

(a) The enthronement of Gregory IX in the Lateran on the day of his election.
(b) His consecration in St Peter's, about which only one point is recorded – the imposition of the *pallium*. The phrase 'symbol of omnipotence', is a summary of the formula pronounced, on this occasion, by the archdeacon.[40]
(c) Easter Day: a station at the Church of Santa Maria Maggiore, after which the Pope returns to the Lateran, wearing his crown on his head.
(d) Easter Monday: after the stational Mass at St Peter's, the Pope is conducted back to his palace by a great procession.

---

[39] See above, p. 188.
[40] *Pallium, plenitudinem scilicet pontificalis officii*, cf. M. ANDRIEU, *Le pontifical romain*, Vol. II, 1940, p. 374.

From all this it would appear that the author's main intention was to stress the imperial nature of the papacy in the light of the Donation of Constantine. The principal accent is laid on the Lateran Palace, which is mentioned no less than three times, because it is the emblem of the pope-emperor's aspirations. Similarly, all the exterior symbols of the Empire are evoked. So as to ensure that they are put in the limelight, the author does not mingle them, but takes them one at a time and is not afraid to arrange them in an order which sometimes breaks the unity of certain rites. It is, for example, striking that the Pope's coronation, which, according to the Pontifical, takes place on the day of his consecration, does not appear in the description at this point, where it is only the *pallium* which is mentioned. On the other hand, the double diadem already hinted at by the comment about the Pope being covered in gold and jewels, emerges into full light on Easter Sunday and Easter Monday. In the same way, it will be noted that the author keeps his description of the papal procession for the last day, whereas in fact it takes place earlier – on the day of the Pope's consecration.[41]

The Lateran Palace, the mitre and the diadem, the procession and the service of the *strator*; all the imperial insignia are thus presented to the reader in turn so that he may be helped to recognise in Gregory IX the successor of Constantine, and doubtless more as well: he who is described sometimes as the *venerandus princeps*, sometimes as the *summus pontifex*, is in fact the vicar of Christ, the very holy man. And so the papal procession, a replica of that of the Emperor on the day of his coronation, represents in the last analysis the entry of Our Lord Himself to Jerusalem.

XX   FREDERICK II'S CONCEPT OF THE EMPIRE AS A ROMAN INSTITUTION

Declaration made by the Emperor to the Romans after his victory at Corte-nuova. [HUILLARD-BREHOLLES, *Historia diplomatica Friderici II*, Vol. V, I, p. 162 – January 1238.]

For us it is an obligation to exalt during our reign the prestige of the City concerning which the ancient peoples were of the opinion that it would be made greater by the glory of victories, and this obligation is laid on us partly by omnipotent reason which gives orders to kings and partly by the natural order; we proclaim with the greatest solemnity, that we are also legally bound to carry out this mission. Indeed, if a victory is traced back to the nature of its cause, we cannot add to the imperial glory without at the same time promoting the honour of the City in which we recognise the origin of the Empire. But although imperial majesty is beyond all laws, it is not on that account exempt from the judgment of reason which is the mother of the Law. . . . Our will would be acting in contravention of all reason if we were to allow those who shed glory on the splendour of the Roman emperor to be frustrated of their

[41] See the detailed description of the procession in ANDRIEU, *op. cit.*, p. 376.

triumphal joys in a Roman victory, if we were to deprive you of the fruits of the affair which we have conducted in your name, in triumphing over the rebels by invoking the name of Rome,[42] if we were not to hand over our honour and our glory to the royal City, which lately sent us into Germany to acquire the pinnacle of the Empire, like a mother who loosens the embrace in which she held her son.[43]

We attribute to your efforts all that we have, under happy auspices, been able to accomplish in recent times, now that we return, adorned with the glory of a magnificent success, to the City which we left with the fear of a doubtful fate. Thus we cause the ancient Caesars to be revived, those to whom the senate and the people of Rome accorded triumphs and laurel crowns for their mighty deeds accomplished under their victorious insignia; thus by making an example of this our present benevolence, we are preparing from afar the way towards the realisation of your wishes,[44] since, after our victory over Milan, we destined for you, as booty and spoil of beaten enemies, the chariot of that town, capital of the Italian faction: accept it as an advance guarantee of our mighty deeds and our glory; we shall pay over the whole of the remainder to you when we have achieved the pacification of Italy, the seat of our Roman Empire.

Welcome then, with thankfulness, O Quirites, the victory of your Emperor; may it cause a great hope to be born in you for, if we willingly conform to the custom of the ancients in celebrating a feast, we aspire with an even greater will towards the restoration of the ancient nobility of the City.

XXI THE CONCEPT OF THE EMPIRE AS A ROMAN INSTITUTION DURING THE INTERREGNUM

I *Manfred's manifesto to the Romans* [drawn up by the Sicilian notary, Peter of Prezza, *Mon. Germ., Constitutiones*, II, No. 424, pp. 558–65; 24th May, 1265].

EXTRACTS

1 *Manfred's hereditary rights* (paragraph 2, p. 559), '. . . As for us, we are bone of the bone and flesh of the flesh of the highly respected imperial dynasty and we remember with what attentive zeal, what lengthy struggles, the divine emperors of triumphant memory, our father, our grandfather, our great-grandfather, our great-great-grandfather and our great-great-great-grandfather and other ancestors to the total number of twelve, who in the past ruled to the

---

[42] According to the *Annales de Plaisance* (ed. HUILLARD-BREHOLLES, Paris, 1856, p. 169), the war cry of Frederick II's troops at the Battle of Cortenuova was *Miles Roma! Miles imperator!*

[43] This was an allusion to the events of 1211: on the initiative of Innocent III (here passed over in silence), Frederick II was acclaimed emperor by the Romans before he went to Germany.

[44] This is probably a reference to the hopes of a restoration, which are also expressed in the last sentence of the text.

greatest satisfaction of the entire world, devoted their whole care to the increasing glory of the Empire and the republic, to the peace of the world and the welfare of mankind; we direct our glance confidently towards the glorious pinnacle of the Empire in order that, by virtue of the imperial prerogative which we bear in our blood because we have belonged since the beginning to a dynasty of emperors, we may shine with a more brilliant light than the other kings in the world; not that we may be wrapped in a wavering and deceitful sophistry, but that we may be glorified with good fortune and by wearing the imperial diadem, by the grace of divine aid.'

2 *The call to Rome: contrast between the past and the present* (paragraph 17, page 563). After denouncing the scandalous behaviour of which the Church was guilty against the Empire, and declaring the Donation of Constantine null and void, Manfred cries:

'Arise, O Rome! recall how in the past a decree of thy decurions, the authority of the senate and the acclamation of thy people publicly installed thy emperor and how, without any intervention by the prelates of the Roman Church, he was crowned, in the presence of thy proconsuls, by the illustrious prefect of the city. And now, the Roman Church has robbed thee of nearly all that; stripped of thy privileges by its malpractices and encroachments, thou hast lain before it, like an orphan who has not been able to reclaim her rights, even unto these present unhappy days. O fortunate root and creator of the empire, thou gavest birth to the first Caesar, great Rome, head of the world, and now thou lackest a head. Once thou didst command all the countries in the world and now, deprived of the guardianship which the emperor assured to thee, thou art weakened, a prey to civil wars and constantly torn apart by foreign influences. Thou didst govern all the countries in the world and didst assure peace to them by thy rule; now thou canst not even govern thyself, deprived as thou art of the aid of him who governed thee. In former times the permanent seat of thy Holy Church lay within thy walls; there the pontiff was traditionally elected; now foreign cities and other places have caused the Roman Church to lose its usual residence.[45] Consider therefore what thou hast done and blush, remember who thou art and take action; complain about this Church, which gives thee no maternal care but on the contrary behaves towards thy Empire like a true stepmother.'

3 *The Lex Regia* (paragraph 19, p. 564). 'Nor can the *Lex Regia* deny thee thy great powers, O Rome! It declares that the Roman people transferred the Empire and all their rights to the Emperor; it sees to the making of the Law, but not to the election of the Emperor and not to the form of the Empire.'

[45] The argument that the Pope ought to reside in Rome appears frequently at this time when the pontifical court preferred to remain outside of the city: among other evidence, see the words which Matthew Paris attributed to Brancaleone (*Mon. Germ. Scriptores*, Vol. XXVIII, pp. 333 and 336). The theme was to re-appear, with wider connotations, at the period of the Avignon papacy.

4 Accession to the Empire can take place even against the will of the Romans (paragraphs 20 and 21, p. 564). '. . . We read that Julius Caesar found his way to the pinnacle of the Empire by himself; he did not wear the crown by virtue of being elected by any authority and, what is even more important, he held it against the wish of your senate, since, according to Lucan, he is alleged to have said: "We have taken the Roman Empire to ourselves although the senate did not wish us to." [46] If then he, who had not in his favour birth, rank or the power which casts its radiance about our majesty, could thus make innovations, there is all the more reason why we too can do so, for the following reasons: privileged by our imperial birth and the possession of the Empire, we greatly surpass the first Christian Caesar; [47] secondly we are, O Rome! thy neighbour because of the land which is subject to our great power; and lastly it is customary in our family to defend the freedom of the Empire most valiantly and to keep all our promises.

'If you will study the triumphant deeds of our victorious great-great-grandfather, O Romans! you will see that Frederick I became tired of the envious gall of the prelates of the Church, which now is a very hard mother and looks on our majesty with a menacing eye; Milan, too, was not willing to welcome him as emperor; he besieged the town with powerful means and tamed it to such an extent that that city, which had intended to build itself up into a rock hostile to the Empire, was finally broken up by him into three boroughs. Even thou, O Rome, didst refuse to receive him; so, after hard battles, he came to seek thee at thy gates; overcoming many different enemies he penetrated with all his power, victoriously and violently, within thy walls; then he took the crown himself from the altar of St Peter, on the advice of his princes: having first forbidden the clergy to participate in the ceremony, served by the princes, the counts, the barons and the nobles, as is laid down in the *ordo*, he himself placed the diadem on his glorious brow and was then the fortunate emperor of his people and of all those on earth who rallied to him.' [48]

5 Conclusion (paragraph 22, p. 565). 'What German, what Spaniard, what Englishman, what Frank, what Provençal, in a word, what foreigner, could dominate thee, O Rome, against our wish and take over for thy welfare the service of thy administration and the government of thy people and of thy senate? What nation could oppose the arrival of our power and prevent us from ourselves ascending in triumph to the Capitol?'

II *Letter from Pope Clement IV to the Romans.* [MARTÈNE–DURAND, *Thesaurus novus anecdotorum*, Paris, 1717, II, col. 591–2; 3rd May, 1268.]

In this letter addressed to John Anibaldi, 'proconsul of the Romans,' the Pope puts the accent on the spiritual and religious character of Rome's mission,

---

[46] *Pharsalia*, I, 274. [47] Charlemagne.

[48] A tendentious interpretation of the events of 1155, which was meant to constitute a precedent allowing Manfred to realise his dream of acceding to the Empire: i.e. a coronation from which the Pope would be excluded and which would take place with or without the consent of the Romans.

which he contrasts with the domination which the city formerly exercised: since the fall of the Empire, Rome is no longer anything more than the pontifical city. We quote the preamble to the missive.

'From ancient times the city of Rome made rebel nations subject to her and was full of pride and arrogance as a consequence of her victories over numerous kings. Nevertheless, honoured by the presence of the holy apostles and consecrated by their blood, she reached such a degree of pre-eminence that she became the residence of the two supreme powers, the papacy and the Empire; in territory, she is smaller than the world; despite this her present status is greater than that she had formerly when she exercised power which was founded, not on right, but on force. Exalted since then to a greater position, she procured, by the benevolence of the divine will, the honour of the pontifical pulpit, without losing any of the glory of the pre-eminence of the Empire, which she had, however, scarcely deserved. This honour was certainly not due in any way to the men of the past who had spilled innocent blood, but He Whose eyes see everything without veils had foreseen that there would be born in Rome a people faithful and catholic, who would honour the relics of the saints, would render the submissive homage due to the successors of the apostles, would endow and enrich the churches, would maintain their ministers throughout the lands subject to their authority and would develop the worship of God. All this was fulfilled in the happy course of time, according to Providence, which makes no mistakes in its counsels,[49] since Rome did indeed produce sons and train disciples, who devoted themselves to the tasks of which we have just been speaking, and to other works, with such zeal that she was able to enlighten all the regions of the world with the rays of her goodness. . . . '

XXII   THE POSITIONS TAKEN UP BY BONIFACE VIII TOWARDS THE EMPIRE

1 The Pope receives the ambassadors of Albert of Hapsburg, shortly after the battle of Göllheim in 1298.

'In the following year (1298), Albert of Hapsburg sent two ambassadors to the Pope, Boniface VIII, to announce to him that it was his intention to come to him to receive the imperial crown from the apostolic throne, in accordance with traditional custom. The Pope replied to them that Albert had not been lawfully elected and that he was unworthy of the Empire, having wickedly declared war against his overlord (Adolf of Nassau) and treacherously put him to death. Sitting on a throne, wearing on his head the diadem of Constantine, his right hand on the hilt of the sword with which he was girt, he cried out: "Am I not the supreme pontiff? Is this throne not the pulpit of Peter? Is it not my duty to watch over the rights of the Empire? It is I who am Caesar, it is I who am emperor!" And with these words he sent them away.' (Chronicle of Francesco Pipino, ed. MURATORI, *Rerum Italicarum scriptores*, IX, p. 745.)

[49] Taken from the prayers for the seventh Sunday after Whitsun.

A similar account can be found in the chronicle of Ferreto of Vicenza in which the following suggestions are also attributed to the Pope, after he has rejected Albert's candidature: 'Let him command in Germany; for our part, we shall reign over the Latin nations which are subject to our authority.' (MURATORI, *op. cit.*, p. 994.)

Even though it may not be completely reliable from a historical point of view this passage does provide valuable evidence of the way in which Boniface VIII appeared to be pope-emperor to his contemporaries. The words which Ferreto de Vicenza attributed to him reflect the general opinion concerning the inherent dualism of the Empire; perhaps we should also see a connexion between them and the plan which the Pope cherished at that time to make his nephew Peter Caetani a patrician of Rome and to nominate him procurator of the vacant imperial throne.[50]

2 At Anagni on the 8th September, 1303, Boniface VIII, 'abandoned by the cardinals, . . . declared to those accompanying him that, betrayed as Christ was, . . . he wished at least to die as a pope. He made them bring him the mantle of St Peter[51] then he sat down on the pontifical throne, wearing on his head the crown of Constantine, holding in his hand the keys and the cross', to await the arrival of Sciarra Colonna. (Chronicle of G. Villani, Book VIII, chapter xxxiii, in MURATORI, *Scriptores*, Vol. XIII.)

XXIII   THE LEGEND OF CONSTANTINE INTERPRETED BY JACQUES DE VORAGINE

(JACQUES DE VORAGINE: *The Golden Legend, life of St Sylvester.*)

Constantine, as a punishment for his persecutions and his tyranny, fell ill of an incurable disease, and became a leper; at length, following advice given by the priests of the idols, he had three thousand children brought together that they might be put to death and that he might bathe in their blood. But when he went out to make his way to the place where the bath was to be prepared, the mothers of the children ran to meet him, their hair dishevelled, lamenting and crying loudly. At that, Constantine wept, ordering his chariot to stop and said: 'Hear me, all you who are my companions in arms and all people who are here! The Empire of Rome became worthy of respect because it had its origins in pity[52] and pity gave us that ordinance which decrees that whoever kills a child in war will be punished by sentence of death. And it would surely be a great cruelty to do to our own children what we do not allow to be done to the

---

[50] C. C. BURDACH, *Rienzo und die geistige Wandlung seiner Zeit*, p. 436.

[51] This mantle is no other than the 'crimson *chlamys*' given by Constantine to Sylvester, Peter's successor, the *cappa rubea* which a pope received immediately after his election, from the archdeacon who then pronounced the following words: *Investio te de papatu romano ut praesis urbi et orbi.*

[52] *De fonte nascitur pietatis*: to be understood here in the sense of humanity.

children of strangers: what good would it do us to conquer the barbarians, if we were in turn conquered by our own brutality? For while it is through the strength of the fighting people that we conquer foreign nations, the ability to conquer vice and sin comes from virtue and good morals. In past wars we have proved stronger than the foreigners, in this particular battle we shall be stronger than ourselves. He who is defeated in this struggle wins a victory, even though he is vanquished; but if pity yields to pitilessness the victor is, indeed, vanquished after the victory. On the present occasion then – let pity triumph! We shall be able to conquer all our adversaries if we ourselves are conquered by pity alone; for he who demonstrates that he is the slave of pity is thereby established as lord over all . . .' Thereupon, he ordered that the children be returned to their mothers and he gave them gifts of money.

XXIV   THE TWO SUNS

[Dante, *Purgatory*, XVI, lines 66–114, translated by Dorothy L. Sayers (Penguin Classics, 1955, pp. 190–1).]

The poet interrogates Marco Lombardo on the cause of evil – is it to be located in heaven or here on earth? This is the reply he receives:

'Brother, the world is blind,
   And thou art of it, sure enough,' said he.

'By you who live, causation's all assigned
   To the sole stars, as though they could compel
   Into their own fixt paths all things combined.

If that were so, it would destroy free will
   Within you, and it were unjust indeed
   You should have joy for good or grief for ill.

Promptings of motion from your stars proceed –
   I say not all, but if I did, what then?
   Light's given you to know right from wrong at need.

And free will, so its stuff can stand the strain
   Of its first tussles with the stars, will fight,
   If nourished well, to win the whole campaign;

For of a nobler nature, mightier might,
   You're the free subjects – might which doth create
   A mind in you that's no star's perquisite.

So, if the world now goes with crooked gait
   The cause is in yourselves for you to trace;
   I'll be thy scout therein to set thee straight

Forth of His hands whose brooding tenderness
    Loves her or ere she comᵉs to be, is brought,
    Laughing and weeping, like a babe that plays,

The simple, infant soul, that, all untaught,
    But moved by a glad Maker, turns with pleasure
    To this or that by which her fancy's caught.

First she's attracted by some trifling treasure,
    Then runs, beguiled, in hot pursuit to scour,
    Save manage sway her love with the curb's pressure.

Hence we did need the curb of legal power,
    And need a ruler, one that could, and should,
    Glimpse the true city, or at least the tower.

The laws are there, but what hand makes them good?
    None; for the shepherd that goes on before
    Parts not the hoof, though he can chew the cud.

Therefore the flock, seeing their guide set store
    By such goods only as themselves have craved,
    Batten on these, and look for nothing more.

Clear cause, then, why the world's so ill-behaved
    Is that it's governed after an ill mode,
    Not that the nature in you is depraved.

Of old, when Rome reformed the world, she showed
    Two suns to lighten the twin ways that went
    One with the other; world's road and God's road;

But one has quenched the other; the sword's blent
    Now with the crook; when one and other meet
    Their fusion must produce bad government;

For one fears not the other when one seat
    Holds both; believ'st thou not that this is so?
    The plant's known by its fruit – look to the wheat!'

Chronological Tables

Chronological Tables

395 Death of Theodosius. The Roman Empire is divided into two parts.

406 Start of the Germanic invasions of the West.

410 Capture of Rome by Alaric's Visigoths.

414 Alaric's successor, Ataulf, marries Galla Placidia, sister of the Emperor Honorius.

440–61 Pontificate of Leo the Great. The primacy of the Roman Church, declared by him, is contested in the East (Canon 28 of the Council of Chalcedon, 451).

451 The Huns invade the West. Battle of Châlons.

455 Death of Valentinian III. Sack of Rome by the Vandals.

476 Deposition of Romulus Augustulus by Odovacar. Italy suffers the same fate as the rest of the West, at that time completely in the hands of the barbarians.

484–519 First schism between the Western and Eastern churches, caused by the policy of the emperors in relation to Monophysism.

492–6 Pontificate of Gelasius I.

493–526 Theodoric, King of the Ostrogoths, but also in control of the militia and a patrician.

481–511 Clovis, King of the Franks, conqueror (in 507) of the Visigoths, comes to Tours, where he is accorded an honorific Roman title by the Emperor Anastasius.

526 Pope John I at Constantinople; quasi-imperial reception accorded to the pontiff.

527–65 Reign of Justinian; partial restoration of the Western Empire.

537–55 Pontificate of Vigilius; the papacy humbled by the imperial government.

568 The Lombards in Italy. Beginning of a conquest finally completed in the middle of the seventh century; partition of Italy into two zones.

590–604 Pontificate of Gregory the Great. Beginning of the conversion of the Anglo-Saxons.

633–44 Beginning of the Arab conquests (Syria, Egypt, Persia).

638–81 Fresh break of Rome with the East. Monothelism dispute.

663 The Emperor Constans in Rome. Last visit of a Roman emperor to the West.

692 'Quinisextus' Council of Constantinople; hostility towards Roman customs.

696–708   The Arabs conquer Africa.

708–15   Pontificate of Constantine I; in 710–11 he is received at Byzantium with the highest honours.

711   The Arabs conquer Spain; collapse of Visigoth rule.

726   Beginning of the Images Dispute; edict issued by the Emperor Leo III.

726–30   Italian revolution. Encouraged by Gregory II, Rome and Ravenna break free from Byzantine domination.

731–51   The Lombards, under their kings Liutprand and Aistulf, once more menace Rome; they take possession of Ravenna.

733   Victory of Charles Martel over the Arabs near Poitiers.

741–7   Saint Boniface, apostle of Germany, reforms the Frankish church.

751   Accession of the Carolingian dynasty; anointing of Pepin by St Boniface.

754   Stephen II's voyage to Francia; the papacy and the Carolingian dynasty form an alliance. The Pope anoints Pepin a second time, also his two sons, conferring the title of Roman patrician on all three. In the East, the Emperor Constantine V condemns the worship of Images.

755–6   The Franks carry out expeditions into Italy. The papal state takes shape.

c. 756–60   The Donation of Constantine is composed.

768   Charlemagne succeeds to the throne; beginning of a reign directed towards a simultaneous aggrandisement of the Kingdom of the Franks and *dilatatio imperii christiani.*

773   At the request of Pope Hadrian I, Charlemagne declares war on the Lombards.

774   Easter: Charlemagne's first visit to Rome; he is received in the style of an emperor or his representative. He promises a donation to Hadrian. June: fall of Pavia; annexation of the Kingdom of Lombardy.

781   In Byzantium, Constantine VI succeeds to the throne under the guardianship of his mother Irene. The King of the Franks makes his second stay in Rome; plans for a marriage between his daughter Rothrude and Constantine.

785   Hadrian I decrees prayers of thanksgiving for the victory of Charlemagne over the Saxons.

787   The worship of Images re-instituted by the Second Nicene Council.

788   Charles's third visit to Rome; anti-Byzantine policy.

790–2   Preparation of the Caroline Books.

794   Council of Frankfurt, representing the Western church.

795   Accession of Leo III. Strengthening of the alliance between Charles and the papacy.

796   Leo III sends the standard of the city of Rome to the King of the Franks.

797   Constantine VI blinded and deposed on the orders of Irene; the imperial throne is declared vacant.

798   All papal instruments are dated in Rome according to the years of Charlemagne's reign. The Pope has the two famous mosaics executed in the apse of St Susanna and the triclinium of the Lateran.

799   Insurrection in Rome against Leo III; the Pope visits Francia and appeals to Charlemagne for his support. Meeting at Paderborn.

800   Charlemagne's fourth visit to Rome.

23rd December: the Pope takes an oath disclaiming the charges made against him. Arrival of an embassy from the Patriarch of Jerusalem, bringing Charlemagne the keys of the Holy Sepulchre and of the city. 25th December: coronation of the Emperor.

801   In Rome, Charlemagne sits in judgment on the authors of the revolt against Leo III, in accordance with the *Lex Romana*.

802   Dethronement of Irene in Constantinople; accession of Nicephorus I.

804–10   Conflict between the two empires in Venetia and Dalmatia.

806   *Ordinatio Regni*. No mention of the Empire. The notion of the unity of the *Regnum* is nevertheless maintained despite the projected partition.

811   Accession of Michael I.

812   Peace between the two empires.

813   Louis the Pious is made the Emperor's associate.

814   28th January: death of Charlemagne. Accession of Louis the Pious.

816   Pope Stephen IV anoints Louis the Pious emperor at Rheims.

817   *Ordinatio Imperii*. Lothair is made the Emperor's associate.

823   Paschal I anoints Lothair at Rome.

824   *Constitutio romana:* organisation of the Emperor's supreme authority at Rome.

843   Treaty of Verdun.

847   The Saracens plunder St Peter's at Rome; Leo IV fortifies the Leonine city.

850   Louis II anointed emperor.

855   Death of Lothair.

858–68   Pontificate of Nicholas I.

869   Charles the Bald, King of the Western Franks, is anointed King of Lorraine at Metz.

871   Louis II's letter to the Emperor Basil I.

875   Death of Louis II. Pope John VIII raises Charles the Bald to the imperial throne.

876   Italy and Western Francia confirm the Pope's initiative. Charles the Bald defeated at Andernach by the sons of Louis the German.

877   Death of Charles the Bald.

881   Charles the Fat, last of the sons of Louis the German, anointed emperor by Pope John VIII.

880–7   Reconstitution of the former Carolingian Empire followed by its definitive dismemberment into a number of kingdoms.

891   Guy and Lambert of Spoleto accede to the Empire.

896   Arnulf, King of Germany, who had seized Rome by force, is anointed emperor by Pope Formosus.

899   Death of Arnulf.

901   Louis of Provence is anointed emperor.

917   Alfonso III, King of León, is referred to as emperor in a document issued by his successor.

919   The Carolingian dynasty extinguished in Germany. Accession of Henry I of Saxony.

924   Death of the Emperor Berengar of Friuli; the imperial throne unoccupied.

925   Union of Lorraine and the Kingdom of Germany.

924–30   Athelstan, King of England; the title of emperor makes its appearance in England.

926   Henry I acquires the Holy Lance.

924–54 Alberic's principate in Rome.

'Renovation' of the institutions of the past within the city.

933 Henry I's victory over the Hungarians in Thuringia.

936 Otto I's accession; he is anointed king at Aix-la-Chapelle.

940–50 Otto I intervenes in French affairs on several occasions.

942 Otto imposes his guardianship, if not sovereignty, on the Kingdom of Burgundy.

c. 950 Adso of Montiérender composes his treatise on the Antichrist.

951 Otto becomes King of Italy.

955 August: Otto I's victory over the Hungarians at the Lechfeld.

October: Otto's victory over the Slavs at Recknitz.

December: accession of John XII at Rome.

955–83 Christianity and Germanism advance between the Elbe and the Oder and even beyond (Otto gains sovereignty over the Warthe region).

962 2nd February: Otto I crowned emperor.

963 Accession of Nicephorus Phocas in Byzantium.

966 In Southern Italy the princes of Capua and Benevento recognise Otto I's sovereignty; cause of conflict between the new empire and Byzantium.

967 Pope John XIII places the imperial crown on the head of Otto II.

968 Military defeat of Otto I at Bari. Liutprand of Cremona goes on a mission to Byzantium.

969 Revolution in Constantinople: Nicephorus assassinated and replaced by John Zimisces.

972 Celebration of the marriage in Rome of Otto II and Theophano, niece or great-niece of John Zimisces.

973 23rd March: Assembly of Quedlinburg.

7th May: death of Otto I and accession of Otto II.

974 The Romans revolt against the imperial pope Benedict VI. The position is restored with difficulty.

978 King Lothair's expedition to Aix-la-Chapelle; Otto II beneath the walls of Paris.

982 Otto II beaten by the Saracens at Cape Colonna.

983 General rising among the trans-Elbe Slavs.

Assembly of Verona, at which Otto III is proclaimed king.

Death of Otto II.

983–91 Regency of Theophano; situation gradually restored.

984 John Crescentius assumes the title of patrician, in Rome; the city is *de facto* independent of the Empire.

987 Accession of Hugh Capet in France.

996 Otto III starts to rule in person.

First Italian expedition.

Gregory V becomes pope and crowns Otto.

John Crescentius is exiled, but returns after the Emperor has departed.

997 Battles against the Liutizes of Brandenburg.

Adalbert, former bishop of Prague, undertakes a mission in Prussia and there suffers martyrdom.

Gerbert at the imperial court.

998–9 Otto's second visit to Italy.

Renovatio Imperii Romanorum.

999 Gerbert becomes pope under the name of Sylvester II.
1000 Otto III's pilgrimage to the tomb of St Adalbert in Gnesen.
The Polish church is established; Boleslav, duke of Poland, becomes co-adjutor of the Empire.
Otto opens Charlemagne's tomb at Aix-la-Chapelle.
1001 Otto III visits Italy again.
The Donation of Constantine is denounced.
A king's crown is sent to Stephen of Hungary.
The Emperor is driven out of Rome by a revolt starting in February and a number of movements in opposition to him make themselves felt.
1002 24th January: death of Otto III and accession of Henry II – end of the dream of universality.
1014 Henry II crowned emperor.
Rome in the hands of the House of Tusculum.
The beginning of Church reform.
1018 Last appearance of the title of emperor in England.
1024–39 Reign of Conrad II; the Empire supreme in Europe.
1027 Conrad II crowned by John XIX, in the presence of Rudolf, King of Burgundy, and Canute, King of Denmark.
Increasing Romanisation of the concept of empire.
1033 The Kingdom of Burgundy incorporated in the Empire.
1037–65 Ferdinand I, King of León and Castile; the title of emperor is attributed to him.
1039–56 Reign of Henry III.
1046 Henry intervenes in the affairs of the Roman Church; three rival popes are deposed and a new pontiff, Clement II, is nominated, who crowns Henry emperor. Henry also takes possession of the insignia of the order of patricians.
1048–54 Pontificate of Leo IX; the party in favour of Church reform seizes the Holy See.
1054 Schism of Michael Caerularius, patriarch of Constantinople.
1056 Accession of Henry IV; difficulties during his minority; troubles in Germany.
1057 Death of Victor II, the last of the series of German popes which had begun in 1046.
Election of Stephen IX.
Cardinal Humbert's treatise *Adversus simoniacos.*
1059 Nicholas II's decree on papal elections.
1060 The papacy enters into an alliance with the Norman princes of Southern Italy.
1073 Accession of Gregory VII.
Dictatus papae.
1076 Start of the Investiture Contest.
The German Synod of Worms declares Gregory VII deposed from the pontificate. Gregory VII deposes Henry IV.
1077 Canossa. Henry IV's German opponents elect Rudolf of Rheinfelden king.
Civil war in Germany.
Alfonso VI, King of León and Castile, takes the title of emperor in official documents.

1080 Henry IV presides over the Synod of Brixen, which deposes Gregory VII and names as his successor Guibert of Ravenna (Pope Clement III).

1081–4 Henry IV faces Rome.
Composition of the false prerogatives of Investiture.
The Ravenna jurist, Peter Crassus, draws up his Defence of Henry IV.

1084 Henry IV in control of those parts of Rome which lie on the left bank of the Tiber.
He is crowned emperor by Clement III.
The Normans enter the town after he leaves it.

1085 Death of Gregory VII at Salerno.

1086 *Ad Heinricum* by Benzo of Alba.

1088–99 Pontificate of Urban II; victory of the Gregorian reform.

c. 1088 Foundation by Irnerius of the Bologna School of Roman Law.

1095 Urban II preaches in favour of a Crusade at the Council of Clermont.

1106 Death of Henry IV. Accession of his son, Henry V, who with the support of Pope Paschal II had been in revolt against his father since 1104. Conflict immediately breaks out again.

1110–17 Alfonso the Battler takes the title of emperor.

1111 Concordat of Sutri; Henry V crowned emperor; receives from Paschal II the prerogative of investiture.

1118 Irnerius, in Henry V's service, reads out the forged prerogatives of investiture to the people of Rome.

1122 Termination of the Investiture Contest. Concordat of Worms.

1125 Accession of Lothair of Supplinburg, very devout supporter of the Church.

c. 1126 onwards Increasing use of the title of emperor by Alfonso VII, King of León and Castile.

c. 1130 Writings of Honorius *Augustodunensis.*

1135 Alfonso VII crowned emperor.

1137 Accession of Conrad III, first ruler of the Hohenstaufen dynasty.

c. 1140 The treatise by Pseudo-Turpin records that, in accordance with a decision made by Charlemagne, the Kingdom of France, successor of the former country of Gaul, is independent of all foreign domination.

1143 The Commune of Rome takes shape.

1143–6 Otto of Freising writes his history of the Two Cities.

1145 Arnold of Brescia in Rome.

1149–50 Conrad III enters into an alliance with the Byzantine Empire against Roger II, King of Sicily.

c. 1150 The *Kaiserchronik* is written by a Ratisbon cleric.

1152 Accession of Frederick I Barbarossa, who immediately uses the title of emperor in a number of official documents.

1154 The Emperor's first contact with the School of Bologna.

1155 18 June: Frederick I crowned emperor.

1156 Rainald of Dassel becomes Frederick's chancellor.

1157 Diet of Besançon: the papal doctrine of empire, put forward by Cardinal Roland, clashes with the concept of empire held by Frederick and Rainald.
A letter to the Emperor from Henry II, King of England.
Death of Alfonso VII; disappearance of the title of emperor in Spain.

1158 Frederick's second Italian expedition.
Diet of Roncaglia.

1159 Two papal elections: Alexander III (Roland) and Victor IV (of moderate views).

1160 Meeting at the instigation of the Emperor, the Council of Pavia proclaims Victor IV.

1162 Diet of Dole: Rainald proclaims Victor IV as lawful pope, in the name of the emperor who rules over Rome. Frederick is unable to persuade Louis VII to support him.

1163 Third Italian expedition; imperial sovereignty is re-established over Tuscany.

1164 Death of Victor IV. Rainald has Paschal III elected.
Diet of Vienna.

1165 Meeting at Würzburg, the majority of the German bishops decide to support Paschal III.
29th December: canonisation of Charlemagne at Aix-la-Chapelle.

1167 Fourth Italian expedition; Frederick in control of Rome; an epidemic of plague in his army compels him to leave the town.

1176 Fifth expedition: Frederick defeated at Legnano by the towns of Lombardy.

1177 The Emperor makes his peace with Alexander III at Venice.

1180 Accession of Philip Augustus in France.

1186 Henry, the Emperor's second son, is crowned King of Italy (*electus Romanorum Imperator*) at Milan, and celebrates his marriage with Constance, heiress to the Kingdom of Sicily.

1187 Treaty of Toul: alliance between the Emperor and Philip Augustus.

1188 At the Diet of Mainz, Frederick takes up the cross, i.e. vows to go on a crusade.

1190 Death of the Emperor, drowned in the Saleph in Cilicia.

1191 Henry VI crowned emperor.

1193 Richard Lionheart, Henry VI's prisoner, pays homage to him for England and receives the Kingdom of Arles in fief.

1195 Henry VI takes up the cross. His brother, Philip of Swabia, marries Irene Angelus.

1195-6 Henry VI prepares a plan designed to ensure that the empire will remain the hereditary right of the House of Hohenstaufen, but the Pope and the German princes refuse to co-operate; all Henry can achieve is the election of his young son, Frederick, as King of the Romans.

1197 28th September: death of Henry VI at Messina.

1198 8th January: accession of Innocent III. Collapse of imperial sovereignty over Italy; the commune of Rome seized by the Pope: Sicily breaks away from the Empire.
Two kings elected in Germany: Philip of Swabia and Otto of Brunswick.

1201 Innocent III accords recognition to Otto, who has paid homage to the Church from the outset.

1202 When Philip's electors make a strong protest (on the grounds that the elections should be independent) Innocent replies with his Decretal *Venerabilem*: the doctrine of the *Translatio*.
Death of Joachim of Floris, the great visionary from Calabria.

1202-8 Civil war in Germany: period of conflict between Plantagenets and Capetians.

1204 Decretal *Per Venerabilem*, giving legal recognition of the complete sovereignty of the King of France.

1209 Otto IV, crowned emperor by Innocent III, endeavours to reinstate imperial domination in Italy. The Pope excommunicates him and raises up a rival in the person of Frederick II, King of Sicily.

1211 Frederick II acclaimed emperor at Rome and elected king at Frankfurt.

1214 Philip Augustus, Frederick II's ally, defeats Otto IV at Bouvines – a victory for the French Carolingian concept.
Frederick II is soon in control of Germany.

1220 Frederick II receives the imperial diadem from Honorius III, Innocent's successor, having first had his son Henry elected king in Germany.

1225 Frederick (who took up the cross in 1215) marries Isabella of Brienne, heir to the Kingdom of Jerusalem, and immediately adopts the title himself.

1211–27 The *Mirror of the Saxons* (*Sachsenspiegel*) is written: the *ordo* of the world is conducted by Two Swords, which are equal.

1226–70 Reign of St Louis.

1227 Accession of Pope Gregory IX, who breaks with the Emperor.

1228–9 Frederick's crusade. He achieves the restitution of the Holy Places to the Christians and crowns himself king at the Holy Sepulchre.

1234 King Henry rebels against his father in Germany and the latter declares war on the league of the Lombardy towns.

1237 Conrad IV is elected king at Vienna.
Frederick vanquishes the Lombardy towns at Cortenuova.

1239 The Emperor is excommunicated for the second time by Gregory IX.

1245 Innocent IV, Gregory's successor, deposes Frederick at the Council of Lyons.

1246 Innocent IV supports some princes who elect Henry Raspe King of the Romans.

1247 On the death of Henry Raspe, William of Holland is elected.

1250 13th December: death of Frederick II after five years of bitter fighting in Italy.

1252 Brancaleone dictator of Rome; electors in Brunswick pronounce their views on the election of kings.

1256 Death of William of Holland; Alfonso X proclaimed King of the Romans and emperor, at Soria in Castile.

1257 Alfonso of Castile and Richard of Cornwall both elected king in Germany. Beginning of the Great Interregnum.

1258 Frederick II's son, Manfred, crowned King of Sicily.

1261 Richard of Cornwall and Manfred both elected to the Roman Senate.
Accession of Pope Urban IV.

1263–4 The Kingdom of Sicily granted in fief to Charles of Anjou by Urban IV.
August 1263. Charles of Anjou becomes a Roman senator for the first time.

1265 Accession of Pope Clement IV.
Manfred proposes himself as candidate for the Empire.

1266 Charles of Anjou, having defeated Manfred at Benevento, conquers the Kingdom of Sicily.

1267 Henry of Castile becomes a Roman senator.
Charles of Anjou acts as 'peacemaker' in Tuscany.

1268 Conradin's expedition.
Charles of Anjou again elected a Roman senator. The Carolingian legend becomes attached to him. The Guelf party wins a victory.

1271 Accession of Pope Gregory X, who seeks to find a formula for a settlement.

1273 End of the Interregnum.
Defeat of the first French candidate for the imperial throne.
Rudolf of Hapsburg is elected King of the Romans and receives his title from Gregory X.

1275-6 The *Mirror of the Swabians* (*Schwabenspiegel*) acknowledges the Pope's right to possess the Two Swords.

1278 Pope Nicholas III produces his 'Constitution', *Fundamenta militantis Ecclesiae*, and has himself elected a Roman senator in his personal capacity.

1280 Proposal by Rudolf of Hapsburg to give the Kingdom of Arles in fief to Charles of Anjou.

1281 Accession of Pope Martin IV. Alexander of Roes writes his *Memoriale*.

1282 30th March: The Sicilian Vespers at Palermo. Charles of Anjou loses Sicily which passes into the hands of Peter III of Aragon, a kinsman of the Hohenstaufens.
The Ghibelline party aroused in Italy.

1285 Death of Charles of Anjou.
Accession of Philip the Fair in France.

1287 Meeting of the German Council of Würzburg where apprehensions are openly expressed about possible changes in the structure of the Empire.
Alexander of Roes writes his *Noticia*.

1292 Adolf of Nassau elected King of the Romans.

1296-7 First phase of the conflict between Boniface VIII (elected in 1294) and the King of France.

1298 Adolf of Nassau deposed by the German princes; election of Albert of Hapsburg who defeats and kills the former king at the battle of Göllheim. Boniface VIII appoints himself judge of the matter.

1300 First Roman Jubilee.

1301-2 The struggle between Boniface VIII and Philip the Fair enters its acute phase. The King of France opposes the theocratic doctrine, and proclaims his own absolute sovereignty.

1302 18th November: the Bull *Unam Sanctam*.

1303 Boniface VIII proclaims Albert king and in April replies to the King of France by declaring the universal authority of the Emperor of the Romans, who is himself a vassal of the papacy.
7th September: the attack at Anagni.

1305 Clement V, second pope after Boniface VIII; did not ever reside in Rome; established from 1309 in Avignon.

c. 1307 Pierre Dubois, jurist in the service of Philip the Fair, draws up his *De recuperatione Terrae sanctae*.

1308 Death of Albert of Hapsburg; failure of Charles of Valois's candidature for the Empire. Election of Henry VII, count of Luxemburg.

c. 1308 Treatise: *De ortu, progressu et fine Romani Imperii*, by Engelbert of Admont.

1310 October: Henry VII sets off for Italy. He has already made a number of very solmn promises to the Pope and concluded an agreement with Philip the Fair stipulating absolute parity between the two signatories.

1311 Œcumenical Council meets at Vienne.
Bernard Gui submits a memorandum beforehand proposing that national kingdoms should replace the empire.

1312 29th June: Henry VII is crowned emperor; the following day the Emperor declares Robert, King of Naples, guilty of the crime of *lèse-majesté* and enters into a struggle with him. Great display of polemics in both camps.

1313 The Romans rise in support of Henry VII.
24th August: death of the Emperor.

c. 1313 Dante's *De Monarchia*.

1313–14 Clement V and Robert of Naples argue against the concept of empire.

1314 Election of two kings in Germany: Frederick of Austria and Louis of Bavaria.

1316 Accession of Pope John XXII.

1317 John XXII declares the imperial throne vacant, reserves the administration of the Empire to himself and appoints Robert of Naples the Emperor's representative in Italy.

1322 Battle of Mühldorf: Louis of Bavaria, victor over Frederick of Austria, immediately renews his relations with the Ghibellines of Italy.

1323 Beginning of the conflict between John XXII and Louis of Bavaria.

1324 Sachsenhausen Appeal. Charles IV the Fair, King of France, appears for a brief period as a candidate for the Empire.

1326 Marsilius of Padua, who completed his *Defensor pacis* in 1324, takes refuge at the court of Louis of Bavaria.

1327 Roman revolution: dictatorship of Sciarra Colonna.

1328 17th January: Louis of Bavaria receives the imperial diadem from the Roman people.
April–May: John XXII deposed, with the encouragement of the Emperor, and the antipope Nicholas V elected.

1330–1 ⎫
1334–7 ⎭ Louis of Bavaria seeks a compromise with the court of Avignon.

1338 The struggle enters an acute phase; the Emperor is greatly influenced by the leaders of the Minorites who are in revolt against the papacy (William of Occam).
May: states of the realm meet at Frankfurt; the 'Constitution' *Fidem Catholicam*.
July: Decree on the method of electing a king of the Romans, issued by the electors at Rhens.
6th August: the imperial 'Constitution' *Licet juris*, general declaration on the Law of the Empire.
September: Diet of Coblenz; alliance between Louis of Bavaria and Edward III of England.

1339 A new declaration, made by the Emperor at the Diet of Frankfurt, reduces the coronation of the Emperor to a simple ceremony.

1340 Lupold of Bebenburg writes his treatise *De Jure regni et Imperii Romani*.

1342 Accession of Pope Clement VI.

1346 13th April: the Pope proclaims the dethronement of Louis of Bavaria.
11th July: Charles of Moravia, grandson of Henry VII, elected king.

1347   20th May – 15th December: Cola di Rienzo, tribune at Rome.
October: death of Louis of Bavaria; to oppose Charles IV, his party puts up an anti-king Günther of Schwarzburg, who dies in 1349.

1349   25th June: Charles IV anointed king at Aix-la-Chapelle.

1350   Second Jubilee year.
Rienzo unable to persuade Charles IV to assume the role of messianic emperor.

1354   Konrad von Megenberg dedicates his treatise *De Translatione Imperii* to Charles IV.
October: Cola di Rienzo returns to Rome, charged by Pope Innocent VI with the task of re-establishing the Pope's authority in the town. He dies in a riot.

1355   Charles IV crowned emperor.

1356   Charles IV issues the Golden Bull.

Short Reading List of Books in English

The last days of the Roman Empire and the formation of the barbarian kingdoms are covered in F. Lot, *The End of the Ancient World and the Beginning of the Middle Ages*, London, 1931, and in A. H. M. Jones, *The Later Roman Empire (284-602)* 3 vols., Oxford (Blackwell), 1964. There are lives of *Charlemagne* by H. W. C. Davis, London, 1900, and by Richard Winston, London, 1956 (popular). The significance of his coronation is discussed briefly in F. L. Ganshof, *The Imperial Coronation of Charlemagne*, Glasgow, 1949, and in *The Coronation of Charlemagne: What did it signify?*, edited R. L. Sullivan, Boston, 1964, a series of excerpts from eminent historians on the subject. H. Fichtenau, *The Carolingian Empire*, trans. P. Munz, Oxford, 1963, is important. See also K. F. Morrison, *The Two Kingdoms, Ecclesiology in Carolingian Political Thought*, Princeton, 1964. For the Donation of Constantine, C. B. Coleman, *Constantine the Great and Christianity* (for the text, H. Bettenson, *Documents of the Christian Church*, Oxford, repr. 1956, pp. 135 ff.); see also E. H. Davenport, *The False Decretals*, Oxford, 1914.

On the Holy Roman Empire, Lord Bryce's study *The Holy Roman Empire*, London, 1964, and frequently reprinted, remains a classic. A modern survey is F. Heer, *The Holy Roman Empire*, trans. Janet Sondheimer, London, 1967, pp. 1-121. J. W. Thompson, *Feudal Germany*, Chicago, 1928, is still useful. Geoffrey Barraclough, *Medieval Germany*, 2 vols., Oxford (Blackwell), 1938, is valuable, especially Vol. II, an important selection of essays by German historians. See also G. Barraclough, *The Origins of Modern Germany*, 2nd ed., Oxford, 1947; *The Holy Roman Empire, Idea and Reality* (Historical Association Pamphlet, repr. 1964). There are good lives of *Frederick II* by E. Kantorowicz, trans. E. O. Lorimer, London, 1931, and by Georgina Masson, London, 1957; on messianic prophecies relating to him, N. Cohn, *The Pursuit of the Millennium*, London, 1957, chapter V. On the later empire see C. C. Bayley, *The Formation of the German College of Electors*, Toronto, 1949; W. M. Bowsky, *Henry VII in Italy*, Lincoln, Nebraska, 1960; H. S. Offler, 'Empire and Papacy, the Last Struggle', *Transactions of the Royal Historical Society*, 5th ser., VI, 1956, pp. 21-47.

Political thought is treated *passim* in the massive work of R. W. and A. J. Carlyle, *A History of Medieval Political Theory in the West*, 6 vols., Edinburgh, 1903-36, and briefly in W. Ullmann, *A History of Political Thought, The Middle Ages*, Penguin, 1965. W. Ullmann, *The Growth of Papal Government in the Middle*

Ages, London, 1955, has much of value on the concept of empire; see also his *Principles of Government and Politics in the Middle Ages*, London, 1961. In *Trends in Medieval Political Thought*, ed. B. Smalley, Oxford (Blackwell), 1965, the essays by J. M. Wallace-Hadrill on 'The *Via Regia* of the Carolingian Age', by K. J. Leyser on 'The Polemics of the Papal Revolution' and by M. Reeves on 'Marsiglio of Padua and Dante Alighieri' are especially relevant. Also important are G. Tellenbach, *Church, State and Christian Society in the time of the Investiture Contest*, trans. R. F. Bennett, Oxford (Blackwell), 1948; Fritz Kern, *Kingship and Law in the Middle Ages*, trans. S. B. Chrimes, Oxford (Blackwell), 1939; Michael Seidlmayer, *Currents of Medieval Thought (with special reference to Germany)*, trans. D. Baker, Oxford (Blackwell), 1960; E. Kantorowicz, *The King's Two Bodies: A Study in Medieval Political Theology*, Princeton, 1959, and C. T. Davis, *Dante and the Idea of Rome*, Oxford, 1957. M. J. Wilks, *The Problem of Sovereignty in the later Middle Ages*, Cambridge, 1963, deals with some aspects of later medieval theory. E. Lewis, *Medieval Political Ideas*, Vol. II, London, 1954, has two chapters on the Regnum and Sacerdotium and the Problem of the Empire.

Some original sources in translation include Einhard's 'Life of Charlemagne', trans. in A. J. Grant, ed., *Early Lives of Charlemagne*, London, 1905; *Gregory VII, A Selection of Letters*, trans. E. Emerton, Columbia Records, 1932; 'Henry IV's Letters', Wipo's 'Life of Conrad II' and the anonymous 'Life of Henry IV', trans. T. E. Mommsen and K. F. Morrison, *Imperial Lives and Letters of the Eleventh Century*, Columbia Records, 1962; C. C. Mierow, Otto of Freising's *The Deeds of Frederick Barbarossa*, New York, 1953; Dante, *De Monarchia*, trans. D. Nicholl, London, 1954; Marsilius of Padua, *Defensor Pacis* in Vol. II of A. Gewirth, *Marsilius of Padua*, New York, 1956.

For the relevant Spanish background, R. Ménendez Pidal, *The Cid and his Spain*, trans. H. W. Sutherland, London, 1934; and for Anglo-Saxon England, Eric John on 'Orbis Britanniae and the Anglo-Saxon kings' in *Orbis Britanniae and Other Studies*, Leicester, 1966, pp. 1–63.

V. H. H. G.

Further Bibliography

So much has been published about the concept of empire that the author has had to make a selection from the many works which explicitly or implicitly deal with the subject. The reader will, therefore, find in the list below the titles of those studies which are likely to be most useful to him and to offer the greatest amount of information on the questions with which this book is concerned. For ease of reference the titles are grouped under headings and arranged in an order which, in general, follows that in which the various subjects arise in the book.

I THE CONCEPT OF EMPIRE BETWEEN THE FIFTH AND THE FIRST HALF OF THE EIGHTH CENTURIES

(a) Elements which compose the concept of empire

C. Erdmann: *Forschungen zur politischen Ideenwelt des Frühmittelalters*, Berlin, 1951.
E. Stengel: *Kaisertitel und Souveränitätsidee*, *Deutsches Archiv*, III, 1939.
G. Tellenbach: *Römischer und christlicher Reichsgedanke in der Liturgie des frühen Mittelalters*, Heidelberg, 1934. See also reading list.

(b) The concept of empire in Byzantium

L. Bréhier: *Les institutions de l'Empire byzantin* (*Evolution de l'Humanité*, Vol. 32b), Paris, 1949.
P. Lemerle: *Le monde byzantin*, *Revue historique*, Vol. 204, 1950 (Bibliographical Supplement to the preceding work).
A. Grabar: *L'empereur dans l'art byzantin* (Publications of the Faculty of Letters in the University of Strasbourg, 75), Paris, 1936.

(c) Evolution of the papacy

H.-X. Arquillière: *L'Augustinisme politique*, Paris, 1934.
E. Caspar: *Geschichte des Papsttums*, I and II, Tübingen, 1933.
U. Gmelin: *Auctoritas, Römischer Princeps und Päpstlicher Primat* (*Forschungen zur Kirchen und Geistesgeschichte*, XI), Stuttgart, 1937.
W. Levison: *Konstantinische Schenkung und Silvesterlegende*, in F. Ehrle, *Miscellanea*, II, Rome, 1924.

P. E. Schramm: *Sacerdotium und Regnum im Austausch ihrer Vorrechte*, in *Studi gregoriani*, ed. Borino, II, Rome, 1947.

(d) Barbarian kingdoms: christianisation, relations with the Empire

M. Bloch: *Les rois thaumaturges* (Publications of the Faculty of Letters in the University of Strasbourg, 19), Paris, 1924.
W. Levison: *England and the Continent in the Eighth Century*, Oxford, 1946.
H. Löwe: *Von Theodorich zu Karl d.G.*, in *Deutsches Archiv*, IX, 2, 1952.
G. Tellenbach: *Germanentum und Reichsgedanke im früheren Mittelalter*, in *Historisches Jahrbuch*. 62–9, 1949. See also reading list.

II THE CONCEPT OF EMPIRE IN THE CAROLINGIAN ERA

(a) General evolution

A. Kleinclausz: *L'Empire carolingien, ses origines et ses transformations*, Dijon and Paris, 1902.
L. Halphen: *Charlemagne et l'Empire carolingien* (*Évolution de l'Humanité*, Vol. 33), Paris, 1947.
— *L'idée d'État sous les Carolingiens*, in *A travers l'histoire du Moyen-Age*, Paris, 1950.
H. Fichtenau: *Das Karolingische Imperium*, Zürich 1949.
H. Mitteis: *Der Vertrag von Verdun im Rahmen der Karolingischen Verfassungspolitik*, in Th. Mayer, *Der Vertrag von Verdun*, Leipzig, 1943.

(b) The coronation of Charlemagne as emperor: the two empires

K. Heldmann: *Das Kaisertum Karls des Groszen, Theorien und Wirklichkeit*, Weimar, 1928.
L. Levillain: *Le couronnement impérial de Charlemagne*, in *Revue d'Histoire de l'Église de France*, XVIII, 1932.
E. Caspar: *Das Papsttum unter fränkischer Herrschaft*, in *Zeitschrift für Kirchengeschichte*, 54, 1935.
F. L. Ganshof: *The imperial coronation of Charlemagne* (Glasgow University Publications, 79), Glasgow, 1949.
— *La fin du règne de Charlemagne*, in *Zeitschrift für schweizerische Geschichte*, 28, 1948.
C. Erdmann: *Forschungen*, see above, under I (a).
P. E. Schramm: *Die Anerkennung Karls des Groszen als Kaiser*, Munich, 1952 (reprinted from *Historische Zeitschrift*, Vols. 172–3, 1951).
— *Die zeitgenössischen Bildnisse Karls des G.*, Leipzig, 1928.
F. Doelger: *Europas Gestaltung im Spiegel der fränkisch-byzantinischen Auseinandersetzung*, in Th. Mayer, *Der Vertrag von Verdun*, Leipzig, 1943.
W. Ohnsorge: *Das Zweikaiserproblem im früheren Mittelalter*, Hildesheim, 1947.

III ROME AND THE CONCEPT OF THE EMPIRE AS A ROMAN INSTITUTION

(a) General works

A. Graf: *Roma nella memoria e nelle immaginazioni del medio evo*, 2 vol., Turin, 1882–3.
F. Gregorovius: *Geschichte der Stadt Rom im Mittelalter*, 8 vol., Stuttgart, 1875 *et seq*. English translation 1894–1902.
F. Schneider: *Rom und Romgedanke des Mittelalters*, Munich, 1926.
E. Dupré-Theseider: *L'idea imperiale di Roma nella tradizione nel medioevo*, Milan, 1950.

(b) Particular studies dealing with the Roman concept during certain periods

E. Pfeil: *Die fränkische und die deutsche Romidee des frühen Mittelalters*, Munich, 1929.
P. E. Schramm: *Kaiser, Rom und Renovatio*, 2 vol., Berlin, 1929.
E. Jordan: *Dante et la théorie romaine de l'Empire*, in *Nouvelle Revue historique de Droit français*, Vol. 45, 1921, pp. 353–96; 4th series, I, 1922, pp. 191–232 and 333–90.
P. Schmitthenner: *Die Ansprüche des Adels und des Volkes der Stadt Rom auf Vergebung der Kaiserkrone während des Interregnum* (Historische Studien, 155), Berlin, 1923.
E. Schoenian: *Die Idee der Volkssouveränität im Mittelalterlichen Rom*, Leipzig, 1919.
C. Burdach: *Rienzo und die geistige Wandlung seiner Zeit* (Vom Mittelalter zur Reformation, II, 1), Berlin, 1913.
C. Burdach, P. Piur: *Briefwechsel des Cola di Rienzo* (same collection, II, 3).

IV THE CONCEPT OF EMPIRE, DISSOCIATED FROM ANY CONNEXION WITH ROME

(a) General works

Those of C. Erdmann and of E. Stengel, see under I (a) above.

(b) The imperial title of the Anglo-Saxon kings

E. A. Freeman: *The History of the Norman Conquest of England*, I (3rd edn.), London, 1877.
W. de Gray-Birch: *Index of the Styles and Titles of English Sovereigns* in *Report of the first annual meeting of the Index Society*, London, 1879.
J. E. A. Jolliffe: *The Constitutional History of England*, 2nd edn., London, 1948.

(c) The concept of empire in the Spanish kingdoms

J. Beneyto-Perez: *España y el problema de Europa, contribucion a la historia de la idea de Imperio*, Madrid, 1942.

H. J. Hueffer: *Das spanische Kaisertum der Könige von Leon-Kastilien*, Münster, 1931.

R. Menendez-Pidal: *La España del Cid*, 2 vol., Madrid, 1929. See also reading list.

— *El Imperio hispanico y los cinco reinos*, in *Rivista di estudios politicos*, Vols. 29 and 30, 1950.

P. Rassow: *Die Urkunden Kaiser Alfons VII von Spanien*, in *Archiv für Urkundenforschung*, Vol. 10, 1929.

P. E. Schramm: *Das Kastilische Königtum und Kaisertum während der Reconquista*, in *Festschrift für G. Ritter*, Tübingen, 1950.

V LITURGY AND ICONOGRAPHY OF THE EMPIRE

M. Andrieu: *Le Pontifical romain au Moyen-Age* (*Studi e Testi*, Vols. 86–9), Rome, 1938–41.

M. David: *Le serment du sacre*, I (extract from the *Revue du Moyen-Age latin*, Vol. VI), 1950.

E. Eichmann: *Die Kaiserkrönung im Abendland*, 2 vol., Würzburg, 1942.

E. H. Kantorowicz: *Laudes regiae* (University of California Publications in History, Vol. 33), Berkeley, 1946.

H. W. Klewitz: *Die Festkrönungen der deutschen Könige*, in *Zeitschrift für Rechtsgeschichte, Kanonistische Abteilung*, 28, 1939.

P. E. Schramm: *Die deutschen Kaiser und Könige in Bildern ihrer Zeit*, 2 vol., Leipzig, 1928. (Referred to in this study under the abbreviation *Kaiserbilder*.)

— *Die Ordines der mittelalterlichen Kaiserkrönung*, in *Archiv für Urkundenforschung*, Vol. 11, 1930.

— *Sacerdotium und Regnum*. See under I(c) above.

VI PAPACY; IMPERIAL NATURE OF THE POPE'S AUTHORITY FROM THE END OF THE ELEVENTH CENTURY

(a) General works on the reform of the Church

H.-X. Arquillière: *Saint Grégoire VII, essai sur sa conception du pouvoir pontifical*, Paris, 1934.

A. Fliche: *La Réforme grégorienne*, 3 vol., Louvain-Paris, 1924–37.

G. Tellenbach: *Libertas, Kirche und Weltordnung im Zeitalter des Investiturstreits* (*Forschungen zur Kirchen und Geistesgeschichte*, VII), Stuttgart, 1936.

(b) Penetration of the concept of empire

H.-X. Arquillière: *Origine de la théorie des Deux Glaives*, in *Studi gregoriani*, ed. Borino, I, Rome, 1947.

C. Burdach: *Rienzo*. See under III(b) above.

K. Jordan: *Die Entstehung der römischen Kurie*, in *Zeitschrift für Rechtsgeschichte, Kanonistische Abteilung*, 28, 1939.

H. W. Klewitz: *Die Entstehung des Kardinalkollegiums*, ibid., 25, 1936.

— *Die Krönung des Papstes, ibid.,* 30, 1941.

— *Papsttum und Kaiserkrönung,* in *Deutsches Archiv,* IV, 1940.

G. Laehr: *Die Konstantinische Schenkung in der abendländischen Literatur des Mittelalters,* Berlin, 1926.

W. Levison: *Die mittelalterliche Lehre von den beiden Schwertern,* in *Deutsches Archiv,* IX, 1, 1951.

A. Michel: *Die folgenschweren Ideen des Kardinals Humbert und ihr Einfluss auf Gregor VII,* in *Studi Gregoriani,* I, 147.

J. B. Saegmueller: *Die Idee von der Kirche als Imperium Romanum im Kanonischen Recht,* in *Theologische Quartalschrift,* Vol. 88, 1898.

P. E. Schramm: *Sacerdotium und Regnum.* See under I(c) above.

VII THE ROMANO-GERMANIC EMPIRE

(a) Imperial biographies

R. Holtzmann: *Geschichte der sächsischen Kaiserzeit,* Munich, 1943.

K. Hampe: *Deutsche Kaisergeschichte in der Zeit der Salier und Staufen* (7th edn.), Leipzig, 1937.

E. H. Kantorowicz: *Kaiser Friedrich II,* I (2nd edn.), 1936, II, 1931. Eng. trans. E. O. Lorimer, London, 1931.

K. Hampe: *Geschichte Konradins von Hohenstaufen* (3rd edn.), Leipzig, 1942.

F. Schneider: *Kaiser Heinrich VII,* 3 vol., Leipzig, 1924–8.

(b) Confrontation of the Empire and Byzantium

W. Ohnsorge: *Das Zweikaiserproblem.* See under II(b) above.

(c) Aspects of the concept of empire

H. Beumann: *Widukind von Korvei, Untersuchungen zur Geschichtsschreibung und Ideengeschichte des 10. Jahrhunderts,* Weimar, 1951.

M. Bloch: *La Société féodale* (*Évolution de l'Humanité,* Vol. 34b), II, Paris, 1940. Eng. trans. L. A. Manyon, London, 1961.

— *L'Empire et l'idée d'Empire sous les Hohenstaufen,* in *Revue des cours et conférences,* 1928–9, II, pp. 481–93, 577–82, 759–68.

A. Brackmann: *Gesammelte Aufsätze,* Berlin, 1941.

K. Burdach: *Walther von der Vogelweide,* Leipzig, 1910.

C. Erdmann: *Forschungen.* See under I(a) above.

— *Das ottonische Reich als Imperium Romanum,* in *Deutsches Archiv,* VI, 1943.

R. Folz; *Le souvenir et la légende de Charlemagne dans l'Empire germanique médiéval* (Publications of the University of Dijon, VII), Paris, 1950.

— *Études sur le culte liturgique de Charlemagne dans les églises de l'Empire* (Publications of the Faculty of Letters in the University of Strasbourg, 115), Paris, 1951.

R. Holtzmann: *Der Weltherrschaftsgedanke des mittelalterlichen Kaisertums und die Souveränität der europäischen Staaten,* in *Historische Zeitschrift,* 159, 1939.

M. Lintzel: *Die Kaiserpolitik Ottos des Groszen,* Munich and Berlin, 1943.

W. Ohnsorge: 'Kaiser' Konrad III, in *Mitteilungen des oesterreichischen Instituts für Geschichte,* 46, 1932.

P. Rassow: *Honor Imperii, Die neue Politik Friedrich Barbarossas*, Munich, 1940.
P. E. Schramm: *Kaiser, Rom und Renovatio*. See under III(b) above.
H. Wieruszowski: *Vom Imperium zum nationalen Königtum*, Munich, 1933.

(d) The Empire in the first half of the fourteenth century

F. Bock. *Reichsidee und Nationalstaaten*, Munich, 1943.
E. Stengel: *Avignon und Rhens*, Weimar, 1930.

(e) Evolution of the German nation-state

H. Mitteis: *Der Staat des hohen Mittelalters* (3rd edn.), Weimar, 1944.
— *Die deutsche Königswahl. Ihre Rechtsgrundlagen bis zur goldenen Bulle* (2nd edn.), Baden near Vienna, 1944.

VIII THE CONCEPT OF EMPIRE IN FRANCE

P. Fournier: *La monarchia de Dante et l'opinion française*; The French Catholic Committee for the celebration of the sixth centenary of the death of Dante: *Bulletin du Jubilé*, No. 3, 1921.
W. Kienast: *Deutschland und Frankreich in der Kaiserzeit*, Leipzig, 1943.
P. E. Schramm: *Der König von Frankreich*, 2 vol., Weimar, 1939.
G. Zeller: *Les rois de France candidats à l'Empire*, in *Revue historique*, Vol. 173, 1934.

IX WORKS DEALING WITH THE CONTROVERSY
OVER THE EMPIRE

A. Dempf: *Sacrum Imperium*, Munich and Berlin, 1929.
E. Gilson: *La philosophie au Moyen-Age*, 2nd edn., Paris, 1944. Eng. trans. London, 1955.
G. de Lagarde: *La naissance de l'esprit laïque au déclin du Moyen-Age*, I (An assessment of the Thirteenth Century), 1934; II (Marsilius of Padua); IV (W. of Occam and his time), 1942.
V. Martin: *Les origines du gallicanisme*, 2 vol., Paris, 1939.
J. Rivière: *Le problème de l'Église et de l'État au temps de Philippe le Bel*, Louvain and Paris, 1925.

X IMPERIAL ESCHATOLOGY

C. Erdmann: *Endkaiserglaube und Kreuzzugsgedanke*, in *Zeitschrift für Kirchengeschichte*, 51, 3, F.2, 1932.
F. Kampers: *Kaiserprophetien und Kaisersagen im Mittelalter*, Munich, 1895.
— *Die deutsche Kaiseridee in Prophetie und Sage*, Munich, 1896.
— *Vom Werdegang der abendländischen Kaisermystik*, Leipzig, 1924.
E. H. Kantorowicz: *Kaiser Friedrich II*. See under VII(a) above.
E. Sackur: *Sibyllinische Texte und Forschungen*, Halle, 1898.

Index

The figures in brackets after the names of popes and emperors give the dates of their pontificates and reigns.
The letter D. followed by a Roman numeral indicates the Document in which the reference occurs.

233